NORTH AMERICAN WILDLIFE

 Marshall Cavendish
Reference
New York

Marshall Cavendish

Copyright © 2011 Marshall Cavendish Corporation

Published by Marshall Cavendish Reference
An imprint of Marshall Cavendish Corporation

Website: www.marshallcavendish.us

Other Marshall Cavendish Offices:

Marshall Cavendish International (Asia) Private Limited, 1 New Industrial Road, Singapore 536196 • Marshall Cavendish International (Thailand) Co Ltd. 253 Asoke, 12th Flr, Sukhumvit 21 Road, Klongtoey Nua, Wattana, Bangkok 10110, Thailand • Marshall Cavendish (Malaysia) Sdn Bhd, Times Subang, Lot 46, Subang Hi-Tech Industrial Park, Batu Tiga, 40000 Shah Alam, Selangor Darul Ehsan, Malaysia

Marshall Cavendish is a trademark of Times Publishing Limited

All websites were available and accurate when this book was sent to press.

Library of Congress Cataloging-in-Publication Data
North American wildlife.
    p. cm.
  Includes index.
  ISBN 978-0-7614-7938-3
  1. Animals--North America--Juvenile literature. I. Marshall Cavendish Reference.
  QL151.N67 2011
  591.97--dc22
                    2010012074

Printed in Malaysia
14 13 12 11 10   1 2 3 4 5

MARSHALL CAVENDISH
Publisher: Paul Bernabeo
Production Manager: Mike Esposito

THE BROWN REFERENCE GROUP PLC
Managing Editor: Tim Harris
Designer: Lynne Lennon
Picture Researcher: Laila Torsun
Indexer: Ann Barrett
Design Manager: David Poole
Editorial Director: Lindsey Lowe

CONTENTS

FOREWORD

For most people, the term *wildlife* conjures images of large mammals or fish, animals that we hunt and capture for food or recreation. However, wildlife is much more and includes the full diversity of animal species. Diversity of wildlife is a component of biodiversity, considered by many to be associated with the tropics, but there is a grandeur and richness of life to be found even in our own backyards.

North America boasts an incredible ecological diversity. The variety of habitats—streams, lakes, boreal forest, Carolinian forests, pinewoods, mountains, prairies, deserts, tundra, and oceans—is mirrored by that of its wildlife. The continent is host to some of the most spectacular wildlife phenomena on the planet. The boreal forests are home to an estimated 2–3 billion nesting songbirds, and during the fall exodus to the south this number reaches an astounding 5 billion migrants as populations are swelled by the young of the year. Millions of salmon return unerringly to the streams of their birth after years at sea to begin their life cycle again. The largest concentrations of reptiles in the world occur in central North America, as garter snakes gather by the thousands at dens suitable for a long hibernation to endure the harsh winter.

With a sampling of over 80 animals and animal groups, this book captures the breadth of North American wildlife diversity by introducing the large and small, invertebrates and vertebrates, herbivores and carnivores. The species profiles and impressive photographs put the animals into a larger context by comparing their life histories with relatives from around the globe. Sidebar summaries provide distribution maps and outline classification, introducing a cornerstone of biology and the language that scientists use to communicate. Common names for animals vary by language and even from person to person, whereas scientific names are standardized—the animal called a moose in English North America is known as an elk in Europe, but among scientists anywhere, it is *Alces alces*.

It is almost impossible to introduce the diversity of wildlife without noting the many factors that threaten to diminish it. Over the 550 million years of the history of multicelled life, the Earth has been in constant flux, and well over 95 percent of all species that have ever existed are extinct. Changes in our environment are happening in a different way than in the past. The dominant agent is likely the human one, and some scientists estimate that 50 species of animals disappear each day as humans gobble up more space and resources. Climate change is altering habitats and the distribution of even familiar animals. Many of the accounts in this book note the impact humans have had on animal populations, and these are not universally negative.

Much of today's society lives apart from the natural world, inhabiting forests of concrete and plains of asphalt. It has been suggested that city dwellers suffer from nature deficit disorder, a condition of higher anxiety and lower emotional connection with people and other living creatures. Paraphrasing Jane Goodall, a scientist made famous through her work on chimpanzees, we will only care about our wildlife if we understand it. The diversity of wildlife is something to celebrate and understand, not only despair its loss. This book contributes to that celebration and understanding.

Randall D. Mooi, Ph.D.
Randall Mooi is Curator of Zoology at the Manitoba Museum, Winnipeg, MB, Canada.

Additional related information is available in the 22-volume print set *International Wildlife Encyclopedia*, third edition, and the corresponding online database at www.marshallcavendishdigital.com.

FACT FILE COLORS

▲ Mammal

▲ Amphibian

▲ Bird

▲ Fish

▲ Reptile

▲ Invertebrate

ALLIGATOR

THERE ARE TWO SPECIES of alligators, reptiles which, with the caimans, belong to a family closely related to the crocodiles. Alligators and crocodiles look extremely alike.

The main distinguishing feature is the teeth. In a crocodile the teeth in its upper and lower jaws are in line, but in an alligator, when its mouth is shut, the upper teeth lie outside the lower ones. In both animals the fourth lower tooth on each side is perceptibly larger than the rest. In the crocodile this tooth fits into a notch in the upper jaw and is visible when the mouth is closed, whereas in the alligator, with the lower teeth inside the upper, it fits into a pit in the upper jaw and is lost from sight when the mouth is shut. In addition, the alligator's head is broader and shorter, and the snout consequently blunter, than in the crocodile. Otherwise, especially in their adaptations to an aquatic life, alligators and crocodiles have much in common.

It is sheer accident that two such similar reptiles should have been given such different common names. The reason is that when the Spanish seamen, who had presumably no knowledge of crocodiles, first saw large reptiles in the Central American rivers, they spoke of them as lizards, *el largato* in Spanish. The English sailors who followed later adopted the Spanish name but ran the two into one to make "allagarter," which was later further corrupted to "alligator."

Smaller than they were

One of the two species of alligators is found in North America, the other in China. The Chinese alligator, *Alligator sinensis*, averages a little over 4 feet (1.2 m) in length. The American alligator, *A. mississippiensis*, is much larger, with a maximum recorded length of 20 feet (6 m). This length, however, is seldom attained nowadays because the American alligator is legally harvested for its skin. Whenever there is intense persecution or hunting of an animal, the larger ones are quickly eliminated and the average size of the remaining population drops slowly. However, adult male American alligators of 13 feet (4 m) in total length are still fairly common.

An American alligator eating a raccoon in the Florida Everglades. Mature adults feed mainly on fish, but they will also capture small mammals that come to drink at the water's edge.

AMERICAN ALLIGATOR

CLASS **Reptilia**

ORDER **Crocodylia**

SUBFAMILY **Alligatoridae**

GENUS AND SPECIES *Alligator mississippiensis*

LENGTH
Adult male: normally less than 13 ft. (4 m); occasionally up to 16⅔–20 ft. (5–6 m)

DISTINCTIVE FEATURES
Adult: bony nasal bridge; large, broad, robust skull; no osteoderms (bony deposits) in belly scales; upper teeth lie outside lower teeth when mouth shut. Juvenile: black skin with 4 or 5 yellow crossbands on body and 10 or 11 bands on tail; crossbands fade with age.

DIET
Adult: other reptiles, fish, small mammals and birds; also large mammals (very large crocodiles only). Juvenile: insects, mollusks and freshwater shrimps.

BREEDING
Age at first breeding: 6 years; breeding season: late April–early June; number of eggs: around 40; hatching period: 62–66 days; breeding interval: 1 year

LIFE SPAN
Probably up to 50 years

HABITAT
All available aquatic habitats including swamps, rivers, lakes, tidal zones and ponds

DISTRIBUTION
Southeastern U.S. from Virginia border and North Carolina south to southern Florida; range extends west to Rio Grande, Texas, and northwest to southern Arkansas and McCurtain County, Oklahoma

STATUS
Locally common; estimated population: 800,000 to 1,000,000

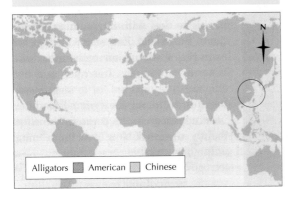

Alligators American Chinese

Female Chinese alligator, eastern China. In addition to persecution by humans, this species is suffering from habitat destruction. Very few individuals remain in the wild.

Long lazy life

Alligators are more sluggish than crocodiles and this possibly affects their longevity. They spend most of their time basking in swamps and on the banks of lakes and rivers. There are records of alligators having lived for more than 50 years.

The American alligator is restricted to the southeastern United States from the Virginia border and North Carolina to southern Florida. Its range then extends west to the Rio Grande in Texas and northwest as far as southern Arkansas and McCurtain County, Oklahoma. The Chinese alligator, meanwhile, is found only in the Yangtze River Basin in China.

Alligators' food changes with age. The juveniles feed on insects, mollusks and freshwater shrimps. As they grow older they take more frogs, snakes and fish. Mature adults live mainly on fish but will catch muskrats and small mammals that go down to the water's edge to drink. They also take a certain amount of waterfowl. Very large alligators may occasionally pull large mammals such as deer or cows down into the water and drown them, and will also attack humans.

Alligator nests

The female alligator plays the more active role in courtship and territorial defense. The males spend much of the breeding season quarreling among themselves, roaring and fighting. The roaring attracts the females to the males, as does a musky secretion from glands in the male's throat and cloaca. Courtship usually takes place at night and is slow and protracted. The pair bump against each other, pressing on the head and neck. The male pushes the female under the water before mounting, with his lower abdomen curled under hers for a couple of minutes.

A large nest-mound is made for the reception of the eggs. The female scoops up mud in her jaws and mixes it with decaying vegetation. The mixture is then deposited on the nest site until a mound 3 feet (90 cm) high is made. The eggs are hard-shelled and number 40 on average. They are laid in a depression in the top of the mound and covered with more vegetation. The female remains by the eggs until they hatch 62–66 days later, incubated by the heat of the nest's rotting vegetation.

Sex determination

Whether the young hatch as males or females is decided by temperature, as in many reptiles. Different parts of the mound experience different temperatures due to exposure to the sun and so eggs placed in different parts of the mound will develop into different sexes. This system leaves the possibility that the sex ratio may be determined by the mother, although this is not proven.

The hatchling alligators peep loudly and the female removes the layer of vegetation over the nest to help them escape. Baby American alligators are 8 inches (20 cm) long when first hatched

and grow approximately 1 foot (30 cm) a year, reaching maturity at 6 years. However, it may be several years before they breed for the first time.

Threats to survival

Young alligators are taken by predatory fish, birds and mammals, and at all stages of growth they are attacked and eaten by larger alligators. This natural predation was, in the past, just sufficient to keep their numbers steady. Then came the fashion for making shoes, handbags and other ornamental goods of alligator skin. This was the driving force behind the decrease in alligator numbers, as well as those of other crocodilians worldwide, in the early part of the 20th century. However, with careful, sustainable harvesting of wild populations, legally conducted throughout the entire range of the American alligator, numbers have increased greatly. The continued survival of this species has probably been ensured, although land drainage and pollution are now the main threats to alligators.

The Chinese alligator is a far more serious case. Its flesh is eaten and many parts of its body are used as charms and aphrodisiacs, and for their supposed medicinal properties. In addition, the recent further damming of the Yangtze River continues to threaten the future of the Chinese alligator. Few individuals are thought to remain in the wild. There are captive breeding programs in both China and the United States.

Pets down the drain

There was for a while another commercial interest detrimental to the alligator: while the fashion for skins from larger individuals was at its height, a fashion for alligator pets set in. Baby alligators were netted in large numbers for pet shops.

This fashion had its disadvantages for owners as well as the alligators. Obviously, the alligator achieves much too large a size for it to be convenient in a modern house or apartment. Most people who invested in an alligator found it necessary to dispose of the animal soon after, and zoos proved unable to deal with the quantity offered them. Brookfield Zoo near Chicago, for example, built up an enormous herd from unwanted pets. It is often said that alligators are disposed of in such a way that they end up in the sewers. Headlines have appeared in the press to the effect that the sewers of New York are teeming with alligators that prey on the rats and terrorize sewer workers. However, such reports are no doubt exaggerated.

Male alligators fighting in the breeding season, St. Augustine, Florida.

ANEMONE

THE WORD ANEMONE, from the Greek for wind, was first used for a flower in 1551. At first these marine animals, which superficially resemble flowers due to their long tentacles and bright and varied colors, were called "plant-animals." The name sea anemone was not used until 1773. Today, marine zoologists almost invariably speak of them as anemones. That they are truly animals is not in doubt, although the superclass to which they were assigned is still called the Anthozoa, that is, plant-animals.

An anemone has simple sense organs, takes solid food and, surprisingly, is capable of locomotion. The most outstanding feature of anemones is the variety of their colors and, in many species, the striking and attractive patterns these make.

Many species

There are thought to be several thousand species of anemones, found worldwide. They live in the seas and oceans, from the tidal zone to depths of more than 33,000 feet (10,000 m). They are most abundant in warm seas where the largest and most colorful species are also found. The largest anemones are of the genus *Stoichactis* and can reach more than 3 feet (90 cm) across. In temperate seas, dense carpets of anemones may cover rocks exposed to strong currents, and one, *Metridium senile*, is often the most obvious colonizer of shipwrecks. The smallest sea anemones are little more than a pin's head in size.

Voracious feeders, anemones will eat any animal flesh they can catch and swallow, and they may swallow prey items larger than themselves. It is not unknown for one anemone to swallow another. They can, however, survive for a long time without food, gradually dwindling in size until quite minute. This may be one of the secrets of their longevity: anemones have been kept in aquaria for as long as 100 years.

Sedentary but mobile

Sea anemones seldom move but are by no means rooted to the spot. There are even burrowing species. Those that are normally seen fixed to a rock move by gliding on their base. Others somersault, bending over to take hold of the rock with their tentacles, then letting the base go and flipping this over to take hold beyond. A few species lie on their side to glide along, or inflate themselves, let go with their foot, and float away.

Simple anatomy

An anemone is a cylindrical bag with a ring of tentacles surrounding the oral disc, or mouth, on the upper surface. The opposite end is flattened and forms a basal disc, or foot, by which the animal sticks to a solid support. Its interior is one large stomach, sub-divided by curtains of tissue, or mesenteries, which hang down, partially dividing the stomach into eight compartments.

The body wall of an anemone is made up of two layers of cells. There is, however, a set of longitudinal muscles running from the foot to the tentacle bases, and a set of circular muscles running around the body. By the lengthening and contraction of these muscles the body can be drawn out or pulled in. There is also a series of retractor muscles that assist in the sudden withdrawal of body and tentacles.

Stinging tentacle feeders

Food is caught by the tentacles, which are armed with stinging cells. When a small animal, such as a shrimp or a fish, touches a tentacle the stinging cells come into action, paralyzing and holding it. Adjacent tentacles bend over and continue to hold and sting the prey, eventually drawing it into the mouth.

The stinging cells, or nematocysts, are double-walled capsules, filled with poison, set in the outer surface of the tentacles. Each contains a coiled hollow thread, sometimes barbed at the base. At the outer end of the capsule is a thornlike trigger. When this is touched, the coiled thread is

Anemones feed on almost any animal matter they can catch with their tentacles. Pictured is a gem anemone, Bunodactis verrucosa.

Beadlet anemones exposed at low tide, with their tentacles retracted. These anemones can be extremely aggressive, often inflicting serious damage on one another.

shot out. It turns inside-out as it is ejected, its fine point pierces the skin of the prey and the paralyzing poison flows down the hollow thread. Some kinds of nematocysts stick to the prey instead of piercing the skin, and in a third type the thread wraps itself around the victim. Some nematocysts are triggered by the presence of certain chemicals as well as by touch.

Some aggressive species

Predators of anemones include large sea slugs, sea spiders, fish and sometimes starfish and crabs. The common beadlet anemone, *Actinia equina*, can be very aggressive to members of its own species and fights lasting several minutes have been observed. The loser can often be quite visibly damaged by the stinging cells of the victor, and usually moves away. It has been found that the more common red variety almost always triumphs over the less common green variety.

Sexual and asexual reproduction

Anemones display a great variety of sexual and asexual breeding methods. Most anemones are either male or female, but some are hermaphroditic. In some, eggs and sperm are shed into the surrounding water, in others the larvae develop inside the parent body. The fertilized eggs sink to the bottom and divide, or segment, to form oval larvae. These move about the seabed but finally each comes to rest, fastens itself to the bottom, grows tentacles and begins to feed.

Other species, for example in the genus *Anemonia*, split longitudinally to form separate individuals, or grow a ring of tentacles halfway down the body, after which the top half breaks away to give two anemones where there was one

ANEMONES	
PHYLUM	**Cnidaria**
SUPERCLASS	**Anthozoa**
CLASS	**Hexacorallia**
ORDER	**Several, but mainly Actiniaria**
GENUS	***Actinia, Anemonia, Stoichactis, Metridium* and many others**
SPECIES	**Several thousand species**

ALTERNATIVE NAME
Sea anemone

LENGTH
Typically ¾–4 in. (2–10 cm) across; larger species up to 3¼ ft. (1 m) across

DISTINCTIVE FEATURES
Flowerlike appearance due to many feeding tentacles, usually in concentric rings around mouth; often brightly colored

DIET
Small animals and pieces of detritus

BREEDING
Great variety of sexual and asexual breeding methods, including budding and splitting

LIFE SPAN
Many species live for a long time, perhaps up to 100 years or more

HABITAT
On rocks, stones and seaweed or buried in sand and gravel; from intertidal zone out to deep sea

DISTRIBUTION
Worldwide, though not common in estuaries or intertidal, sandy areas

STATUS
Many species common

before. Alternatively, young anemones may be formed by fragmentation, or laceration. In fragmentation small anemones, complete with tentacles, arise from the base of a parent, become separated and move away. Laceration occurs in some of the more mobile species, such as those of the genus *Metridium*. As the anemone glides over the rocks, pieces of the base are ripped away and, being left behind, regenerate to form minute but otherwise perfect anemones. In other species young anemones are formed asexually inside the parent and are subsequently spat out as perfectly formed miniatures.

ANOLE LIZARD

NOLE LIZARDS ARE ANY of approximately 250 species in the genus *Anolis*, one quarter of the total number of species in the iguana family of lizards. Because the genus is so large, some authorities split it. Under this scheme, the green anole of the southeastern United States remains in the genus *Anolis*, but the Jamaican anole is placed in another genus, *Norops*.

The anoles' heads are triangular with elongated jaws, and their bodies are slender, ending in a long, whiplike tail. Like the geckos, the toes have sharp claws as well as adhesive pads. These enable the anoles to climb tree trunks and sheer walls. Males have a flat throat sac, or dewlap, which they expand by muscular action when they are excited. This expands the folds of skin to reveal a pattern of colors between the scales, often green, red, white, yellow and black in many combinations.

Anoles are small lizards, most ranging in length from 5 to 10 inches (13–25 cm). A few species are larger than this, the knight anole, *Anolis equestris*, of Cuba being 18 inches (45 cm) in length. Of this, two-thirds is tail, so the knight anole is by no means a large lizard. It is, however, a striking reptile: pale green with white markings on its body, a braided yellow pattern on its head and patches of blue around the eyes. The male's throat sac is pale pink.

The best-known anole is the green anole, *A. carolinensis*, from the southeast of the United States. It is about 6–7 inches (15–18 cm) long, with a pale green body, the male having a throat sac spotted with red and white. The leaf-nosed anole of Brazil gets its name from the sideways, flattened structure that projects beyond its snout for a distance equal to the length of its head.

Tree-dwelling lizards

Anole lizards are found only in the Americas, where they range from North Carolina to southern Brazil and Chile, and are particularly abundant in the Caribbean. Most of them live in trees, running along the branches with the aid of their long, delicate toes and adhesive pads. A few species have enlarged toe pads that act as tiny parachutes, enabling them to jump from considerable heights. Other anoles have become associated with humans, living in houses and gardens where they often become quite tame.

Three of the more unusual anoles (*A. lionotus*, *A. poecilopus* and *A. barkeri*) live along the banks of streams, diving into the water and hiding under stones when frightened. Living in Cuba are two cave-dwelling anoles. One of these, a pale, translucent lizard with brick-red stripes running across its body, lives in limestone caves frequented by bats. Anole lizards are mainly insect eaters, but will take fruit and plant material when it is abundant.

Able to change color

The green anole is commonly called the American chameleon because, like most species of anoles, it is adept at changing color. Experiments and observations in natural conditions show that anole lizards change color mainly in response to temperature and light intensity. Background color (the principal factor in chameleon color changes) will affect the color of an anole to some extent, but if it is kept cool, at about 50° F (10° C), it will go brown, whatever the background. If the temperature is raised to 70° F (21° C) it turns green, but only so long as the light is dim. If the light is bright it stays brown. In normal conditions the green anole tends to be green at night and brown by day. Color changes in anoles are also sometimes associated with aggression. For example, the male green anole becomes bright green if he wins a fight but brown if he loses.

Anole lizards change color in response to changes in temperature or light intensity. This compares with the chameleons, in which background color is the most important factor.

Male anoles, such as this brown anole, Anolis sagrei, *have a brightly colored throat sac that they expand during territorial displays or courtship.*

The mechanism of color change varies among reptiles. For example, in chameleons, the pigment-containing cells in the skin, responsible for color changes, are controlled by nerves. As a result, chameleons can change color quite rapidly. However, in anoles the cells are controlled by a hormone, a chemical messenger called inter-medin, which is secreted into the blood by the pituitary gland. This is a slow process compared with the action of the nervous system, and anoles can take up to 10 minutes to change color.

Breeding behavior

The male anole is larger and more brightly colored than the female. He holds a territory that he defends against other males by displaying the colors of his throat sac and, at times, by fighting. The throat sac is also used to attract the female which, if willing, turns her head to one side. The male approaches her from the rear, grabs her neck with his jaws, slips his tail under hers, and mates. The eggs are nearly always laid in the ground, the female coming down the tree to dig a hole with her snout. She lays the eggs into the hole, which she then fills in. The cave anoles lay their eggs in narrow crevices in the cave walls, or between stalactites. Anoles often lay only one or two eggs at a time. The eggs, which are not guarded, hatch after 42–70 days.

Many enemies

Predators of anoles include hawks, cats and mongooses. In one experiment, 200 anoles were marked and released. A year later only four had survived. Like many abundant animals, there is a very rapid turnover of population, very few anoles even reaching maturity. The maximum age an anole can reach in captivity is over 6 years, but they probably live only 2 or 3 years in the wild.

ANOLE LIZARDS

CLASS **Reptilia**

ORDER **Squamata**

SUBORDER **Sauria**

FAMILY **Iguanidae**

GENUS *Anolis*

SPECIES **About 250 species**

ALTERNATIVE NAME
Green anole: American chameleon

LENGTH
Most species: 5–10 in. (13–25 cm); a few species larger than this

DISTINCTIVE FEATURES
Small size; triangular head; elongated jaws; long claws; most species have adhesive pads on their digits; extensible dewlap (throat sac) on underside of throat (male only); most species can change color

DIET
Mainly insects; also plant material

BREEDING
Varies according to species. Hatching period: 42–70 days.

LIFE SPAN
Most species: 2–3 years in the wild, or up to 6 years in captivity

HABITAT
Most species in trees; a few species in caves and suburban areas

DISTRIBUTION
Americas from North Carolina south to southern Brazil and Chile; also on many Caribbean islands

STATUS
Generally abundant; on some Caribbean islands anoles achieve densities greater than for any other lizards worldwide

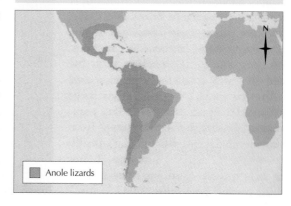

Anole lizards

ARMADILLO

THERE ARE 20 SPECIES of armadillos, grouped in eight genera. They all have a protective covering of armor, brown or pinkish in color, and are stout, short-legged animals with strong claws. Armadillos are distributed through the tropical and subtropical Americas from Argentina to the southeastern corner of the United States. Most live in open areas but some are found in forests. Although they belong to the order Edentata, meaning "no teeth," armadillos do have primitive teeth.

The three-, six- and nine-banded armadillos belong to the genera *Tolypeutes*, *Euphractus* and *Dasypus*, respectively. They are named for the number of movable bands on their armor. The best known of these is one species of nine-banded armadillo, *Dasypus novemcinctus*. It ranges northward from South America into Kansas and Missouri in the United States.

Armadillos, large and small
The giant armadillo, *Priodontes giganteus*, of the forests of eastern South America, is the largest species. It has a 3-foot (90-cm) body and can weigh up to 130 pounds (60 kg). It is unusual in having up to a hundred small teeth, more than twice the normal number for a mammal.

This compares to the smallest armadillo, the lesser fairy armadillo or pichiciago, *Chlamyphorus truncatus*. It is just 9 inches (23 cm) in length, including its 3-inch (7.5-cm) tail, and weighs 4 ounces (113 g). This species, found only on the plains of western Argentina, has less armor than the others. The carapace (back armor) is made up of bands hinged together and is attached to the armadillo's body only by a narrow ridge of flesh running down its spine. There is another flat shield consisting of a single plate covering its rump, and its armored tail sticks through this. The rest of its body is covered with a fine, soft, white fur. The fairy armadillo is molelike, having powerful front legs and small eyes. It spends more time underground than other armadillos.

Roll into a ball
The naked-tailed armadillos, genus *Cabassous*, of Central and South America, have five large claws on their front feet. The middle claw is especially large and sickle-shaped. The three-banded armadillo or apara, *Tolypeutes matacus*, of Bolivia, Argentina and Brazil, is the only armadillo to have its carapace separated from the skin around the sides of its body. As a result it is also the only species that is able to roll up into a complete sphere. The separation of the carapace from the

skin means there is room for its head, legs and tail when it rolls up. Other species are able to roll up to some extent, but not so completely.

The pygmy armadillo or pichi, *Zaedyus pichiy*, is a common resident of Patagonia and the Argentinian pampas. It is said to hibernate.

Dig burrows
Armadillos are mainly nocturnal and live in burrows when not active. They might be found alone, in pairs or in small groups. Nine-banded armadillos will only share burrows with other animals of the same sex. Armadillos are good at digging and their burrows are usually 2–3 feet (60–90 cm) beneath the surface.

Rivers are no obstacles to armadillos, for although they are proportionately heavy due to their coats of armor, they gain added buoyancy by swallowing air to blow up the intestine. The nine-banded armadillo, for example, is said to be able to submerge for 6 minutes.

Some species of armadillos have an unusual gait. The soles of their hind feet are pressed to the ground as they walk, but their forefeet are raised up on the strong pointed claws.

The nine-banded armadillo, Dasypus novemcinctus, *is the only armadillo found in the United States. Its behavior and habits are better known than those of other species.*

The hairy armadillo uses its head as a drill to get at grubs and other insects, forcing it into the ground, then twisting its body to make a hole.

Omnivorous feeders

Armadillos live on a wide variety of food, such as insects and other invertebrates, plants, carrion and small vertebrates such as snakes and lizards. Naked-tailed armadillos feed mainly on ants and termites, cutting open their nests with their sickle-like claws and extracting the insects with their long, extensible tongues.

Legend has it that the giant armadillo sometimes digs into new graves to get at human corpses. The peludo or hairy armadillo, *Chaetophractus villosus*, is known to burrow under, and sometimes into, carcasses to get at maggots. It will also dig into soft soil for grubs and other insects in a most unusual manner. It forces its head into the ground, then twists its body round to make a conical hole. These armadillos have also been seen killing snakes by cutting them with the hard edges of their carapaces.

Delayed implantation

Except for the nine-banded armadillos, breeding habits are not well known. Male armadillos mark their home range with urine, in much the same way as a domestic dog or cat. After mating, females exhibit delayed implantation, that is, the development of the embryo does not take place immediately. Instead, the single egg is fertilized and then lies free in the uterus for a period of time before becoming embedded in the uterine wall. At this point development can continue.

Gestation periods vary with species thereafter. In nine-banded armadillos mating takes place in July and August, the female lying on her back during courtship. Gestation takes around 120 days in this case, but is known to be just 65 days in the hairy armadillo.

ARMADILLOS

CLASS	**Mammalia**
ORDER	**Edentata (alternatively Xenarthra)**
FAMILY	**Dasypodidae**
GENUS	**Nine-banded armadillos, *Dasypus*; six-banded armadillos, *Euphractus*; three-banded armadillos, *Tolypeutes*; fairy armadillos, *Chlamyphorus*; naked-tailed armadillos, *Cabassous*; hairy armadillos, *Chaetophractus*; giant armadillo, *Priodontes*; pygmy armadillo, *Zaedyus***
SPECIES	**20 species**

WEIGHT
Fairy armadillos: 3–4 oz. (85–113 g).
Giant armadillo: up to 130 lb. (60 kg).

LENGTH
Lesser fairy armadillo. Head and body: up to 6 in. (15 cm); tail: 3 in. (7.5 cm).
Giant armadillo. Head and body: up to 3 ft. (90 cm); tail: 1⅔ ft. (50 cm).

DISTINCTIVE FEATURES
Armor-plated back and head; soft fur on underparts; protruding ears; short legs with powerful claws; tapering, conical tail

DIET
Invertebrates, lizards, snakes, rodents, carrion, fruits and other plant matter

BREEDING
Gestation period: delayed implantation, then up to 120 days, according to species; number of young: 1 to 4 (most species)

LIFE SPAN
Varies according to species

HABITAT
Savanna, pampas (grassland) and forest

DISTRIBUTION
Southern U.S. to southern South America

STATUS
Some species common; 6 species threatened

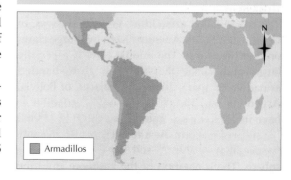

Armadillos

Identical young

One to four young are normally born each year, depending on the species. In some species the female might bear up to 12 identical young, all of which develop from a single egg.

In the nine-banded armadillos there are four in a litter and, as in other armadillos, the young are all identical, in sex as well as other characteristics. Armadillo young of the same litter are always identical because they all come from the same fertilized egg. All are attached by umbilical cords to a single placenta. This is the area of the uterine wall specialized for transferring nutrients between the blood of the mother and that of the embryos. In other mammals such multiple births are accidental and therefore rare, but identical young are the rule in armadillos.

The young are born with a soft leathery skin that hardens with age. They reach sexual maturity at around 1 year of age in the three-banded species. Life spans vary with species. Giant and nine-banded armadillos live for some 12 to 15 years. One six-banded armadillo lived for 18 years in captivity.

Protective armor

The name armadillo is derived from the diminutive of the Spanish word *armado*, meaning one that is armed. Body armor in mammals is generally made of compressed hair, as in the plates of pangolins and the horns of rhinos, but the armor of armadillos is made up of small plates of bone, each covered by a layer of horny skin and separated from its neighbors by soft skin, from which sparse hairs grow.

The carapace, or back armor, hangs down over the body, protecting the soft underparts and limbs. It is divided into two shields, one covering the forelimbs and one the hind limbs, the two being linked across the middle of the back by a series of transverse bands of plates that allow the carapace to be flexed. The number of transverse bands varies between species. In some they are sufficiently flexible to allow the animal to curl up. The head is also armored and in most species the tail is protected by a series of transverse, bony rings. The softer underparts are covered with a dense layer of hair and scattered, small bony scales.

Defensive behavior

If cornered, armadillos will defend themselves with their sharp claws, but they are more likely to run away, some species moving surprisingly fast. They will also attempt to burrow into the ground if they cannot find a hole. Armadillos such as the pichi will draw in their feet and wedge the surrounding carapace firmly into the ground. This ruse is effective against birds and some mammals, but not against coyotes, which can pierce their armor. The three-banded armadillo is more effectively protected by being able to roll itself into a complete sphere. Nonetheless, large predators such as the jaguar have a large enough gape to crack even this protective shell.

Becoming rare

Some species of armadillos are agricultural pests, tearing up crops in search of insects, but they can also be beneficial to farmers because they eat unwanted insects. This is not their only use to humans. Armadillos are the only other known mammals to carry leprosy, so are often used in medical research and vaccine development.

In addition, armadillos are hunted across their range for their flesh. Their armor has also been used to make items such as baskets, and the nine-banded armadillo, in particular, is increasingly meeting the hazard of motor traffic.

These factors and others are starting to have an impact on armadillo populations. The already rare lesser fairy armadillo is becoming rarer with the spread of agriculture. The giant armadillo, greater fairy armadillo, *Chlamyphorus retusus*, and several other species are also listed as being vulnerable or endangered as a result of disturbance and persecution by humans.

Reproduction in armadillos is unusual in that the young of a litter all spring from a single fertilized egg. As a result the offspring are identical in sex and other characteristics.

BALD EAGLE

ONE OF THE GROUP KNOWN as sea eagles, the bald eagle of North America is specialized in hunting fish. Bald eagle is an inaccurate name, but an impression of baldness is given by the bird's snow-white head and neck, contrasting with the brownish black plumage of the rest of its body. Its tail is also white and it has a large, yellow bill and yellow eyes and legs. Adults reach up to 3⅗ feet (1.1 m) in length, with a wingspan of perhaps 11½ feet (3.5 m). Bald eagles do not get their white feathers until they are 4 or 5 years old and might be mistaken for golden eagles up until this point. The remainder of the juvenile's plumage is lighter and more mottled than that of the adult.

The bald eagle has become one of the most familiar of eagles from its use on the seal of the United States of America.

No longer endangered

At one time bald eagles bred extensively throughout North America. Formerly, the northern boundary of their range extended east from Bering Island and Alaska, following a line down to the south of Hudson Bay in northern Canada, then back to Labrador in Newfoundland. The southern boundary extended from lower California in the west to Florida in the east. However, extensive use of the pesticide DDT (which results in sterility) in the 1960s, coupled with shooting and habitat destruction, caused serious declines in the 48 state populations outside Alaska. By the end of the 1960s, as few as 417 nesting pairs remained outside the Alaskan stronghold, but this number climbed by 2006 to 9,789 breeding pairs. In 1999, the bald eagle was removed from the endangered species list of the U.S. Fish and Wildlife Service, and yearly tracking was suspended in 2000. There are two subspecies: the northern and southern bald eagles. The differences between these are not great. The southern form is now confined to South Carolina, Florida, the states around the Gulf of Mexico and Texas.

Like many other raptors (birds of prey), bald eagles spend much of their time perching motionless, taking in every movement within their wide range of vision. They are generally found close to inland or coastal waters, but may be seen in more mountainous regions during migration. They are solitary birds, occasionally seen roosting together in a tree but otherwise being found in large numbers only where there is a plentiful source of food. Up to 4,000 have been recorded congregating along a 10-mile (16-km) stretch of the Chilkat River, Alaska, during winter, attracted there by abundant salmon.

Mainly fish eaters

Bald eagles take many kinds of prey, and will also feed on carrion. For most of the year, however, fish provide the bulk of their diet, including dead fish that have been washed ashore.

A bald eagle in flight. Adult bald eagles have a wingspan of up to 11½ feet (3.5 m).

A bald eagle with its catch, Kachemak Bay, Alaska. Bald eagles are skilled fishers, but often prefer to rob ospreys of their prey.

BALD EAGLE

CLASS	**Aves**
ORDER	**Falconiformes**
FAMILY	**Accipitridae**
GENUS AND SPECIES	***Haliaeetus leucocephalus***

ALTERNATIVE NAMES
American eagle; white-headed sea eagle

WEIGHT
7¾–11 lb. (3.5–5 kg)

LENGTH
Head to tail: 2⅘–3⅗ ft. (0.85–1.1 m); wingspan: 6½–11½ ft. (2–3.5 m)

DISTINCTIVE FEATURES
Adult: snow-white head and tail; brownish black body; yellow eyes, bill and legs. Juvenile: lacks white areas; lighter and more mottled elsewhere.

DIET
Mainly fish; also waterfowl, shorebirds, small mammals and carrion

BREEDING
Age at first breeding: 4–5 years; breeding season: October–February in southern states, later farther north; number of eggs: 2 or 3; incubation period: 35 days; fledging period: 72–75 days; breeding interval: 1 year

LIFE SPAN
Up to 20 years

HABITAT
Usually close to inland or coastal waters; also in mountains during migration

DISTRIBUTION
Throughout most of U.S. and Canada, from Alaska south to Florida and California

STATUS
Locally common in parts of Alaska and northern Canada; uncommon elsewhere

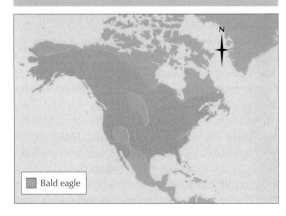

Bald eagle

The bald eagle's method of catching live fish varies. It is highly adaptable and able to take advantage of almost any opportunity for feeding. Sometimes it fishes in the same manner as the osprey, circling over the water, hovering on rapid wingbeats as it spies its quarry, then dropping onto its prey. At other times it will search a lake by flying leisurely just above the surface, or will wait patiently in a nearby tree until it sees a fish.

A more spectacular and regular habit of the bald eagle is that of systematically robbing ospreys. The eagle, sitting on a suitable perch near the osprey's hunting ground, waits for the other bird to appear laden with its prey. On seeing the eagle, the osprey attempts to escape but the eagle, not being weighed down by a fish, soon overtakes it and harries the bird until it is forced to drop its catch and flee. The eagle then hurtles down to retrieve the fish. Occasionally the bald eagle will even snatch prey away from the osprey using its talons.

When fish are not so plentiful, bald eagles turn to other prey such as rabbits, squirrels, waterfowl, shorebirds, puffins and rats. Larger mammals are sometimes caught and the remains of young caribou, mule deer and lambs have been found around eagle nests. However, it is likely that most of these died from other causes and were picked up by the birds as carcasses. Nevertheless, some farmers assert that bald eagles take sheep, and will shoot them.

The methods employed to catch waterfowl also show the bald eagle's adaptability. Most frequently waterfowl are pounced upon, on land or in the water, and carried off, but the eagle is also capable of forcing them down while in flight. Ducks and other diving birds may be forced by the eagle to dive again and again until exhausted, and are then easily captured. Even more remarkable is a method of catching geese on the wing. The eagle dives under the goose, rolls over and sinks its talons into its breast.

Lifelong partnership

Bald eagles mate for life and also cling tenaciously to their nesting site. The nest is used year after year, and the eagles will stay put even if humans begin to develop the area.

In Florida the breeding season begins very early, in October or November. The reason for this early nesting is thought to be the abundance of waterfowl in winter, which can provide ample food for the growing eaglets. It may also be an advantage for the chicks to have grown an insulating layer of feathers to keep them cool before the weather becomes too hot. In other southern states breeding takes place between November and February, but it starts later farther north.

In the south the nests are in lone trees, usually some 45–70 feet (14–21 m) above the ground, pines being preferred. In Alaska, beyond the tree line, the eagles build their nests on rocky cliffs or pinnacles. Being used many years running, with additions every year, bald eagle nests become impressive edifices. They are made up of a great pile of sticks, some of them 6 feet (1.8 m) long, with a mass of weeds, stubble and adhering earth in the middle. During the season the whole of the nest becomes trampled flat, so each year a new, 1-foot (30-cm) high rampart is built.

Only one chick survives

The normal clutch is of two or three eggs. They are white or pale blue, and 2½ inches (6.5 cm) long. Incubation takes 35 days. Both parents take part in brooding and, later, in feeding the chicks. It is very rare for three to survive, and usually only one chick fledges, having bullied its nest mates out of their share of the food.

As the eaglets grow they are guarded only in bad weather, when one parent will stand over them with wings spread. Gradually they are taught to tear up their own food, and as their feathers develop they begin flying exercises, flapping their wings and even flying up a few feet. Eventually the parents lure them into proper flight with food as a reward, but they still return

to the nest until the end of the summer, when their parents drive them away. Generally the fledging period is between 72 and 75 days and the young birds reach sexual maturity at 4 or 5 years.

Mobbed by other birds

Apart from humans bald eagles have no real predators, but several birds are known to mob them. Ospreys sometimes hit back as they are being robbed of their fish, and crows will repeatedly fly at raptors in order to protect their nests, eggs and chicks and themselves. They will harass the eagles, even landing on their backs and pecking at their heads. Small birds, such as kinglets and gnatcatchers, fearlessly pester any eagle that comes too near their nests.

The national emblem

On June 20th, 1782, the citizens of the newly independent United States of America adopted the bald or American eagle as a national emblem. At first the heraldic artists depicted a bird that could have been a member of any of the larger species, but by 1902 the bird portrayed on the seal of the United States of America had assumed its proper white plumage on the head and tail.

Although eagles are traditionally used as emblems of power, the choice of the bald eagle came in for some criticism. Benjamin Franklin preferred the wild turkey and said the bald eagle "like those among men who live by sharping and robbing... is generally poor and often very lousy." This was an allusion to its robbing ospreys, and its habit of eating carrion was also held against it. Nevertheless, the bald eagle's noble appearance has preserved its status as America's national bird.

The bald eagle, the only eagle confined to North America, was adopted by the United States as a national emblem in 1782. Large numbers of bald eagles gather at favored feeding grounds during the winter.

BALTIMORE ORIOLE

The Baltimore oriole's nest is like a basket hanging from a branch, with the entrance near the top. Here a male feeds its young.

THE MELODIC, FLUTELIKE song of the Baltimore oriole is one of the welcome sounds of spring in many parts of North America. With its black hood and bright orange underparts, rump and tail, along with its black-and-white wings, the Baltimore oriole is also one of the most attractive new arrivals each April and May. The species is found right across the United States east of the Rockies, and from northwestern British Columbia to Nova Scotia in Canada.

Like the other New World orioles, the Baltimore oriole is a member of the Icteridae family, the 104 members of which include species as diverse as the eastern meadowlark, *Sturnella magna*, and the brown-headed cowbird, *Molothrus ater*. Seven species of orioles are found in the United States and Canada, the Baltimore oriole being the most common of these.

The origin of the Baltimore oriole's name goes back to early colonial times. When George Calvert, an early English colonist and the first Baron of Baltimore, saw the species he was so impressed with its bright colors that he adopted it for his coat of arms. The bird was later named after him and is now the state bird of Maryland.

Long-distance migrant

The Baltimore oriole migrates long distances between its winter quarters and the areas in which it breeds. The species winters in Central America and South America, leaving there between mid-March and mid-April. It reaches the southern United States early in April and the Canadian border late in the month. By late May

it has reached its most northerly breeding grounds in British Columbia. The males arrive about a week earlier than the females.

Research done on birds killed on migration in the autumn suggests that adult males migrate on a narrower path than either adult females or young birds. Juveniles begin to leave the breeding grounds as early as the first half of July, with migration gathering pace during August. Most have left by September.

Small numbers of Baltimore orioles winter in southern California and along the east coast of the United States from Virginia to Florida, while a few birds have braved the winter conditions as far north as Ontario, Canada. However, the vast majority spends the winter months from southeastern Mexico south to northern Colombia and northern Venezuela. Most of these migrant birds move southeast through the Caribbean slope of Mexico in autumn, but in spring more of the returning birds make the sea crossing over the western Caribbean. However, the species is rarely found east of Jamaica.

Return year after year

The interesting thing about the Baltimore orioles that winter in the southeastern states is that birds return there year after year. This fact has been discovered by programs of trapping and banding. So site-faithful are some that one individual was trapped at the same place in six years out of seven. The trend for spending the winter in the United States seems to have been encouraged by an increase in the number of people putting out bird feeders. Some ringing recoveries are most peculiar. A bird ringed in Rhode Island in October 1963, for example, was found a month later many miles to the northeast, in Newfoundland. It should have migrated in the opposite direction! Several birds have also crossed the Atlantic Ocean to western Europe in the autumn.

Singing frenzy

When they reach the breeding grounds in spring, the male Baltimore orioles start up an almost continuous frenzy of singing. The interval between bursts of this flutelike song may be just 4 seconds. Once they find a mate, the singing tails off. By late May most of the birds that are still singing continuously are unpaired males fledged the previous summer. Rarely, females also sing, though their song is not as melodic.

While it is thought that virtually all females mate, including one-year-old birds, few males of this age are successful. So while the mating

BALTIMORE ORIOLE

CLASS	**Aves**
ORDER	**Passeriformes**
FAMILY	**Icteridae**
GENUS AND SPECIES	***Icterus galbula***

ALTERNATIVE NAME
Formerly known as northern oriole

WEIGHT
1–1⅔ oz. (25–47 g)

LENGTH
Head to tail: 8⅔ in. (22 cm)

DISTINCTIVE FEATURES:
Male: black head and back; bright orange rump; black wings with orange epaulet (shoulder patch) and wide, white wing bar; mainly orange tail. Female: duller orange below; browner wings.

DIET
Insects, especially caterpillars; also berries and sometimes flower nectar

BREEDING
Age at first breeding: 1–2 years; breeding season: eggs laid April–late June; number of eggs: usually 4 or 5; incubation period: 12–14 days; fledging period: 12–14 days; breeding interval: 1 year

LIFE SPAN
Up to 12 years

HABITAT
Open woodland, riverside trees and parks, including in suburban areas

DISTRIBUTION
Breeding: U.S. east of the Rockies and Canada from northwestern British Columbia to Nova Scotia. Winter: southeastern Mexico to Colombia and Venezuela.

STATUS
Common

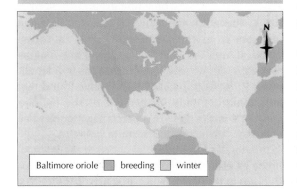

Baltimore oriole ▮ breeding ▮ winter

system is broadly monogamous, males will also mate outside the established pairing. The technical name for this is opportunistic polygyny.

Hanging nests

The Baltimore oriole's nest is an interesting construction, a pendant basket hanging from a branch with the entrance at the top. A big problem for many North American songbirds is that of parasitism by cowbirds. These birds lay their eggs in the nests of other bird species, particularly smaller ones. Once hatched, the young cowbirds tend to have a competitive advantage over their hosts' nestlings, so the cowbirds prosper and the hosts suffer. The break-up of large tracts of forest by roads and other development has enabled cowbirds to reach far more birds' nests than previously, as they are reluctant to venture more than ⅗ mile (1 km) away from the forest margin.

The fact that Baltimore orioles have hanging nests does not prevent cowbirds laying their own eggs in them, but unlike many species the orioles can recognize the alien eggs, and they get short shrift. The oriole stabs the cowbird eggs with its bill and throws them from the nest. This ability to deal with the parasite is doubtless one reason why the Baltimore oriole population has remained stable in most areas, unlike many other songbirds.

Caterpillar lovers

Baltimore orioles have also benefited from having a varied diet. Although they have a particular fondness for caterpillars taken from leaves, and will take even very hairy ones that other birds avoid, they also consume berries, nectar and fruits. One was seen to kill a ruby-throated hummingbird, presumably to eat, but this is exceptional behavior.

An immature male Baltimore oriole. While all females mate, even at 1 year of age, males are rarely successful at this age. As a result, the courtship song of unpaired young males may still be heard into late May.

BASS

THE MANY SPECIES of fish commonly known as bass are members of two entirely unrelated families, which has frequently given rise to confusion. One of these groups contains freshwater fish native to North American lakes and rivers. This family is the sunfish, or Centrarchidae, and it includes species such as the largemouth bass and the smallmouth bass. The other group consists mainly of marine fish found throughout the world's tropical and temperate waters, but it also includes a few freshwater species. This family is the sea bass, or Serranidae. Among its members are the common bass of the eastern North Atlantic, Mediterranean and Black Sea, and the giant sea bass, which is found on the western coastline of North and Central America.

Although unrelated, the fish in these two families share a number of characteristics. They are generally large and of athletic build, with prominent, spiny fins. All are voracious predators, hunting a wide range of smaller fish, as well as crustaceans and other aquatic animals. Several species of bass are important sport fish because they have delicious flesh and are strong, putting up a determined fight against anglers. However, overfishing is a growing problem and fishing quotas are enforced for some species.

Common bass

The common, or European, bass is at the root of all the confusion surrounding the names of these various fish. The name bass was originally taken overseas by emigrants from Britain, with the result that it has been applied, with or without some qualifying word, to a number of spiny-finned fish that live in a variety of both marine and freshwater habitats.

The fins of the common bass are so spiny that some of them can pierce human flesh, and the species also has spines on the gill-covers. Its large mouth is equally well armed. Besides the usual teeth in the jaws, the common bass has teeth on every surface of the mouth, including even the tongue. It is uniformly silver gray, with a slight tinge of pink at the bases of the fins. The common bass bears a superficial likeness to the Atlantic salmon, *Salmo salar*, and like that species its flesh is slightly pink.

Common bass feed largely on smaller fish, especially sardines, sprats and sand eels, and

supplement this diet with crustaceans, including prawns, shrimps and crabs. They move inshore in June and remain there until October, when they return out to sea. In the summer common bass may enter estuaries, particularly on the southern and western coasts of Britain, where they are caught by a bait towed behind a boat or by casting from the beach.

Spawning takes place either at sea or in brackish (slightly salty) water in estuaries, from May to the end of August. In the sea the eggs are just buoyant enough to float, whereas in fresh water they sink. They hatch in 6 days. The young fish, known as fry, grow rapidly, and by the fall are 4–6 inches (10.2–15.2 cm) long. They follow the adults in their migration out to sea.

Other species of sea bass

The giant sea bass frequents the shore, and is extremely popular with the anglers of the West Coast. It is a ruthless predator and can grow to a huge size. Another species of sea bass, the stone bass, is widely distributed in the Atlantic and Mediterranean. It has a habit of swimming beside any wreckage and among floating logs, planks and boxes, and also frequents wrecks lying on the seabed. Also known as the wreckfish, it regularly reaches weights of 100 pounds (45 kg). It is highly aggressive, often attacking and killing fish larger than itself.

Sea bass gather in large shoals off the western seaboard of North America and are one of the main targets of sport fishers.

A formidable hunter, the largemouth bass lies unseen in wait for passing prey.

BASS

CLASS	Osteichthyes
ORDER	Perciformes

FAMILY (1)	Sea bass, Serranidae
GENUS	Several, including *Morone, Stereolepis* and *Polyprion*
SPECIES	Common bass, *M. labrax*; giant sea bass, *S. gigas*; others

FAMILY (2)	Sunfish, Centrarchidae
GENUS	Several, including *Micropterus*
SPECIES	Largemouth bass, *M. salmoides*; smallmouth bass, *M. dolomieui*; others

WEIGHT
Sea bass: up to 880 lb. (400 kg).
Sunfish: up to 22 lb. (10 kg).

LENGTH
Sea bass: up to 9¾ ft. (3 m).
Sunfish: up to 31½ in. (80 cm).

DISTINCTIVE FEATURES
Robust body; prominent, spiny fins

DIET
Sea bass: fish and crustaceans. Sunfish: fish, amphibians and aquatic invertebrates.

BREEDING
Varies according to species

LIFE SPAN
Usually up to 10 years

HABITAT
Sea bass: marine habitats, some species in fresh water. Sunfish: lakes and rivers.

DISTRIBUTION
Sea bass: worldwide. Sunfish: North America.

STATUS
Common; often locally abundant

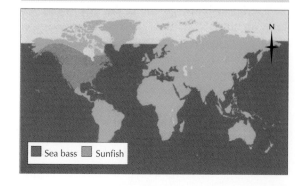

Sea bass   Sunfish

Largemouth bass

The best-known member of the North American sunfish family is the largemouth bass. As its name suggests, it differs from its close relative the smallmouth bass in having a larger mouth and body size. Its powerful jaws reach further back than the level of the eyes. The largemouth bass has the belligerence of the marine wreckfish, hunting a wide range of fish, tadpoles, worms, snails, crayfish and amphibians. Largemouth bass are also cannibalistic, often taking smaller individuals of their own species.

Unlike sea bass, the largemouth bass and its relatives in the sunfish family tend to build nests for their eggs. Breeding takes place in summer, when the male digs a shallow scrape in the bed of the lake or river. After spawning, the female leaves the male to guard the eggs. Once the eggs have hatched, he continues to guard the young fish, and will readily attack intruders in defense of the offspring. At first the fry feed on insect larvae and other small prey, but as they increase in size the young bass hunt a wider range of prey. The rate at which they grow is dependent on a variety of factors, including water temperature, but they typically reach sexual maturity within 3 years.

Upsetting the balance

The largemouth bass is highly rated by anglers, and its natural distribution has been artificially increased through introductions to other temperate regions, such as Japan and Europe. Such introductions tend to upset the delicate balance of local food chains. Native animals sometimes have no defenses against the alien predators and therefore suffer heavy predation, with devastating effects on their populations.

BEAVER

BEAVERS ARE THE second largest type of rodent, exceeded in size only by the capybara. Stout-bodied, with a large, thickset head and powerful limbs, a beaver can weigh as much as 85 pounds (38.5 kg). It has a blunt muzzle, small ears and five toes on each foot. Those on the front feet are strongly clawed for digging, manipulating food and carrying mud or stones for building. The hind feet are webbed, with two split claws for grooming the fur and spreading waterproofing oil. The beaver's body oil also provides insulation against the cold, as do its dense layer of underfur and its heavy outer coat of coarse hairs, known as guard hairs.

When a beaver submerges, its nostrils and ears are automatically closed by valves, and it can remain underwater for 15 minutes. The tail is used for steering and sometimes for propulsion through the water. It also forms a tripod with the hind legs when the beaver stands up to gnaw trees.

Pair of species

There are two species of beavers, which resemble each other closely in both appearance and habits. The Canadian beaver once occurred throughout North America, from northern Canada south to beyond the United States–Mexico border. Today it is found in severely depleted numbers from Canada into parts of the northern United States. The European beaver must at one time have been plentiful throughout Europe, but has long been extinct in England and survives in relatively small numbers elsewhere, mainly in Scandinavia, on rivers in European Russia and in the valleys of the rivers Elbe and Rhône. However, where it has been given protection, the species shows signs of increasing.

Waterside lodges

Beavers live in loose colonies comprising a family unit of four to eight, or sometimes up to 12, individuals. Each colony has a dominant breeding pair, which mates for life, and the young remain with their parents for 2 years. The colony's home is either a burrow dug into a bank, with an underwater entrance, or a lodge in a beaver pond, a pool made by damming a river until it overflows. The beavers make secondary dams upstream of the lodge to help control the flow of water and relieve some of the strain from the main dam, and usually add another secondary dam downstream of their pond. They obtain the branches they need for building by felling young trees, using their chisel-like incisors to chew chips out of the trunks until the trees fall. The beavers cut the trees up and carry the timber to the building site. If necessary, they dig canals to float logs to the pond.

Feats of engineering

The typical beaver lodge is a conical pile of logs, branches and sticks compacted with mud and stones. It may reach 36 feet (11 m) in width, and its upper section projects up to 2½ feet (2 m) above the water surface. From an engineering standpoint, the beaver lodge could hardly be improved. It has a central chamber just above water level, one or more escape tunnels leading from the chamber to underwater exits and well-insulated walls. A vertical chimney or ventilating shaft helps to regulate the internal temperature and provides air-conditioning.

Evidence gained from dissecting beaver lodges suggests that they are built by laying sticks more or less horizontally to create a pile. The beavers then chew their way inside to make the entrance tunnels and the central chamber. Finally they add a surface cladding of mud and stones, but stop short about 1 foot (30 cm) from the top of the pile so that the spaces between the sticks provide ventilation.

Beaver dams give way no more frequently than do artificial dams. This is because they are resilient, under constant surveillance, subject to immediate repair and supported by subsidiary

In beavers the jaw bone is unusually wide to accommodate the the large muscles they need for gnawing wood. This European beaver is stripping bark from a felled branch.

Beaver dams (above) and lodges provide excellent examples of a species manipulating its environment for its own benefit.

BEAVERS

CLASS	**Mammalia**
ORDER	**Rodentia**
FAMILY	**Castoridae**

GENUS AND SPECIES **Canadian beaver, *Castor canadensis*; European beaver, *C. fiber***

WEIGHT
Up to 85 lb. (38.5 kg), usually 25–55 lb. (11–25 kg)

LENGTH
Head and body: 24–36 in. (61–92 cm); tail: 10–18 in. (25.5–46 cm)

DISTINCTIVE FEATURES
Large incisor teeth; thickset head; stocky body; muscular limbs with strong claws; very broad, flattened and scaly tail

DIET
Bark, shoots and leaves of birch, aspen and willow; some aquatic vegetation

BREEDING
Age at first breeding: 1–3 years; breeding season: January–June; gestation period: 100–110 days; number of young: usually 2 to 4; breeding interval: 1 year

LIFE SPAN
Up to 24 years, usually 7–8 years

HABITAT
Lakes, rivers and streams in or near to deciduous woodland, preferably with birch or aspen trees

DISTRIBUTION
Canadian beaver: throughout North America. European beaver: patchy range in northern and central Europe and the former U.S.S.R.

STATUS
Canadian beaver: abundant in north of range, common to uncommon elsewhere. European beaver: rather uncommon.

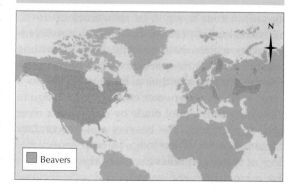

Beavers

dams. Main dams average 25 yards (23 m) in length, but in exceptional cases may stretch for up to 600 yards (550 m) from end to end.

Many people think that beavers are unusually intelligent, largely because their lodges and dams display such fine engineering work. In fact, beavers are instinctive builders following an inborn pattern of behavior. A colony of beavers that occupied an artificial dam made of concrete and stone on a small lake in New York State set about repairing the dam with branches and mud even although it was already fully effective and there was no chance of a leak.

High-fiber diet

Beavers eat the bark, sapwood, shoots and leaves of twigs and small branches, including those cut during building work. They prefer aspen and willow, but also feed on birch and a range of other deciduous trees. The wood that beavers eat is remarkably nutritious. This is because food made in the leaves of a tree is carried in the sap just below the bark, where most of the tree cells that are alive and growing—and therefore contain protein—are also concentrated.

Beavers often store surplus twigs and branches around the base of their lodge. These have always been regarded as being for the winter use of all members of the colony but recent research has shown that the bulk of these are eaten by the young and that older beavers live on their fat and eat little during winter.

Life at the lodge

Beavers are monogamous, and the mating season lasts from January to February. The female gives birth to a litter of two to four young, or sometimes more, in April, May or early June. The young, or kits, have a coat of soft fur and open eyes. At birth each weighs about ½–1 pounds (225–450 g) and is 15 inches (38 cm) long, including 3½ inches (9 cm) of tail. Kits start to find and eat solid food at 1 month, but are not weaned until 6 weeks old. They remain with their parents for about 2 years, becoming sexually mature at 1–3 years of age.

As with all rodents, beavers are hunted by many predators of approximately their own weight or more. Their enemies include the wolverine, lynx, coyote, gray wolf, bobcat, puma and brown bear. A beaver's alarm signal when a predator is in sight is to bring the tail over the back then smack it down with such force on the water that the sound can be heard up to ½ miles (0.8 km) away. Beavers can make fearsome opponents when cornered, turning in their tracks to face the enemy, with the hair on their head and neck standing on end.

Decline of the European beaver

European beavers were on the way to extinction in the 19th century as a result of centuries of hunting by humans. Their extermination was due partly to their valuable fur—beaver pelts were up to six times as valuable as marten, otter, wolf and fox pelts—but particularly to slaughter for the glandular secretion with which beavers mark their territories. This secretion, known as castoreum, enjoyed a vogue as a cure-all in the 16th and 17th centuries. Scientific analysis has shown castoreum to contain salicylic acid, one of the ingredients of aspirin.

Beavers were once common in Switzerland, as shown by the place-names Biberach, Bibersee and Biberstein (*Biber* is German for beaver). Their former presence in England, too, is commemorated by such place-names as Beverley, Beverege, Bevercotes and Beversbrook. The species seems to have survived in Britain until the mid-16th century. At this time Henry IV of France, impressed by the demand for beaver

pelts for hats, trimmings, fur linings and leather for shoes, tried to increase the economic strength of his state by sending troops to Newfoundland and Nova Scotia. In due course the English gained control of this resource, largely through the Hudson Bay Trading Company. It was the search for more furs that led to new areas of Canada being explored by Europeans.

Profit or protection?

The Hudson Bay Trading Company was formed in 1670, and such was the growth of its trade that from 1853 to 1877 it marketed nearly 3 million beaver pelts. Whereas Native Americans killed only mature animals, so that their hunting had little impact on beaver populations, the new trappers killed beavers indiscriminately. Within 150 years the Canadian beaver had been exterminated in the coastal regions of the eastern states, and seriously reduced elsewhere. As more of the North American continent was opened up, so the trade continued unabated, with results similar to those seen in the eastern states.

Beavers were not always killed for profit. At times they became a nuisance by making inroads on timber, invading settled areas, damaging riverbanks and feeding on corn. Nevertheless, the species received legal protection in Maine as early as 1866. By the early 20th century its numbers had increased to such an extent that population controls had to be imposed again. Many beaver conservation initiatives have since been undertaken by landowners, public bodies and state and federal governments. This is because the authorities realized that beaver ponds and dams on the headwaters of mountain streams hold back large quantities of water during the dangerous flood season and equalize the water flow so that during the dry seasons the water supply is greatly increased in the valleys.

A Canadian beaver feeding on willow twigs in the relative safety of its pond.

BISON

BISON ARE LARGE AND oxlike, the adults weighing up to 2,200 pounds (1,000 kg). The largest bison stand 6 feet (1.8 m) at the shoulder, which is raised in a distinct hump, giving a very hunchbacked appearance. The hair on head, neck, shoulders and forelegs is long and shaggy. The broad forehead is flanked by two short, curving horns in both sexes.

The two species of bison extant today are the European bison, *Bison bonasus*, or wisent, and the American bison, *B. bison*, often incorrectly called the buffalo. The latter name strictly belongs to the Cape buffalo of Africa. The European bison has a shorter coat, larger, more curved horns and larger hindquarters than its American relative. There are two subspecies of American bison. The plains bison, *B. b. bison*, of the United States, is smaller and lighter in color than the wood bison, *B. b. athabascae*, of Canada, but its head and shoulders are more stocky. Of the two, the wood bison resembles the European bison more closely.

Divergence of the bison

Bison probably once roamed across Europe, Asia and North America. This theory is supported by the similarity between the wood bison and the European bison, both of which live in woodlands. The European bison is now thought to have crossed into Asia and Europe from North America at the end of the Ice Age, traveling across what is now the Bering Strait but was once a land bridge. This view is contrary to the common assumption that the American species is a descendant of the European species.

Senseless slaughter

Some 50 million bison once roamed North America but by 1889 a mere 540 were left. The massacre of the North American bison is matched by the extinction of the passenger pigeon, *Ectopistes migratorius*, also of North America. Both once appeared to exist in limitless numbers but both succumbed to organized slaughter backed by modern techniques.

When Europeans first settled in North America, bison ranged from northern Canada as far south as the border of Mexico and across the continent east from the Rocky Mountains. The bison were apparently increasing in numbers and it is thought that they would have spread through the passes of the Rockies and onto the plains of the Pacific coast. However, with the coming of Europeans, they were hunted so relentlessly that they nearly became extinct.

Bison had always played a vital part in the economy of Native Americans, but relatively few bison were killed. Native Americans became more efficient bison hunters after the introduction of horses by the Spanish conquistadors. Later, European settlers spread across the plains, killing

Today most North American bison are confined to national parks. This bull is one of the 1,500 to 2,000 bison that live in Yellowstone National Park, Wyoming.

BISON

CLASS	**Mammalia**
ORDER	**Artiodactyla**
FAMILY	**Bovidae**

GENUS AND SPECIES   **American bison, *Bison bison*; European bison, *B. bonasus***

ALTERNATIVE NAMES
B. bison bison: plains bison; B. b. athabascae: wood bison; B. bonasus: wisent

WEIGHT
770–2,200 lb. (350–1,000 kg)

LENGTH
Head and body: 83–138 in. (2.1–3.5 m); shoulder height: 59–79 in. (1.5–2 m)

DISTINCTIVE FEATURES
Hunched back; shaggy hair on neck, shoulders and forelegs; short, curved horns

DIET
Grasses, herbs, bark, shoots and acorns

BREEDING
Age at first breeding: 2–4 years; breeding season: July–September; number of young: 1; gestation period: 285 days (American bison), 260–270 days (European bison); breeding interval: 1–2 years

LIFE SPAN
Up to 40 years

HABITAT
American bison: prairie, mountains and forest. European bison: woods and grassland.

DISTRIBUTION
American bison: mainly western and central North America. European bison: Poland, Lithuania, Belarus and European Russia.

STATUS
American bison: population at least 100,000. European bison: endangered; population: 2,700.

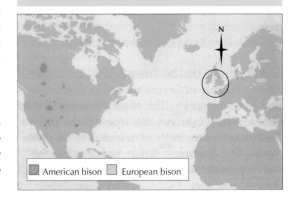

American bison ▮ European bison ▯

Bison calves stay with their mother for 2–3 years. They are born in late spring and soon develop the thick coat that will protect them in the coming winter.

bison for meat and hides, and large-scale hunts were organized to get meat for railroad construction workers. The railroads opened up a new market in the East for bison hides and tongues, while bison bones were ground to make fertilizer for the corn-growing prairies.

Bison were also killed for sport. Daily bags of 50 or 60 seem to have been common, and totals of more than 100 bison shot by a single hunter in one day were claimed. The carcasses were usually left to rot, without any meat or a single hide being collected. The effect of this slaughter is not mitigated by the fact that the spread of agriculture would eventually have decimated the herds by taking away their grazing lands.

The European bison also suffered a catastrophic fall in numbers, but its decline occurred over a period of centuries. The principal cause of its demise was the felling of forests in which it roamed. The last truly wild European bison lived in the Bialowieza Forest, Poland, but were devastated in World War I and during the upheavals that followed. Only about 30 bison survived, all of which were in zoos. Careful management enabled numbers of European bison to rise again, reaching 360 in 1959, including a herd in a reserve established in Bialowieza. The population stood at 790 to 800 in 1965, and there are now 2,700 European bison.

Today the future of the North American bison is also more secure. Indeed, the population of the plains bison is sufficiently healthy to allow hunting under license. In Canada the last wood bison are fully protected in a reserve in Alberta, the Wood Buffalo National Park.

Smaller herds

Bison live in herds, in the past numbering thousands of individuals but now much smaller. The basic social grouping comprises a bull together with a cow and her offspring. The cow is the leader of family groups such as this.

North American bison feed mainly on grasses and herbs, making long seasonal migrations to find the best grazing areas, which vary with the seasons. They supplement this diet with the bark and shoots of different trees. Bark is more important to European bison, in particular that of sallow, poplar and aspen trees. The shoots of young evergreens are also sometimes browsed, and in the fall acorns are a favorite food. Both species of bison are fond of wallowing in mud and rubbing themselves against trees and boulders.

Battles for dominance

Mating takes place from July to September, when the males in a herd fight one another. The more successful males tend a female for several days during estrus, the period in which she is receptive, and prevent other males from approaching closer than 26 feet (8 m). Successful males are therefore able to almost monopolize sexual activity through consorting with females.

Bison have a gestation period of about 9 months, the calves being born from April to June. The cow leaves the herd to drop her calf and returns when it is able to walk. The entire herd assists in the defense of calves against their only natural enemy, the gray wolf. The calves are nursed for a year and stay with their mothers until they are sexually mature at 2–3 years.

Relationship with humans

Bison were essential to many Native American tribes. The animals provided meat, both fresh and dried for later use; hides, for clothing, bedding, tents and canoes; dung, for fuel; and bones and sinews, for weapons, tools and utensils. The bison appeared in Native American religions as a powerful figure to be worshiped.

Native Americans had various rituals that were thought to ensure a plentiful supply of bison, for if the bison did not arrive on their annual migration the people would face a lean time. Native Americans believed that "buffalo" sprang up every year, and that it was necessary to lure them to hunting grounds. Bison skulls were considered to be extremely useful for this purpose, and were piled up or displayed in a prominent place because it was thought that the bison would seek out their "white-faced" companions. In other rites, oracles were consulted to find out where the bison were. The medicine men performing these services acquired great merit. They continued their ceremonies and incantations until the bison arrived, an inevitable event if the Native Americans were waiting on a regular migration route.

There came a time when the bison did fail to arrive. By the late 19th century Europeans had contrived virtually to wipe out North America's vast bison herds and the Native Americans starved as a result. To Native Americans, wanton killing of bison was a serious crime punishable by death. The loss of their livelihood combined with the loss of their territory caused them to resort to an armed struggle. Some enlightened Europeans sought to safeguard both the Native Americans and the herds of bison on which they depended, but others claimed that the extermination of bison was the only way of "civilizing" Native Americans.

Huge herds of North American bison are a thing of the past, and compact family units are now the norm.

BOBCAT

AMONG THE VARIOUS species of cats found in the United States, including the puma and lynx, the bobcat is relatively small and comparable to the European wildcat. Bobcats weigh 9–34 pounds (4–15 kg) on average, though there is one record of a very large individual weighing 40 pounds (18 kg). The body is 26–41 inches (65–105 cm) long, with the short, thick tail accounting for about 6 inches (15 cm). The tail's stubbiness gives the bobcat its name, although the name probably also refers to the species' lolloping gait, which is reminiscent of a rabbit.

Body coloration varies considerably between the different races of bobcats, and is often linked with habitat. In general, the coat is a shade of brown spotted with gray or white, but buff-colored bobcats are common in desert country, and those from forest regions tend to be darker. The ears are tipped with pointed tufts of hair. Experiments suggest that these tufts improve the efficiency of the bobcat's ear in collecting sounds and that captive bobcats with clipped ear tufts do not respond so readily to sounds.

The bobcat is distinguishable from the closely related lynx by its lighter build, proportionately shorter legs, shorter tail and less prominent ear tufts. Lynx favor thick coniferous forest and tundra, whereas bobcats have less specialized habitat preferences. Bobcats occur in a wide variety of landscapes, including thick forest, open woodland, rocky deserts, scrub and even swamps.

Natural loners

Bobcats are solitary animals that hunt mainly at night, and therefore they are not often seen. The size of their home range varies with the abundance of food and with their gender. Females maintain exclusive home ranges, and keep out neighboring females. The home ranges of male bobcats overlap. Males roam areas of 2½–40 square miles (6–105 sq km) while females range over 3½–17 square miles (9–45 sq km).

Bobcats leave several indications of their presence. The trails regularly used by bobcats can be traced, not only by footprints in mud, soft earth and snow but also by scratches on tree trunks where the cats have stretched and sharpened their claws just as domestic cats do. They also have favorite spots for defecating and urinating, covering their feces and urine by scratching a mound of earth over them.

Bobcats are found in most areas of the United States, except for the Ohio Valley and the Upper Mississippi Valley. They are also found in southern Canada and in northern Mexico. The combination of small size, retiring habits and a varied diet has enabled bobcats to adapt to the spread of agriculture much more successfully than lynx. Indeed, farming can sometimes benefit bobcats by providing a ready supply of food in the form of calves and lambs.

Versatile hunter

The wide range of food taken by bobcats is usually cited as a major reason for their continued abundance in areas where the face of the countryside has been greatly changed.

The bobcat is distributed widely across the United States but, as a wary night hunter, is rarely seen.

Spots and flecks on the bobcat's coat break up its outline, helping it sneak up on prey unseen.

BOBCAT

CLASS	**Mammalia**
ORDER	**Carnivora**
FAMILY	**Felidae**
GENUS AND SPECIES	***Felis rufus***

WEIGHT
9–34 lb. (4–15 kg)

LENGTH
Head and body: 26–41 in. (65–105 cm); shoulder height: 18–20 in. (45–50 cm)

DISTINCTIVE FEATURES
Short, stubby tail; black, tufted ears; coat variable, but usually has dark flecks

DIET
Mainly rabbits, rodents, bats and birds; also livestock, deer, snakes, insects and fruits

BREEDING
Age at first breeding: 2 years; breeding season: November–August; number of young: usually 2; gestation period: 60–70 days; breeding interval: usually 1 year

LIFE SPAN
Up to 32 years

HABITAT
Forests, mountains, semideserts and brushland; occasionally also swamps

DISTRIBUTION
Southern Canada south through most of U.S. to Mexico

STATUS
Fairly common; population: up to 1 million

Rabbits, jack rabbits and rodents, such as deer mice, wood rats and squirrels, form the bulk of a bobcat's diet. Grouse, quail and other ground-dwelling birds are also eaten. Occasional food items include snakes, skunks, opossums, bats, grasshoppers and, very rarely, fruits.

Bobcats attack porcupines when there is a shortage of other food and porcupine quills have been found in bobcat feces, but the cats usually emerge second best in such an encounter. Bobcats with quills in their paws and mouths are likely to die of starvation, as a mouthful of quills makes eating impossible.

Bobcats are strong for their size and will attack and kill adult pronghorn antelope, deer, and livestock. The bobcat stalks its prey before leaping onto the animal's back, biting at the base of the victim's skull and tearing with its claws.

Protected at last

Bobcats begin breeding at 2 years of age. Their young, or kits, may be born during any month of the year, but usually in late February or March. Twins are usual, although litters range in size from one to six kits and occasionally a bobcat will have two litters a year. The kits are blind for their first week. Breeding dens are located in caves, among rocks, under logs or even under barns and sheds. Females defend their young vigorously and fathers are kept well away until the kits are weaned, at which point they help the females to bring food for the young.

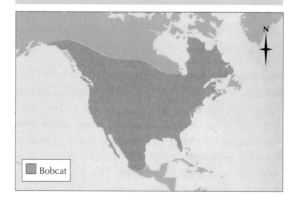

Bobcat

Young bobcats fall prey to foxes and great horned owls, but adults have only one natural predator, the puma. Humans have long hunted bobcats for their soft fur, for sport and because they kill livestock. However, 11 U.S. states have granted the species complete legal protection.

BROWN BEAR

The brown bear was formerly widespread throughout Europe but is today found only in remote forests on the continent. This bear was photographed in Finland.

THE BROWN BEAR IS a heavily built member of the order Carnivora. It is practically tailless, with broad, flat feet, each of which has five toes armed with nonretractile claws. The brown bear's eyesight is relatively poor, but its smell and hearing are both acute. The snout is well developed, with a wet nose, or rhinarium, which heightens its sense of smell. The usual coat color is a shade of brown, but bears found in central Asia are reddish and those that occur in western China and Tibet have blackish brown hairs frosted with slate gray.

It is a matter of opinion whether there are several species of brown bears distributed over Europe, Asia and North America, or whether there is only one. Half a dozen species, as well as many subspecies, have been recognized by various authorities in the past. This is now accepted as being too many, given that all brown

bears have a similar habitat, behavior and life history, and that their skeletons and general anatomy are not significantly different. Today the consensus is that the grizzly bear and the other brown bears of North America, such as the giant Kodiak bear of Alaska and northern Canada, belong to the same species as the smaller brown bears found in Europe, the former Soviet Union, the Middle East and Central Asia.

Regional variation

The historical list of species and subspecies of brown bears was based mainly on differences in coat color and size. Body coloration is variable in many mammals, however, and so size was considered more important. The Kenai and Kodiak bears can weigh as much as 1,700 pounds (770 kg), whereas Siberian brown bears weigh 330–550 pounds (150–250 kg) and the grizzly

BROWN BEAR

CLASS	**Mammalia**
ORDER	**Carnivora**
FAMILY	**Ursidae**
GENUS AND SPECIES	***Ursus arctos***

ALTERNATIVE NAMES
Grizzly bear (*U. a. horribilis*); Kodiak bear
(*U. a. middendorffi*); European brown bear
(*U. a. arctos*); Tibetan brown bear
(*U. a. pruinosus*)

WEIGHT
Up to 1,700 lb. (770 kg)

LENGTH
Head and body: 5⅔–9⅕ ft. (1.7–2.8 m);
shoulder height: 3–5 ft. (0.9–1.5 m);
tail: 2–8 in. (6–21 cm)

DISTINCTIVE FEATURES
Prominent shoulder hump; long fur and claws

DIET
Mainly grasses, roots, berries, fish, insects,
honey, mammals and carrion

BREEDING
Age at first breeding: 4–6 years or over;
breeding season: May–July; number of
young: usually 2; gestation period: 180–270
days; breeding interval: 2–4 years

LIFE SPAN
Up to 50 years in captivity

HABITAT
Tundra, alpine meadows, coasts, coniferous
forest (Siberia), montane woodland (Europe)

DISTRIBUTION
Western North America; Scandinavia east
to easternmost Asia and Japan; mountains
of Iberia, central Europe and Balkans

STATUS
Numbers vary greatly according to area;
population: 100,000, Eurasia; 50,000,
Canada and Alaska; 1,000, rest of U.S.

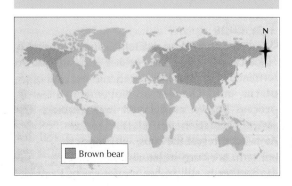

Brown bear

bears of Yellowstone National Park weigh only
225–715 pounds (100–325 kg). In 1904 J. G.
Millais, naturalist and author, wrote that "no
terrestrial mammal varies so greatly, both in size
and pelage [coat coloration], as this animal."

*Although cubs and
young bears can climb
trees with relative ease,
adults do not often
attempt such a feat.*

Loners
Brown bears live in forests, the northern tundra
and wild, mountainous country. They wander
singly or in family parties over home ranges that
have an average radius of 20 miles (32 km),
although individuals may stray beyond their
usual range. Brown bears normally walk on all
fours, at times standing erect and shuffling for
a few paces. Young bears climb trees well,

although slowly and deliberately, but adults rarely do so. Bears feed intensively during the summer and fall, storing fat in their bodies. This enables them to sleep for most of the winter in dens, located among rocks and inside hollow trees, or dug into hillsides.

Brown bears are not normally aggressive to humans except under extreme provocation, when they are injured, or when a person comes between a female and her cub. The strength of brown bears is demonstrated by the fact that a grizzly bear can fell an American bison larger than itself with one blow of its paw, breaking its neck. The bear is also strong enough to drag away the carcass.

Omnivorous carnivores

Despite the fact that brown bears are classified in the order Carnivora, or flesh-eaters, their diet varies greatly with the individual. Some are wholly vegetarian, others wholly flesh-eating, but most eat both plant and animal foods.

The diet of brown bears typically consists of berries, fruits, roots, insects and other small animals, honey and the grubs of wild bees. Fish may be taken, flipped from the shallows onto the bank with the forepaws, or seized in the water, as is the case in the salmon runs of western North America. Sometimes young deer are killed and eaten, and larger mammals, such as bison and moose, are also taken. Occasionally brown bears will kill livestock and even the smaller American black bears.

Tiny cubs

Brown bears lead an existence similar to that of black bears. Mating takes place in June, but the fertilized egg is not implanted into the wall of the uterus until October or November, a bodily process known as delayed implantation. The overall gestation period is therefore 180–266 days. As a result the cubs, which normally number two, are born in January or February, while the mother is still in her winter sleep. Each cub weighs 1–1½ pounds (450–680 g) at birth and is 8 inches (20 cm) long, almost hairless, blind and toothless.

Brown bear cubs are tiny compared with the size of adult females, and an ancient belief was that they were born shapeless and that the mother licked them into shape, hence the well-known saying. The reference here is to the licking the mother gives each cub after birth to clean them of the birth fluids, as in most true mammals. The mother rouses herself from her sleep to do so. A brown bear cub weighs 54 pounds (24 kg) when a year old, and will stay with its mother until at least that age. Females usually breed at 4–6 years of age, and individual bears have been known to live for up to 50 years.

Shrinking range

In the Old World brown bears once ranged in considerable numbers from Britain east to Japan, and as far south as the Mediterranean, the Himalayas and northeastern Africa. By the 11th century the last bear had been killed in Britain and today, in Europe, the surviving descendants are largely confined to inaccessible forests in the Pyrenees, the Swiss Alps, the Carpathian mountains, the Balkans and areas of Scandinavia. Brown bears are more numerous in some regions of Asia, particularly parts of the former Soviet Union, but even there numbers are steadily declining. The North African brown bear population became extinct in the 19th century.

It is evident that persecution, particularly hunting, radically reduces the maximum sizes reached in a species, especially when the hunters' ambition is to collect record trophies. Brown bears were killed for their flesh and their fat, and because their tempers were unpredictable. Above all, however, their shaggy coats were coveted prizes for hunters. Today C.I.T.E.S. (Convention on International Trade in Endangered Species of Wild Flora and Fauna) lists all U.S. populations of *Ursus arctos* as threatened, and the Mexican brown bear (*U. a. nelsonii*), Tibetan brown bear (*U. a. pruinosus*) and Italian populations of *U. arctos* as endangered. The I.U.C.N. (World Conservation Union) classifies *U. a. nelsonii* as extinct.

The cave bear

Bones of the now-extinct cave bear, *U. spelaeus*, have been found in caves throughout western Europe. This species denned in caves during the winter and females may also have given birth in

caves. The cave bear was primarily herbivorous, although it would occasionally have eaten meat; it had a large head and massive canine teeth. The cave bear also possessed powerful front legs and paws and large, broad claws, which suggests that it dug for much of its food. The root-beds of plants buried in deep glacial silt must have formed a large part of its diet.

When the large glaciers that covered much of western Europe melted, the cave bear began to reduce in size. It may have become smaller because of a decrease in the amount of root-beds due to low glacial silt production. The growing populations of brown bears in Europe during the late Pleistocene (the last ice age) may also have competed with cave bears for food resources, driving the species to eventual extinction.

The rich food supplies and favorable climate around Kodiak Island, Alaska, have enabled the Kodiak brown bear to attain the largest size and weight of the species.

BULLFROG

The bullfrog favors marshes, ponds and slow-flowing rivers. It rarely moves far from water except during unusually wet weather.

THE BULLFROG IS ONE of the largest species of North American true frogs and may grow up to 8 inches (20 cm) long. The tadpoles are the largest in North America, commonly reaching a size of 1½–3½ inches (4–9 cm). The bullfrog is named for its deep, resonant croak. It is native to the United States, and is found east of the Rockies, and on the northern borders of Mexico. The species has also been introduced to the western states, as well as to Canada, Hawaii, Mexico, Cuba, Jamaica, Italy and Japan. The bullfrog has flourished in Europe, often at the expense of the native wildlife.

The North American bullfrog is similar in appearance to the much smaller edible frog of Europe; its skin is usually smooth but sometimes it is covered with small tubercles. On its upperparts the frog is usually greenish to black, sometimes with dark spots, while the underparts are whitish with tinges of yellow. The females are more highly spotted than the males and are browner in color; males have a yellower throat than females. It is also possible to distinguish the sexes by comparing the size of the eye and the eardrum, which is exposed. In females they are equal; in males the eardrum is larger than the eye.

Bullfrogs are usually found in or near water, but venture further afield during very wet weather. They prefer to live near ponds, marshes and slow-flowing streams, and may be found lying along the water's edge under the shade of shrubs and reeds. In winter they hibernate near water, under logs and stones or in holes on the banks. The duration of their hibernation is dependent on the climate. Bullfrogs are often the first amphibians in an area to retire at the approach of winter and the last to emerge in the spring. In the northern parts of their range bullfrogs usually emerge around the middle of May, but in Texas, for example, they may emerge in February in mild weather. In the southern areas of their range they may not hibernate at all.

Voracious appetite

The bullfrog feeds mainly on insects, earthworms, spiders, crayfish and snails. Many kinds of insects are caught, including grasshoppers, beetles, flies, wasps and bees. The bullfrog captures its prey by lying in wait and then leaping forward as its victim passes. Its tongue is rapidly extended by muscular contraction and wraps around the prey. The frog then submerges to swallow its victim. A voracious carnivore, the bullfrog takes active adult insects as well as the slow-moving larvae and immobile pupae.

The bullfrog also takes larger prey, including other frogs, fish, small terrapins, newly hatched alligators, turtles and small mammals, such as mice and shrews. Small garter snakes and even venomous coral snakes are eaten. There is one recorded case of a coral snake measuring 17 inches (43 cm) being taken by a bullfrog. The bullfrog also captures small birds, especially ducklings. Even swallows, flying low over the water, are not safe from the bullfrog's voracious appetite and considerable

BULLFROG

CLASS	**Amphibia**
ORDER	**Anura**
FAMILY	**Ranidae**
GENUS AND SPECIES	***Rana catesbeiana***

ALTERNATIVE NAMES
American bullfrog; jug o' rum (archaic)

WEIGHT
2–9 oz. (50–250 g)

LENGTH
3½–8 in. (9–20 cm)

DISTINCTIVE FEATURES
Large size; usually greenish olive, paler below; female browner than male

DIET
Mainly insects, earthworms, snails, spiders and aquatic animals, including tadpoles and crayfish; larger prey includes turtles, snakes, small mammals, birds and other frogs

BREEDING
Age at first breeding: 2–3 years (male), 3 years (female); breeding season: February–August, earliest in south; number of eggs: up to 25,000; hatching period: about 7 days; larval period: up to 2 years; breeding interval: 1 or 2 clutches per year

LIFE SPAN
Up to 16 years in captivity

HABITAT
Fresh water with dense aquatic vegetation, often in prairies, chaparral, farmland and woodland

DISTRIBUTION
U.S. east of Rocky Mountains. Introduced to western U.S. and Canada, Hawaii, Mexico, Cuba, Jamaica, Italy and Japan.

STATUS
Common

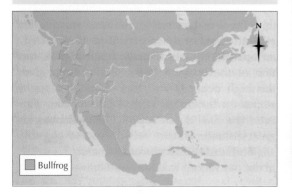

Bullfrog

leaping ability; adult bullfrogs can leap over 3 feet (0.9 m). This indicates that the bullfrog is both an opportunistic feeder and a powerful predator.

Unusual mating call

When the water temperature reaches about 70° F (21° C), mating takes place. This condition arises about February in the south of the bullfrog's range, and in June or July in the northern parts. At night the males move out from the banks to call, while the females stay inshore. They join the males only when their eggs are ripe.

The bullfrog utters a distinctive hollow, booming call during the mating season. The sound is made three or four times within a few seconds and repeated after an interval of about 5 minutes. The call is produced by air being passed back and forth along the bullfrog's windpipe, from lungs to mouth, with the nostrils closed. Some air enters the air sacs in the floor of the mouth which swell out like balloons and act as resonators, amplifying the sound so that the noise can be heard ½ mile (0.8 km) away. The bullfrog's call sounds similar to the words "jug o' rum" enunciated in a gruff tone, and gave rise to one of the bullfrog's traditional names.

After mating the female bullfrog lays 10,000 to 25,000 eggs, which float in a film on the surface of the water among water plants. The size of the clutch depends on the size of the female. Including its envelope of jelly, each egg is just over ½ inch (1.5 cm) in diameter. It is black above and white below. The eggs usually hatch within a week of being laid. If the temperature is low, however, they may take over 2 years to metamorphose into an adult frog, by which time they are 2–3 inches (5–8 cm) long. The young bullfrogs feed on algae and decaying vegetation, though they occasionally take small pond animals. Approximately 2 years later the young are almost fully grown and are ready to breed.

It is possible to distinguish male and female bullfrogs by their coloring. The females are browner and more highly spotted than the males.

BURROWING OWL

THE BURROWING OWL stands 9 inches (23 cm) high, about the same size as the little owl, *Athene noctua*, of Europe and Asia. The upperparts are brown with white markings, while the underparts are off-white and bear darker marks. It is largely a terrestrial creature, perching and hunting on the ground, and accordingly has a very short tail and proportionately long legs compared to the larger forest owls, such as the screech owl, *Otus asio*, of North America. The burrowing owl's habit of bobbing up and down is characteristic of the species. As its name implies, it nests in holes in the ground rather than in trees. These holes are sometimes excavated by the owls themselves but are often adapted from dens abandoned by burrowing mammals.

Threatened by agriculture

At one time the burrowing owl was common on the plains and prairies of North America, but the steady encroachment of agriculture has greatly restricted the range of the species. Plowing ruined the owls' burrows, and many owls were shot because of the chance that horses and cattle might break their legs in the holes. Families of burrowing owls have also been killed indiscriminately by the poison gas used against ground squirrels. However, providing that the terrain is not altered too greatly, the burrowing owl is under no real threat. Farmers have realized that, like other species of owl, it is mainly beneficial to humans because it preys on pests such as mice and insects.

The burrowing owl ranges from the Pacific coast of North America east to Minnesota and Louisiana. It breeds as far north as British Columbia and Manitoba and south to Tierra del Fuego, though it does not occur in the forests of the Amazon Basin. To the east it is found in Florida and on some of the Caribbean islands. In winter some burrowing owls migrate from the northern parts of the range and the Florida population disappears outside the breeding season.

Hunts by day

Like the little owl of Eurasia, the burrowing owl is more diurnal in its habits than most owls. Its vision is not believed to be as sharp as that of other owl species. The outcome of experiments on the keenness of sight in owls showed that whereas the barn owl, *Tyto alba*, could locate mice in light intensities equivalent to one candle located nearly 2,000 feet (610 m) away,

The burrowing owl's long legs and short tail are adaptations to its ground-dwelling lifestyle.

The burrowing owl's white and brown markings break up its outline, providing excellent camouflage.

BURROWING OWL

CLASS	**Aves**
ORDER	**Strigiformes**
FAMILY	**Strigidae**
GENUS AND SPECIES	***Athene cunicularia***

LENGTH
Head to tail: 9–10 in. (23–25 cm); wingspan: 19½–22½ in. (50–57 cm)

DISTINCTIVE FEATURES
Long legs; short tail; pale brown facial disc with prominent white eyebrows; sandy-brown above with white markings

DIET
Mainly small mammals including rodents, ground squirrels and young prairie dogs, and invertebrates such as large spiders, beetles and grasshoppers; large numbers of newly fledged birds in breeding season; also lizards, snakes and scorpions

BREEDING
Age at first breeding: 1 year; breeding season: most of year, depending on region; number of eggs: 7 to 9; incubation period: 28 days; fledging period: not known; breeding interval: 1 year

LIFE SPAN
Usually up to 9 years

HABITAT
Arid and semiarid open country including prairies, rough grassland and golf courses

DISTRIBUTION
Western North America and Florida south through parts of Central America and Caribbean to southern South America as far as Tierra del Fuego. Absent from much of Amazon Basin.

STATUS
Locally common; has declined in many agricultural areas

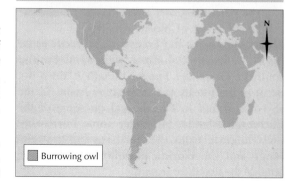

Burrowing owl

burrowing owls found it difficult to locate prey in far greater light intensities. Their sensitivity to light is in fact about the same as that of humans.

Hunting does take place at night, but is mainly carried out during the day. Burrowing owls pounce on prey, burying their talons into the victim's back. Prey species include mice, sage rats and other small rats, ground squirrels, young cottontail rabbits, chipmunks and even bats. Insects represent a large proportion of the diet, especially large beetles and grasshoppers, which are caught in the air in the talons. Large numbers of newly fledged birds, especially larks, are taken during the breeding season, but few other birds are eaten at other times. Other animals occasionally feature in the diet, and the remains of scorpions and centipedes are sometimes found near burrows. Crayfish are also eaten by burrowing owls living near water, which may simply take advantage of crayfish cast up on the banks or exposed by a drought.

Empty burrows taken over
Burrowing owls dig holes by scraping with their talons, but also frequently take advantage of burrows made by a wide variety of other animals. The holes of prairie dogs, groundhogs, American badgers, armadillos, foxes, skunks and many other burrowing creatures are taken over, and enlarged if necessary.

The nesting chamber, lined with grass, feathers, the stalks of weeds and other materials, is usually made at the end of a tunnel about

5 feet (1.5 m) long. The tunnel is about 5 inches (13 cm) wide and often turns sharply along its length to help conceal the eggs and chicks.

Both parents incubate the eggs, for about a month. The young leave the nest before they can fly and roost near the entrance, rushing forward whenever a parent arrives with food. When not hunting, the parents stand guard on a favorite mound or low perch, their *cack-cack-cack-cack* alarm call sending the chicks running back into the nest at times of danger. This call, together with the cooing notes used in courting, has led the burrowing owl to be nicknamed the cuckoobird in the Caribbean and South America.

The eggs of burrowing owls are glossier than those of most owls and along with the chicks are particularly vulnerable to predators. Skunks, opossums and snakes, and probably domestic cats, destroy the nests of burrowing owls, unless the owners can drive them away. In the Caribbean, introduced mongooses have wiped out the burrowing owls in Antigua, Nevis, St. Kitts and Marie Galante. When disturbed in the burrow, the young get a certain measure of safety by their rattling hiss, which is very similar to that of a rattlesnake. Burrowing owls formerly bred in colonies but since the end of the 19th century these have largely disappeared. Only in suitable terrain where there is abundant food is it possible to find 10 or more pairs nesting within 3 acres (1 ha).

Unlikely cohabitants

It was once thought that burrowing owls shared holes with viscachas and ground squirrels, or with reptiles such as rattlesnakes and hognose snakes. The burrowing owls were believed to act as sentries, uttering their alarm calls when danger threatened. The snakes were thought to deter or kill any enemy and, it was assumed, the ground squirrels and other rodents provided company and warmth and constructed burrows. However, no scientific observations support these tales. At least a century ago, it was pointed out that burrowing owls move into burrows after the rodent owners have abandoned them. Furthermore, the owls prey on rodents, especially the young. Snakes certainly seek holes and crevices to hide in, but will readily eat the broods of any birds or mammals they may find there.

Prairie and desert are the chief habitats of the burrowing owl. The nesting holes are often adapted from dens abandoned by burrowing mammals.

CARDINAL

A FAMILIAR GARDEN SONGBIRD of North America, the northern cardinal is also known as the red bird. Apart from a black "bib," the male plumage is a mixture of several shades of red, from deep scarlet to an intense reddish orange. The female's plumage is composed of a mixture of pinkish red and tinges of brown. Cardinals are finches, about 8⅔ inches (22 cm) long, with a stout bill which is nearly conical in shape, a conspicuous crest in both sexes and short, rounded wings.

The range of the northern cardinal extends from the temperate zone of the United States south to Mexico and Central America. It has also been introduced to southwestern California, Bermuda and Hawaii. In the latter, it breeds all year round and has become a pest because of the damage it does to fruit. Cardinals are also spreading unaided northward through the United States and are now a fairly common resident around New York and in parts of southern Canada. This spread may, at least in part, be due to the popularity of keeping bird feeders to attract birds into gardens and to provide them with a plentiful source of food in winter. Some cardinals migrate south in winter while others, especially the young birds, stay near the places where they were reared, in flocks of 6 to 24. It has been suggested that the practice of putting out food for birds may also be reducing migration.

The cardinals occur in a range of temperate and tropical habitats. On the arid Marias Islands off Mexico, the birds have to drink early morning dew before it evaporates, and cardinals have been seen drinking from pools formed at the bases of leaves. They prefer to live in open woodlands with clearings or in mixed growth at the edges of woods. Suburban gardens are very popular, providing both open ground and trees.

Accomplished songsters

Apart from their bright red plumage, cardinals are popular birds because of their song, which they perform nearly year-round. The male and female sing equally well so that it is difficult to distinguish the sexes by song alone.

In Tennessee the clear, whistling song of the male cardinal can be heard in January or February, when the ground is still snow-covered. The female starts singing during March; her song is a more muted version of the male's. Cardinal song can be heard throughout the summer and fall, occasionally as even late as November or December. The song is very varied. One male cardinal was recorded as producing 28 songs,

composed of different combinations of syllables. There is also a very quiet song, known as the subsong, which is mainly heard during the courtship season, in February–April.

The song plays an important part in courtship and nesting. As is usual when both sexes sing, both male and female defend the territory. The female drives out intruding females but ignores strange males, which are repelled by her mate. The males sing in order to attract females. Cardinals have a wide range of songs that vary from place to place and which they learn to sing in a particular way by imitating the songs of other cardinals around them. Females do not appear to favor males with one particular song, though it may be that the intensity and duration of the song is important in female choice. Strong singers must be strong birds because in terms of energy singing is very costly for the male cardinal; the equivalent of a human singing at the top of his or her lungs for a few hours. Cardinal males sometimes have two female mates. The nestlings of one female will be provisioned by the male, but the other female's brood will tend to be neglected.

Nest-building starts in March or April. Sometimes the male helps; at other times he accompanies the female while she flies from place to place collecting weeds, leaves, grasses

Female and young male cardinals have a predominantly brown plumage, enlivened by a pinkish red suffusion to the breast.

The male cardinal's gaudy plumage ensures its popularity with humans. By putting out food to attract the species, garden owners have helped it expand northward through the United States.

CARDINAL

CLASS	**Aves**
ORDER	**Passeriformes**
FAMILY	**Emberizidae**
GENUS AND SPECIES	***Cardinalis cardinalis***

ALTERNATIVE NAMES
Northern cardinal; red bird

LENGTH
Head to tail: 8⅔ in. (22 cm); wingspan: 9–12 in. (23–30 cm)

DISTINCTIVE FEATURES
Strong, conical bill; large crest. Male: bright red plumage with black bib. Female and young: brownish plumage, pinkish on breast.

DIET
Seeds, fruits and invertebrates

BREEDING
Breeding season: March–August; number of eggs: 3 or 4; incubation period: 12–13 days; fledging period: 10–11 days; breeding interval: 2 to 4 broods per year

LIFE SPAN
Not known

HABITAT
Woodland edge, thickets, scrub, gardens and swamps

DISTRIBUTION
Southeastern Canada and eastern U.S. south to Mexico, Guatemala and Belize

STATUS
Common or abundant

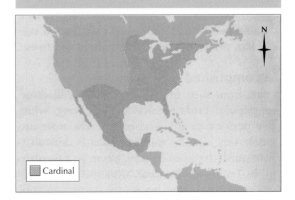

Cardinal

and rootlets, which are then woven into a bowl. The nest itself may be compact and well-lined or a very loose, flimsy structure. It is usually situated in a shady location, such as in a hedge or among the branches of a young evergreen. However, the site of the nest can vary considerably; some are built on the ground, while others are placed high in a tree.

The first clutch is started shortly after the nest is completed, and consists of three or four eggs, though five have been recorded. Clutches laid later in the season usually have only two eggs. Incubation takes 12–13 days, starting when the last egg is laid. The eggs are pale blue in color with brown and pale purple speckles. The chicks leave the nest when 10–11 days old. During this time both parents feed them. As is often the case with fruit-eating birds, at the outset the young are fed on insects, which provide a high-protein diet necessary for rapid growth.

Multiple broods

The cardinal raises two to four broods during the year. In Tennessee, for example, breeding continues from April to August. Further south, breeding may take place year-round. The pair stays together throughout the breeding season and may keep company during the winter. While the female builds a new nest and incubates the next clutch, her mate continues to feed the previous brood, which are finally chased out of the territory when the next brood is hatched.

Young cardinals begin to sing when they are 3–6 weeks old. At first the song is warbling, not at all like the adult song, which is a much-repeated whistle of varying pitch. However, adult phrases are added by the age of 2 months and the full song develops by the next spring.

CHIPMUNK

The eastern chipmunk (above) is larger than the various species of western chipmunks, though its tail is proportionately shorter.

THERE ARE TWO GENERA of chipmunks, *Tamias* and *Eutamias*, among the many kinds of ground squirrels. *Tamias* contains a single species, the eastern chipmunk, *T. striatus*, which is the largest of all the chipmunks. Its fur is reddish brown, with dark stripes on the back, alternating with two lighter stripes. The tail is not as bushy as that of tree squirrels. *Eutamias* contains 17 species, collectively known as western chipmunks. All are smaller than the eastern chipmunk, but they have a similarly sized tail, which is therefore larger in relation to the body. Their fur is lighter and there are five light stripes between the dark stripes on the back. The eastern chipmunk has one upper premolar (grinding tooth) on each side of the jaw, whereas western chipmunks have two. The eastern chipmunk's rufous rump also distinguishes the two genera.

Variety of species

The designations eastern and western refer to the species' distribution in North America. The eastern chipmunk is widespread in the eastern United States north of Florida and Louisiana and also occurs in southeastern Canada. It thrives in forests and shrubland, and frequents fallen logs, rocks and outbuildings.

All but one of the western chipmunks are native to western and central North America, ranging from the Yukon to Sonora in Mexico. The remaining *Eutamias* species, the Siberian chipmunk, *E. sibiricus*, ranges from Siberia to northern China, Korea and northern Japan. Western chipmunks are found in a variety of forest and woodland, as well as in juniper scrub, chaparral and rocky areas. Some species are widespread, while others have very specialized habitat requirements and occur in small ranges.

Burrow systems

Chipmunks are skillful climbers, but prefer to stay on the ground, although the eastern chipmunk sometimes rears its young in trees. They make a complicated system of burrows underground, often running under logs and stones, or delving several feet under the turf. Each burrow

CHIPMUNKS

CLASS **Mammalia**

ORDER **Rodentia**

FAMILY **Sciuridae**

GENUS AND SPECIES **Tamias: eastern chipmunk,
T. striatus. Eutamias: 17 species, including
Townsend's chipmunk, E. townsendii;
least chipmunk, E. minimus; and Siberian
chipmunk, E. sibiricus**

LENGTH
**Tamias. Head and body: 5½–7½ in.
(14–19 cm); tail: 3¼–4¼ in. (8–11 cm).
Eutamias. Head and body: 3¼–6¼ in.
(8–16 cm); tail: 2½–5½ in. (6–14 cm).**

DISTINCTIVE FEATURES
**Pointed head; prominent ears; bushy tail;
brown-gray fur; black and white stripes on
back, extending over eyes in Eutamias**

DIET
**Mainly seeds, fruits, fungi and grasses; also
bird eggs, invertebrates and small vertebrates**

BREEDING
**Age at first breeding: 1 year; breeding season:
February–April and June–August (Tamias),
May–August (Eutamias); number of young:
usually 4 or 5; gestation period: about 31
days; breeding interval: 1 or 2 litters per year
(Tamias), 1 litter per year (Eutamias)**

LIFE SPAN
Usually 2–3 years, sometimes up to 8 years

HABITAT
**Forest, especially coniferous; also open
woodland, scrub, chaparral and rocky scree**

DISTRIBUTION
**Tamias: eastern U.S. and southeastern
Canada. Eutamias: western Canada south
through western U.S. to Mexico; Siberia,
Mongolia, Korea and Japan (E. sibiricus).**

STATUS
Common, sometimes very common

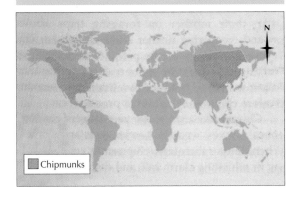
Chipmunks

is owned by one chipmunk which continues digging throughout its life, so that the burrows may reach lengths of 30 feet (9 m) or more. The burrows may have more than one entrance and perhaps several side chambers, one of which may contain a nest of leaves and grasses.

Chipmunks do not hibernate in the strict sense of the word. However, during prolonged spells of bad weather the animals do enter a state of torpor, from which they awake from time to time to feed from caches (stores) of food.

Although adept at climbing, chipmunks spend most of their time near the ground. These are young Townsend's chipmunks.

Cheek pouches

Chipmunks feed mainly on berries, fruits, nuts and small seeds, which are collected after they have fallen to the ground, or which the chipmunks climb trees and shrubs to pick. Fungi, grasses and leaves are also eaten. Chipmunks are sometimes carnivorous, eating slugs, snails and insects. Bird eggs, mice and small snakes are also taken, and in the Sierra Nevada the eastern chipmunk is considered to be one of the chief predators of the rosy finch, *Leucosticte arctoa*.

Food that is not immediately needed is carried in the cheek pouches and cached for use in the winter. The cheek pouches are loose folds of skin, naked inside but not moist, that open into the side of the mouth. To fill its pouches, a chipmunk holds a nut in its paws, neatly bites off

During the fall the least chipmunk, like all chipmunks, devotes a lot of energy to gathering the hoards of food that will last it through the winter.

the sharp point on each end and slips it into one pouch. The next nut is placed on the other side and the pouches are filled alternately. The chipmunk can take up to four nuts in each pouch and another between the teeth.

Expert hoarders

Chipmunks are probably the most accomplished hoarders in the squirrel family, but are selective about the items they hoard. When a chipmunk is collecting its winter store, it selects only nuts, seeds and cones, never any fruit or flesh that would decompose.

The sheer bulk of chipmunk stores is highly impressive. There are reports of caches containing 8 quarts (9 l) of acorns or 32 quarts (35 l) of nuts, and one cache does not constitute a chipmunk's complete winter store. More than one cache may be made in the burrow, and small caches are made in secure hiding places across the chipmunk's home range. In this respect the chipmunk combines the hoarding behavior of the chickaree, which creates one or two large stores, with that of the gray squirrel, which usually makes many small ones.

Like the gray squirrel, the chipmunk sometimes forgets the location of some of its small, scattered stores. These often consist of just a mouthful of nuts buried under leaves or turf. During the winter the chipmunk may find some of the stores by smell; otherwise they remain hidden until they germinate and contribute to the growth of the woodland.

Breeding and predators

Mating takes place during the spring and summer, the males seeking out the females in their burrows. The young, usually four or five in number, are born about 1 month later. They spend a month in the nest, then begin to accompany their mother on foraging trips above ground, venturing further afield each time. The young remain as a group for 6 weeks before starting to forage independently. Eastern chipmunks may produce two litters in a season; western chipmunks only ever produce one.

Chipmunks are a major prey item of coyotes, bobcats, foxes, weasels, hawks, owls and snakes. When danger threatens, chipmunks give a scolding or whistling alarm call, and dash to cover.

CLICK BEETLE

Click beetles can jump up to 12 in. (30 cm) into the air, enduring a higher gravitational force than any other insect.

CLICK BEETLES ARE SMALL, hard-shelled, short-legged, elongated insects, generally about ¼ inch (7 mm) long. Most of the common species are black or dark brown, but some are red, yellow or green. The antennae may be simple or quite elaborately branched.

The harlequin click beetle, *Chalcolepidius zonatus*, is a 2-inch (5-cm) long insect with black and white stripes and is usually found on fallen trees in South American forests. The elegant click beetle, *Semiotus affinis*, is a large and spectacularly colored species, which inhabits the rain forests of the American Tropics.

Jumping beetles

Most click beetles are active at night and hide away in the daytime. Apart from the luminosity of some tropical species, their most notable feature is the ability to jump with an audible click when turned on their backs.

In click beetles the first and second sections of the thorax are hinged, and on the underside of the first there is a spine directed backward, the tip of which rests just over the edge of a cavity in the second. The spine is pressed against this edge, and as the hinge between the two sections moves, it causes the spine to slide until its tip passes over the edge and snaps into the cavity

with enough force to jar the whole body of the insect and throw it into the air. This mechanism is peculiar to the family Elateridae.

If a click beetle is put on its back it can be seen to arch its body using its thoracic hinge just before jumping. The beetle cannot be sure of landing the right way up at the first jump, and in fact often fails to do so, but by repeated jumps it eventually lands on its feet.

The legs of a click beetle are so short that they cannot be used to right the beetle when it is inverted, so the click mechanism must be of considerable value for this reason alone. However, scientists believe that the mechanism may serve another purpose. If caught and squeezed, the beetle always clicks repeatedly. This may be no more than a response to being held off balance but it is quite likely that a young, inexperienced bird or lizard, finding and seizing a click beetle, might be so startled by the strength of the clicks that it will drop its prey, which then has the opportunity for escape.

In common with other insects, click beetles employ another defense mechanism, that of thanatosis, or shamming death. If it is touched or senses danger, a click beetle draws in its legs and lets itself fall to the ground until the danger is past. However, the effectiveness of this act is uncertain. Some predators, such as toads, will take only active creatures, but not all insect-eaters limit themselves to prey that is alive and moving.

Major crop pests

Adult click beetles feed on leaves, mostly at night, and are also attracted to sweet liquids. Some harmful species are trapped by putting out sweet baits to attract them. The larvae of some click beetles live in rotting wood, but those of the most abundant species (*Agriotes* and *Athous*), known as wireworms, feed on the roots, bulbs

and tubers of plants and also on seeds lying in the ground before germination. The larvae are equipped with a hardened cuticle which is resistant to crushing. Wireworms are elongated, cylindrical, tough-skinned larvae, usually yellow in color, and are among the most serious of all insect pests. They attack most cultivated crops, but especially cereals and potatoes.

The eggs are laid in the soil and the larvae develop slowly, taking 2–6 years to reach full size. In the commonest British wireworm, *Agriotes obscurus*, the larval life duration is estimated at 5 years. Only a few weeks are spent as a pupa, but the adult beetles may live for 10 months or a year, overwintering in the soil in temperate and cold climates.

Agriotes and *Athous* wireworms are serious agricultural pests. In land that is already cultivated, some measure of control can be achieved by getting rid of weeds (which support the wireworms between crops), frequent working of the soil and careful use of insecticides. However, of all insects harmful to agriculture, wireworms are among the most difficult to destroy.

When grassland is ploughed it is usual for an economic entomologist to sample the soil and determine the approximate number of wireworms present per acre of the land. If the figure exceeds 1 million, no crop will have a very good chance of success. A figure of over 600,000 wireworms is a serious threat to most crops on light soil, but on heavy soil peas can be planted and also barley, the least susceptible of the cereals. For all crops except potatoes, a figure of 300,000 to 600,000 wireworms per acre is regarded as an acceptable population.

CLICK BEETLES

PHYLUM **Arthropoda**

CLASS **Insecta**

ORDER **Coleoptera**

FAMILY **Elateridae**

GENUS **Many, including *Agriotes*, *Athous*, *Chalcolepidius* and *Semiotus***

SPECIES **About 8,000, including striped elaterid beetle, *Agriotes lineatus* (detailed below)**

ALTERNATIVE NAMES
Skipjack; wireworm (larva only)

LENGTH
Adult: ¼–⅓ in. (7–8 mm)

DISTINCTIVE FEATURES
Adult: elongated body with very hard outer surface; large head; short legs; brownish overall but often covered with grayish microscopic hairs

DIET
Adult: leaves; flower pollen and nectar. Larva: roots and seeds.

BREEDING
Age at first breeding: up to 7 years; breeding season: eggs laid May–June; number of eggs: 150 to 200; hatching period: 25–60 days; breeding interval: 1 generation every 6 years

LIFE SPAN
2–7 years

HABITAT
Most habitats; larva in wood or soil

DISTRIBUTION
Worldwide

STATUS
Abundant

COD

THE COD IS THE second most valuable food fish in the world, after the herring. The cod family contains 150 species, of which about 10 are important food fish, including the coalfish or pollack, haddock, hake and whiting. Cod are marine fish, though there is one entirely freshwater species, the burbot, *Lota lota*, found in northern parts of Eurasia and North America.

The Atlantic cod is round-bodied, up to 100 pounds (45 kg) in weight and 6 feet (1.8 m) long, although those usually sold are 2–25 pounds (1–11 kg). Its typical color is olive green to brown, the back and flanks marbled with spots, the belly white. There are three dorsal and two anal fins, the snout projects over the mouth and there is a prominent, whiskerlike barbel on the chin.

Seasonal movements

The distribution of the Atlantic cod is reflected in the locations of the main fisheries, in the North Sea and off Norway, Bear Island, Iceland, Greenland and Newfoundland. The Arctic cod, *Boreogadus saida*, which is also known as the polar cod, is a slender-bodied species that lives in the northern Pacific.

Within each area the populations of Atlantic cod are self-contained, and several subspecies have been recognized. However, the larger, older fish make long migrations of several hundred miles between the areas, for example from Newfoundland to Greenland and from Greenland to Iceland. In each region the species has distinct seasonal feeding grounds and spawning grounds. In late spring and summer Atlantic cod live in deep waters, at depths of up to 650 feet (200 m). In the fall, the shoals move to shallower waters along coastlines; at times cod can be caught just 50 yards (45 m) offshore.

Atlantic cod also execute a daily movement related to the intensity of light, similar to that found in a number of other shoaling fish. Even when at depths of 600 feet (180 m), the cod form compact shoals during the daylight hours, disperse at sunset and reform at sunrise.

Voracious predators

Cod feed primarily on other fish, especially herring, mackerel and haddock, as well as sand eels and smaller members of their own species. Squid and bottom-living invertebrates such as

shrimps, crabs, mollusks and worms are also eaten. Cod have strong, sharply-pointed teeth, and their digestive juices can dissolve seashells and the shells of crabs. The overlapping upper lip is an adaptation for scooping up worms and other prey from the seabed.

Vast numbers of eggs

There is no marked outward difference between the sexes of Atlantic cod, which become sexually mature at 4–5 years, when 2–3 feet (60–90 cm) long. In the first 3 months of the year adults of breeding age move to the spawning grounds. This may take the fish across very deep water, for example from Norway to Bear Island. The females shed their eggs and the males release milt into the sea; fertilization is random.

A large female cod lays up to 9 million eggs, each 1–2 millimeters in diameter, which float to the surface. Generally these hatch in about 10–20 days and the larvae remain in the surface plankton for the next 60–75 days. When just over ¾ inch (2 cm) long they move down to the bottom, into depths of about 250 feet (70 m), to feed on small crustaceans, amphipods, isopods and small crabs. By the end of the year the young cod are 6 inches (15 cm) long. Young cod of a similar age keep together, and are known as codling.

The Atlantic cod hunts fish and crustaceans in large groups. However, years of overfishing have severely reduced its numbers and the species is now vulnerable.

Cod feed mainly near the seabed, where the chin barbel is used to scoop up invertebrates.

COD	
CLASS	**Osteichthyes**
ORDER	**Gadiformes**
FAMILY	**Gadidae**
GENUS AND SPECIES	***Gadus morhua***

ALTERNATIVE NAMES
Atlantic cod; codling (young only); codfish (archaic)

WEIGHT
Up to 100 lb. (45 kg), usually 5–25 lb. (2–11 kg)

LENGTH
Up to 6 ft. (1.8 m), usually under 3 ft. (0.9 m)

DISTINCTIVE FEATURES
Rounded body; prominent barbel on chin; 3 dorsal and 2 anal fins; body mainly greenish brown with dark mottling on sides, white lateral line and white underside

DIET
**Adult: other fish including smaller cod; wide range of invertebrates.
Young: plankton, larvae and eggs.**

BREEDING
Age at first breeding: usually 4–5 years; breeding season: February–April; number of eggs: up to 9 million; hatching period: 8–23 days at 37–52° F (3–14° C)

LIFE SPAN
Up to 20 years

HABITAT
Mainly near seabed; summer: usually in waters 500–650 ft. (150–200 m) deep; winter: in shallower waters nearer coast

DISTRIBUTION
North Atlantic, Baltic Sea and White Sea (Arctic waters to north of European Russia)

STATUS
Vulnerable; large declines in many areas

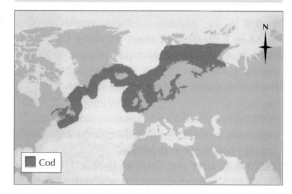

Cod

Place in human history

Atlantic cod have been fished by humans since the 16th century and during the 20th century the annual catch reached 300 million to 400 million fish. As a source of revenue cod have had an important bearing on the course of human history. In the early 16th century, Spanish, Basque, French and English fishers caught cod in the North Sea and North Atlantic. By the middle of that century 300 French ships were fishing on the Grand Banks of Newfoundland. Many of the sailors crewing the fighting ships of the Spanish Armada learned seamanship in cod ships.

England was slow to exploit these "silver mines," as the seemingly inexhaustible supplies of cod off Newfoundland were then known. Early in the 17th century, however, there came a two-pronged attack. Ships from western and southern England were making the long journey and returning with valuable cargoes of salted cod. By 1634 an estimated 18,700 English seamen were working the Newfoundland fishery. The colonists of New England had also discovered this source of wealth and by 1635, one generation after the colony was founded, 24 vessels were exporting up to 300,000 cod a year.

Atlantic cod led the English and the French to Canada, and when the United States was founded a title to the cod-fishing grounds was included in the Act of Independence. The species appears on bank notes, seals, coins and revenue stamps of the New England colonies, and a carved figure of a cod still occupies a place of honor in the Massachusetts State House. The fish left its mark in the form of open strife between the crews of different nations.

Salted cod soon became a standby for seafarers, explorers and armies as Europeans settled the new-found continents. Nothing of the fish was wasted. Its skin yielded glue, its liver was used to produce a high-grade oil and its swim bladder furnished a semitransparent gelatin used as a clarifying agent and in glue and jellies.

CONCH

THE WORD CONCH WAS originally applied to bivalve mollusks but was later taken to include mollusk shells in general, the study of which is still known as conchology. Today the word conch signifies only the sea-snails of the genus *Strombus*. Some other large marine snails are often called conchs, for instance the horse conch of the Florida coast, but these species do not belong to the genus of true conchs.

Large shells

Strombus shells range in length from just ¾ inch (2 cm) to the 13 inches (33 cm) of *S. goliath*. One of the best known species, the queen conch, *S. gigas*, which occurs throughout the Caribbean, reaches a length of about 12 inches (30 cm) and weighs up to 6 pounds (2.5 kg). This mollusk is sexually mature at 3 years, by which time it weighs 2 pounds (1 kg) and is 8 inches (20 cm) long, and continues to grow to its maximum size at the rate of 3 inches (7.5 cm) per year.

In some species of conch the lip of the shell is developed in the adult as a heavy projecting "wing" or fingerlike projection. This serves to stabilize the shell as it lies on the seabed, preventing it from rolling over. A peculiarity of conchs is the two large eyes, often ringed with orange, red or yellow, which are carried on long stalks arising from either side of a stout proboscis. Each stalk has a short tentacle, and the right eye is lodged, when in use, in the so-called stromboid notch in the lip of the shell.

Confined to warm water

Members of the genus *Strombus* are widespread in tropical waters, but are absent from most of the Atlantic. They can survive only in places where the water temperature never falls below 70° F (21° C). The distribution of conchs is therefore similar to that of coral reefs, and few species occur in waters too cool for reef corals.

Conchs are found mainly in the Indian Ocean and the South Pacific, with more than 40 species in the Red Sea, Arabian Sea and East Africa eastward through the Indian Ocean to Hawaii and Easter Island in the Pacific. There are seven conch species in the Caribbean, four on the Pacific side of Central America, and one on the West African coast. Two species live at depths of up to 400 feet (120 m), but most live in shallow water, from low-tide level to 65 feet (20 m).

Jumping shellfish

Conchs move in quite a remarkable way for marine mollusks. When at rest conchs tend to bury themselves in sand or gravel, but when active they push themselves along. The foot of a conch is unlike that of the more familiar terrestrial snails in that only a small part of it is used as a creeping sole in locomotion. The hind end of the foot has a horny plate called the operculum, which in many land snails serves to seal the entrance to the shell when the animal withdraws inside. In conchs the operculum is clawlike, with a sharp, often serrated edge. It is used not only in

Conchs gather in large numbers to spawn and also perform mass migrations when food is scarce.

CONCHS

PHYLUM	**Mollusca**
CLASS	**Gastropoda**
ORDER	**Mesogastropoda**
FAMILY	**Strombidae**
GENUS	***Strombus***
SPECIES	**Over 50, including *S. goliath* and queen conch, *S. gigas***

ALTERNATIVE NAMES
Fighting conch; trumpet shell; stromb shell

WEIGHT
Up to 6 lb. (2.5 kg); male smaller than female

LENGTH
2–12 in. (5–30 cm)

DISTINCTIVE FEATURES
Thick shell, often with a "wing" or fingerlike projections for stability; 2 large eyes on long stalks; right eye stalk protrudes through stromboid notch in outer lip of shell

DIET
Mainly seaweed and algae

BREEDING
Age at first breeding: 2–3 years; number of eggs: tens of thousands to hundreds of thousands; hatching period: 14–21 days; larval period: 14–21 days

LIFE SPAN
Adult: usually 5–6 years

HABITAT
Warm, shallow seas, mainly 35–65 ft. (10–20 m) deep; usually on sand, mud, coral rubble and meadows of seagrass and algae

DISTRIBUTION
Tropical seas that always exceed 70° F (21° C); absent from most of Atlantic

STATUS
Generally common; localized declines due to overfishing

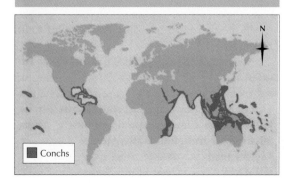

Conchs

defense, as a kind of dagger against crabs and fish, but also to pole the animal along with a leaping action. Each jump carries the conch forward by about half the length of its own shell. The conch pushes the operculum, which looks like a huge fingernail, into the sand or against a firm object and then presses hard.

The shell of a conch is nearly four times the weight of its soft parts and the thrust given by its muscles must be powerful. A conch shell 6 inches (15 cm) long will be carried forward 3 inches (7.5 cm) and lifted 2 inches (5 cm) off the seabed in the process. More expressive of the power of the thrust is the experience of conch divers who gather the shells to sell for food and as tourist souvenirs. The divers often arrive at the surface cut by the sharp edges of the conchs' opercula.

Seaweed grazers

The smaller conchs graze the deposits of seaweed fragments that accumulate on the seabed. Other conchs eat living seaweed. The queen conch, for instance, aligns its vertical slitlike mouth with seaweed fronds, seizing them in its two ribbed lips. Inside the lips is a pair of jaws as well as the usual radula, or horny tongue.

During the warmer months conchs gather in the shallows for spawning. After mating the females lay thousands of eggs in long, jellylike masses, up to 75 feet (23 m) long. The eggs hatch in 1–2 weeks, releasing free-swimming larvae that feed on plankton for up to 10 weeks before settling on the seabed.

The queen conch lives in the Gulf of Mexico and the Caribbean. Its empty shells are often washed up onto the region's beaches.

CORAL SNAKE

The Arizona coral snake is less than half the size of the almost identical common coral snake, and it is seen much less frequently.

CORAL SNAKE IS THE NAME given to many strikingly colored snakes with bold patterns of rings running round the body and tail. The body is slender, and there is no pronounced distinction between head and neck. In North and South America there are several genera of true coral snakes, which are close relatives of the cobras, as are the Oriental coral snakes belonging to the genus *Maticora*. In South Africa some members of the genus *Aspidelaps* are called coral snakes; they are similar in appearance and habits to their American relatives.

Of the 60 species of coral snakes found in the Americas, only two extend as far north as the United States. The two North American species have prominent rings around the body in the same sequence of black, yellow or white, and red. The Arizona, or Sonoran, coral snake, *Micruroides euryxanthus*, is small, having a maximum recorded length of about 20 inches (50 cm). The larger, common coral snake, *Micrurus fulvius*, occasionally reaches 4 feet (1.2 m). The range of the common coral snake extends north from northeastern Mexico, through eastern Texas to the low-lying country of Kentucky and North Carolina and south to Florida. The Arizona coral snake lives in the arid lands of Arizona, New Mexico and northwestern Mexico. Other American species of coral snake range as far south as central Argentina.

Brightly colored banding is not invariable in coral snakes. Those in the genus *Leptomicrurus* have long, thin bodies and short tails, which are dark on the upper side and which have yellow spots underneath.

Feeding and breeding

Coral snakes are nocturnal, lying up during the day in runs under stones and bark or in mossy clumps, though they are sometimes active by day if it has been raining. The jaws of coral snakes do not open very wide and the species can therefore eat only slender prey. Important prey items include small lizards, other snakes and frogs. On Trinidad, mongooses introduced to control the numbers of snakes have not adversely affected the island's population of coral snakes.

The female common coral snake lays 3 to 14 soft, elongated eggs in May or June, in a hollow in the earth or under a log. When the young snakes hatch, after 10–12 weeks, they measure 7–8 inches (18–20 cm) and have pale skins, the colors of which become more intense with age.

Poisonous but rarely dangerous

A coral snake approaches its prey slowly, sliding its head over the victim's skin. The fangs are short and to inject a lethal quantity of venom the snake chews the flesh, lacerating the skin to force in a large amount of poison, which acts on the nervous system and has a powerful effect. In Mexico the common coral snake is called the "20-minute snake" as its bite was traditionally thought to be fatal to humans within that period, though 24 hours is probably a more accurate figure. Relatively few human deaths have been attributed to coral snake bites. If a coral snake senses danger, its initial impulse is to coil itself up and raise its tail, which it moves in an attempt to distract a would-be predator's attention from its more vulnerable head.

Warning colors?

Parallels can be drawn between the brightly colored markings of coral snakes and the bright stripes typical of certain insects, especially some bees and wasps. Conspicuous coloration is a feature of many animals that are toxic or have defensive venom, although many predators of snakes, including mammals, are color-blind. The dramatic light and dark bands of coral snakes would be noticeable to even color-blind species and may serve as a visual warning that these snakes are venomous.

It has been suggested that the banding on coral snakes may serve as a disruptive pattern, breaking up the outline of a coral snake's body, thereby making it less readily seen by would-be predators. Another theory is that the bright coloration may act as sexual signaling. Intense,

NORTH AMERICAN CORAL SNAKES

CLASS **Reptilia**

ORDER **Squamata**

FAMILY **Elapidae**

GENUS AND SPECIES **Common coral snake,** *Micrurus fulvius*; **Arizona coral snake,** *Micruroides euryxanthus*

ALTERNATIVE NAMES
Micrurus fulvius: eastern coral snake; Texas coral snake. *Micruroides euryxanthus*: western coral snake; Sonoran coral snake.

LENGTH
Micrurus fulvius: usually up to 4 ft (1.2 m). *Micruroides euryxanthus*: up to 20 in. (50 cm).

DISTINCTIVE FEATURES
Slender body; small, inconspicuous head; striking pattern of black, white, yellow and red bands

DIET
Mainly other snakes, lizards and frogs; probably also some insects

BREEDING
Micrurus fulvius. Breeding season: usually May–June; number of eggs: 3 to 14; hatching period: 70–84 days.

LIFE SPAN
Not known

HABITAT
Micrurus fulvius: open woodland, scrub and deserts. *Micruroides euryxanthus*: semiarid areas.

DISTRIBUTION
Micrurus fulvius: northeastern Mexico and eastern Texas east to North Carolina and Florida. *Micruroides euryxanthus*: Arizona, New Mexico and northwestern Mexico.

STATUS
Generally locally common

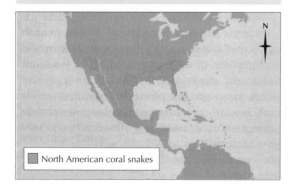

North American coral snakes

gaudy colors may be physiologically costly for a snake to maintain and, if so, it follows that a colorful individual is likely to be fit and healthy. Female coral snakes may therefore use body coloration as a guide to the quality of a potential mate. Parasites and disease may weaken body coloration; pale, faded colors may be a signal that an individual is not genetically strong.

Snake mimics

In the insect world, some harmless insects, such as certain flies and hoverflies, mimic the color patterns of harmful species. By doing so, they gain protection because predators learn to associate the color with an unpleasant taste and refrain from taking insects of that color. Coral snakes may also have their mimics, for there are nonpoisonous snakes with brightly colored rings in the Americas, Africa and Asia.

In the United States some of the reports of coral snakes found in unusual places may be explained as erroneous sightings of other, non-venomous species. These include the common king snake (*Lampropeltis getulus*), the shovel-nose snake (genus *Chinactis*) and several species of milk snakes. All of these snake species, however, have a different sequence of colored bands to that of the common and Arizona coral snakes. In the North American coral snakes each red band always has a yellow or white band on either side. In the "mimics" each red band has a black band on either side.

Scientists disagree as to the purpose of the colored bands typical of coral snakes. They may deter would-be predators, provide camouflage or play a part in mate selection. Pictured is Micrurus nigrocinctus of Costa Rica.

COYOTE

Unlike most predatory mammals found in North America, the coyote expanded its range during the 19th and 20th centuries. It occurs from Canada south to Panama in a wide variety of habitats, from prairies to city suburbs.

THE COYOTE IS CLASSIFIED with wolves and domestic dogs in the genus *Canis*. The name coyote comes from the Mexican *coyotl* and can be pronounced with or without the "e" silent. A coyote weighs 15–50 pounds (7–20 kg) and measures about 4 feet (1.2 m) from nose to tail-tip. The fur is gray or tawny and the tail, bushy with a black tip, droops low behind the hind legs, rather than being carried horizontally in the manner of wolves. The coyote is smaller and hunts smaller game than the gray wolf, though it is larger than the red fox.

Coyotes once lived on plains and in woods to the west of North America; they were known as brush wolves in forested regions and as prairie wolves in open lands. In the 19th century the species' range began to increase despite persecution from humans and coyotes are now one of the most widespread mammals in the Americas, ranging from northern Alaska south to Panama. They have also spread eastward to the Atlantic seaboard. By the early 1900s coyotes had reached Michigan; they were seen in New York State in 1925 and in Massachusetts in 1957. Coyotes had spread to the southern shores of Hudson Bay by 1961. They are now found in most areas of Canada except for the extreme north.

An adaptable species

In the face of persistent harassment by humans most carnivorous animals have retreated. Their habitat has been destroyed and they are hunted mercilessly as vermin or as valuable fur bearers. In contrast, the coyote is extending its range. There is no market for its fur but the coyote has long been shot on sight, or trapped and poisoned, because it has been regarded as an enemy of livestock and competes with humans for game. According to one estimate about 125,000 coyotes have been killed annually for many years, yet the species continues to flourish. The coyote's powers of survival seem to lie in its wariness, its ability to adapt to new circumstances and its broad diet. Generally a solitary animal, it also hunts in packs, which are capable of bringing down larger prey, such as sheep.

The spread of the coyote into the northeastern United States is probably linked with widespread tree-felling and with the regional decline of the gray wolf. The demise of that species left a niche that the coyote was able to fill. Even urban development has not deterred the coyote. It has moved into suburbs where, like the red fox in Britain, it can supplement its diet with gleanings from trash cans and other sources.

COYOTE

CLASS	**Mammalia**
ORDER	**Carnivora**
FAMILY	**Canidae**
GENUS AND SPECIES	***Canis latrans***

ALTERNATIVE NAMES
Brush wolf; prairie wolf (both archaic)

WEIGHT
**Male: 20–50 lb. (9–20 kg);
female: 15–40 lb. (7–18 kg)**

LENGTH
**Head and body: 2½–3 ft. (75–90 cm);
tail: 1–1⅓ ft. (30–40 cm)**

DISTINCTIVE FEATURES
**Resembles gray wolf, but smaller, lighter
and has more slender muzzle; long coat,
usually gray on upper side and paler below**

DIET
**Mainly small mammals, especially jack
rabbits, cottontail rabbits and rodents; some
birds, fish, insects, fruits, nuts and carrion;
occasionally poultry, sheep, goats and deer**

BREEDING
**Age at first breeding: 1–2 years; breeding
season: usually January–March; number of
young: usually 6; gestation period: 58–65
days; breeding interval: 1 year**

LIFE SPAN
Up to 15 years, usually much less

HABITAT
**Varied, including woodland, grassland,
prairie, tundra, chaparral and scrub**

DISTRIBUTION
**Alaska east to Nova Scotia and south to
Panama; range extending southward**

STATUS
Very common

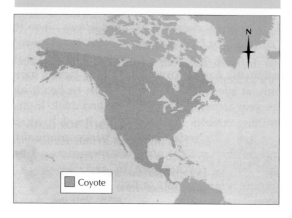

Coyote

Persecuted as a pest

Coyotes are persecuted because of their reputation as killers of livestock and deer. While sheep, goats and deer are occasionally killed, the coyotes' reputation is largely undeserved and has probably arisen due to the commonplace sightings of coyotes feeding on carrion.

In studies to establish whether coyotes pose a major threat to livestock, several thousand dead specimens were examined. Their stomachs were found to contain mainly jack rabbits and cottontails, together with mice, voles and other small rodents. Poultry and livestock made up

*The coyote is the only
wild member of the
dog family that often
barks, although it also
has a range of other
calls, the best known
of which is its
distinctive howl.*

Play among coyote pups helps to hone hunting skills that will be needed as adults.

about one-eighth of the sample. It is probable that, as with other animals that have a varied diet, coyotes will eat whatever is most readily available. If rabbits are abundant, then poultry runs are left alone; however, if a weak calf is found, a coyote will attack it. Coyotes feed on a range of animals: insects, birds, trout and crayfish have all been found in coyote stomachs. They sometimes attack and eat beavers, domestic cats, skunks and even gray foxes. At one time coyotes were a major cause of mortality in the swift, or kit, fox, *Vulpes velox*; coyotes are also known to take red foxes and the rare San Joaquin kit fox, *V. v. mutica*. Sometimes coyotes eat large amounts of vegetable matter, including prickly pears, grasses, nuts and ripe water melons.

Coyotes usually hunt singly or in pairs, and are capable of attaining speeds of over 40 miles per hour (65 km/h). Sometimes they chase deer in relays, one coyote taking over the pursuit as another becomes tired. Another habit is to play dead, waiting for inquisitive, carrion-eating birds such as crows to land and examine the "corpse," at which point the coyote attacks them.

Rearing the young

Breeding begins when coyotes are a year old; a male and female pair for life. They mate during January to March and the pups are born 58–65 days later. The den is usually made in a burrow abandoned by a groundhog, skunk or fox, and is enlarged to form a tunnel up to 30 feet (10 m) long and 1–2 feet (30–60 cm) in diameter, ending

in a nesting chamber that is kept scrupulously clean. In some circumstances, for example in marshlands where tunnels would be flooded, nests are sometimes made on the surface.

Up to 12 pups may be born in a litter, the average number being around six. They are born with their eyes shut and stay underground for over 1 month. The father stays with the family, bringing food first for the mother, then for the pups. The mother regurgitates the food to her young in a partly digested form. Later the family go out on communal hunting trips and the pups learn to hunt for themselves, finally leaving the parents when they are 6–9 months old. Although coyotes are efficient hunters, they are by no means immune to attacks from larger predators, and are known to have been killed by gray wolves and pumas. Golden eagles will sometimes attack young coyotes.

The call of the coyote

The coyote is classified as *Canis latrans*, literally "barking dog," because apart from the domestic dog it is the only member of the dog family that habitually barks. Foxes, wolves and jackals bark only at specific times. Coyotes can be heard all the year round, usually at dawn and dusk. In the evening coyotes sing in chorus. An individual starts with a series of short barks, gradually increasing in volume until they merge into a long yell. Other coyotes join in and the chorus continues for a minute or two. After a pause, the chorus starts again.

CRAYFISH

THE CRAYFISH ARE FRESHWATER crustaceans some 4–19½ inches (10–50 cm) in length. Most are colored sandy yellow, green or dark brown. The head and thorax are covered with a single shell, or carapace, which ends in front in a sharp-pointed rostrum. The eyes are compound and stalked. On the head are a pair of small antennules, which are well supplied with sense organs, and a pair of long antennae. The latter are organs of touch, with excretory organs at the base. Crayfish have strong jaws and two pairs of smaller accessory jaws, or maxillae. The second pair of maxillae drives water across 20 pairs of feathery gills.

On the thorax there are three pairs of appendages, which pass food to the jaws, a pair of stout pincers and four pairs of legs, which crayfish use to walk forward. The abdomen is segmented and has five pairs of limbs on its underside. The first pair are grooved in the male and are used to introduce sperm onto the female. The other four are swimmerets, small appendages that aid locomotion. A crayfish can escape predators by swimming speedily backward with forward flicks of its abdomen, which ends in a fan-shaped tail.

Crayfish are freshwater relatives of lobsters. They usually remain inactive during the day, often hiding under rocks and logs or inside burrows.

Emerge at night

The two families of crayfish are confined almost entirely to temperate regions: the Astacidae in the Northern Hemisphere, the Parastacidae in the Southern Hemisphere. There are no crayfish in Africa, but several species are present in Madagascar. Crayfish are also absent from the greater part of Asia, although they do occur in Korea and in the northern islands of Japan.

Crayfish generally live in rivers, streams and lakes. They are nocturnal and feed on a variety of vegetable and animal matter, including insect larvae, snails, worms, tadpoles and organic detritus. During the day crayfish remain within burrows or under stones and logs. The largest crayfish, *Astacopsis gouldi*, inhabits streams and rivers in northern Tasmania and may weigh up to 9 pounds (4 kg). It is the largest freshwater invertebrate in the world. Another of the Tasmanian crayfish, sometimes known as the land crab, habitually leaves standing fresh water and burrows in damp earth in forests. In Mammoth Cave in Kentucky, there are several crayfish living in the underground waters. These cave-dwelling species are colorless and blind. Their eyes have gone, leaving only the stalks.

The hard shell of a crayfish (Astacus pallipes, above) gives protection but limits the animal's growth. As a result the crayfish must regularly shed its shell and grow a new, larger one.

CRAYFISH

PHYLUM	**Arthropoda**
CLASS	**Crustacea**
ORDER	**Decapoda**
FAMILY	**Astacidae (Northern Hemisphere); Parastacidae (Southern Hemisphere)**

GENUS AND SPECIES   **Many species, including signal crayfish, *Pacifastacus leniusculus*; noble crayfish, *Astacus astacus*; Tasmanian giant crayfish, *Astacopsis gouldi*; and white-clawed crayfish, *Austropotamobius pallipes***

ALTERNATIVE NAMES
Crawfish; crawdad; yabbie (Australia only)

LENGTH
4–19½ in. (10–50 cm)

DIET
Wide range of small aquatic animals and plant matter, including detritus

DISTINCTIVE FEATURES
Resemble small lobsters; hard carapace (shell) covering head and thorax; 2 pairs of long antennae; 1 pair of large pincers; 4 pairs of limbs on thorax and 5 pairs on abdomen; abdomen ends in fan-shaped tail

BREEDING
***Austropotamobius pallipes.* Age at first breeding: 3–4 years; breeding season: usually fall; number of eggs: up to 100; breeding interval: 1 year.**

LIFE SPAN
Up to 15 years

HABITAT
Streams, rivers, canals, lakes, reservoirs and water-filled quarries

DISTRIBUTION
Temperate regions of Americas, Eurasia, Southeast Asia and Australasia, also Japan and Madagascar; absent from Africa

STATUS
Some species relatively common; growing number of species under threat

No larval stage

Crayfish mate in the fall. The male turns the female over and sheds milt through the first pair of abdominal appendages onto her abdomen, where it sticks. The female then enters a burrow to lay her eggs, which may number more than 200, depending on the species. These become attached to bristles on her swimmerets, where they are fertilized by contact with the milt.

The fertilized eggs hatch the following spring. Unusually for crustaceans, crayfish have no larval stage. The newly hatched crayfish are transparent and are tiny replicas of the adults. They grasp the female's swimmerets with their claws and remain attached for some time.

Periodic molts

In common with most crustaceans and insects, crayfish grow by periodic molts. During the process of molting calcium salts—the chalky matter in the old shell—are taken back into the blood, ready to be laid down again in the new shell being formed beneath the old one. The old shell, by now merely a tough cuticle, is shed and the body takes up water and swells. The calcium salts are then laid down in the new cuticle, which gradually hardens.

Molting takes 6 hours, during which time the crayfish fasts and stays in hiding. Many crayfish die during this vulnerable period due both to an increased risk of predation and to the many attendant difficulties of the process itself.

Crayfish plague

Crayfish plague is a disease caused by the fungus *Aphanomyces astaci*, and only affects freshwater crayfish. All native European crayfish species are highly susceptible to the disease. Individuals affected by the plague may show abnormal behavior, such as daylight activity and walking on tiptoe and in more severe cases individuals may be seen struggling on their backs or leaving the water. It is thought that the disease was introduced into Italy in the 1860s and spread rapidly across much of Europe. It devastated indigenous crayfish populations, particularly those of the noble crayfish, *Astacus astacus*.

CROCODILE

C ROCODILES AND THEIR close relatives, alligators, caimans and gharials, are the sole survivors of the great group of reptiles, the Archosauria, that included the dinosaurs. The crocodile family itself includes the dwarf crocodile, *Osteolaemus tetraspis*, and false gharial, *Tomistoma schlegeli*, as well as the dozen or so species of true crocodiles.

The shape of a crocodile's snout offers one means of distinguishing between species. It is long and broad in the Nile crocodile, *Crocodylus niloticus*, the best-known species, short in the Indian marsh crocodile, or mugger, *C. palustris*, and long and narrow in the false gharial. The differences between crocodiles and alligators are discussed in the article "Alligator."

As with many large, powerful animals, the size of crocodiles has often been exaggerated. There is reliable evidence for the Nile crocodile reaching 20 feet (6 m), and specimens of the American crocodile, *C. acutus*, and Orinoco crocodile, *C. intermedius*, have been measured at 23 feet (7 m). At the other extreme, the Congo subspecies

of dwarf crocodile, *O. t. osborni*, has never been recorded as exceeding 45 inches (1.1 m). Crocodiles have been hunted intensively, and large individuals of most species have now become rare.

Temperature regulation

Crocodiles are found in the warmer parts of the world, including the tropical and subtropical regions of Africa, Asia, Australia and the Americas. Unlike alligators, they are often found in brackish (slightly salty) water and have even been known to swim out to sea. The Indo-Pacific crocodile, *C. porosus*, is also known as the saltwater, or estuarine, crocodile because it is particularly common in brackish habitats. It has colonized many of the islands that lie between Asia and Australia.

Reptiles such as crocodiles are said to be cold-blooded because they cannot keep their body temperatures within fine limits in the way that mammals and birds can. A reptile's body temperature is usually within a few degrees of that of its

Crocodiles often rest with their mouths wide open. This may be to regulate body heat, or to allow the mouth to dry out, thereby reducing the chance of fungal infections. Pictured is the American crocodile.

CROCODILES

CLASS **Reptilia**

ORDER **Crocodylia**

FAMILY **Crocodylidae**

GENUS AND SPECIES **14 species, including Nile crocodile, *Crocodylus niloticus*; and American crocodile, *C. acutus***

LENGTH
C. niloticus: up to 20 ft. (6 m); usually less than 16½ ft. (5 m). *C. acutus*: up to 16½ ft. (5 m), usually less than 13 ft. (4 m).

DISTINCTIVE FEATURES
Armor of tough scales and osteoderms (bony deposits); broad snout; long, muscular tail; teeth large and (unlike in alligators) positioned in line; 4th pair of teeth in lower jaw enlarged and protrude when mouth shut

DIET
C. niloticus: wide range of mammals, reptiles, fish and invertebrates. *C. acutus*: mainly fish; also turtles, frogs and mollusks.

BREEDING
Age at first breeding: 12–15 years (*C. niloticus*), 5–10 years (*C. acutus*); breeding season: summer or dry season; number of eggs: 15 to 80; hatching period: about 90 days, depending on temperature

LIFE SPAN
Up to 50 years

HABITAT
Rivers, marshes, swamps, lakes and water holes

DISTRIBUTION
C. niloticus: much of Africa, except north and south; Madagascar. *C. acutus*: southern Florida; Mexico south to northern Colombia and Venezuela; Caribbean islands.

STATUS
C. niloticus: common. *C. acutus*: vulnerable.

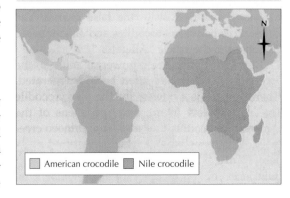

American crocodile ▢ Nile crocodile ▮

The Indo-Pacific, or saltwater, crocodile often occurs in the slightly salty water of estuaries and swamps. By staying submerged in the heat of the day, crocodiles maintain their body temperature within certain limits.

surroundings. It cannot shiver to keep warm or sweat to keep cool. However, many reptiles, including crocodiles, keep their body temperatures from varying too much by following a daily routine to avoid extremes of temperature.

Crocodiles emerge from the water at sunrise to bask in the sun. When their bodies have warmed up, they move either into the shade or back into the water to escape the midday heat. In the late afternoon they bask again, returning to the water by nightfall. Water retains heat more effectively than air, and so crocodiles conserve their body heat by staying underwater at night.

Stones in their stomachs

When crocodiles leave the water, they generally stay near the bank, although occasionally they wander some distance in search of new water and can cause great consternation by appearing in towns. They are generally sluggish but, considering their bulky bodies and relatively short legs, are capable of unexpected bursts of speed. Crocodiles have two distinct gaits. The first is a high walk, in which the body is lifted well off the ground with the legs under the body. The second method is the low walk, which is similar to that used by most other reptiles. In this mode, the crocodile's legs are splayed out and the belly remains close to the ground. This gait is usually adopted only over short distances.

There are two other forms of terrestrial locomotion used by crocodiles. Most can trot and smaller or young crocodiles can gallop at speeds of up to 10 miles per hour (16 km/h) when required. Any increase in speed results in a collapse of leg synchronization and the crocodile ends up sliding on its belly using its legs as paddles. This final method of locomotion is most often used when sliding down an embankment into a river, lake or pool.

Crocodiles float very low in the water, often with little more than their eyes and nostrils showing. They habitually carry several pounds of stones in their stomachs, which help to stabilize their bodies. The stones lie in the stomach, below the center of gravity, and counterbalance the buoyant lungs. This is particularly useful when the crocodiles are fairly young as they are top-heavy and cannot float easily at the surface.

Kill by brute force

During their first year, young crocodiles feed on small animals, including frogs, dragonflies, crabs and even mosquito larvae. A hatchling crocodile swims stealthily toward its prey and then pounces, snapping at its victim with a sideways movement of the jaws. This movement is necessary because the crocodile's eyes are at the side of its head. Young crocodiles have also been seen cornering insect larvae by curving their bodies and tails around them.

As a crocodile grows, the amount of insects in its diet decreases, and it begins to eat water snails and fish. When adult, it continues to catch fish but turns increasingly to trapping mammals and birds. Adult crocodiles capture their prey by lying in wait near game trails and water holes. When a victim approaches, the crocodile seizes it and drags it underwater or knocks it over with a blow from its tail or head. Once the victim is pulled into the water, the crocodile has a definite advantage. Drowning soon stills the victim's struggles and, grasping a limb in its jaws, the crocodile may roll over and over so that the victim is dismembered.

Dangerous to humans?

Crocodiles are widely regarded as being a threat to humans, though this reputation is only partly justified. It may be that only certain individuals attack people. In parts of Africa, crocodiles are not regarded as a menace at all, while elsewhere palisades have to be erected at the edge of streams and rivers to allow people to fetch water in safety. It seems that crocodiles are likely to be more aggressive when their streams and pools dry up so they cannot escape, or when they are guarding their young.

In a crocodile's nest

The Nile crocodile breeds when it is 12–15 years old, by which time it has grown to a length of 7–10 feet (2–3 m). The full-grown males stake out their territories along the banks and share them

The Cuban crocodile, Crocodylus rhombifer, is endangered due to a long history of being hunted and, more recently, to interbreeding with American crocodiles. Hybrids of the two species may now outnumber the pure Cuban species.

Large species such as the Nile crocodile hunt mammals by hiding near a spot where prey comes to drink. When prey is close enough, the crocodile rushes forward and seizes it, dragging it back into the water for the kill.

the female, sometimes the male also, takes the hatchlings in the mouth to carry them to water. The hatchlings disperse when 6–8 weeks old. Young Nile crocodiles are about 1 foot (30 cm) long at hatching and for their first 7 years grow at a rate of about 10 inches (25 cm) a year.

The female crocodile has to be permanently on her guard as many animals feed on crocodile eggs and hatchling crocodiles. The chief predators are monitor lizards, which are bold enough to dig underneath the crocodile as she lies over her nest. Baby crocodiles are also eaten by mongooses, turtles, herons, eagles, predatory fish and other crocodiles. Predators of adult crocodiles include lions and leopards, and hippos attack crocodiles in defense of their young.

Crocodile tears

The phrase "to shed crocodile tears" means to make a false appearance of showing grief or sympathy. The origin of the phrase probably stems from a misguided observation. When James Hawkins stated that "many crocodils" encountered during his explorations throughout the Americas in 1565 "cry and sobbe" he was probably observing osmoregulation. This is a process whereby the balance of water and salts in the body is maintained. Excess salt can be excreted, as a strong solution, from salt glands in the tongue and skin as well as through the urine and feces. Hawkins probably observed this saline solution exuding near to a crocodile's eyes and mistook it for tears.

with younger males and females. They defend the territories by fighting, which may sometimes end in one contestant being killed. Prior to mating, the male crocodile approaches a female and displays to her by thrashing the water with his snout and tail. The two then swim in circles with the male on the outside. He tries to get near to the female so that he can put a forelimb over her body and mate.

Female Nile and marsh crocodiles dig pits 2 feet (60 cm) deep for their nests, and the Indo-Pacific crocodile of northern Australia and Southeast Asia makes a mound of leaves. The nests are built near water and shade, where the female can guard her brood and keep herself cool. During the incubation period she stays by the nest, defending it against predators. These include other crocodiles, although in colonies nests may be only a few yards apart. Up to 90 eggs are laid, depending on species, during the summer or dry season. They hatch about 3–4 months later in the rainy season, when insect prey is plentiful.

The hatchling crocodiles begin to grunt before hatching. This is the signal for the female to uncover the nest. The hatchlings climb out and

Sustainable harvesting

More than half of the world's 21 crocodilian species are currently threatened. However, extensive efforts by conservation organizations, in coordination with representatives from the exotic leather industry, have helped to bring several species back from the brink of extinction. Sustainable harvesting programs, whereby eggs and hatchlings are removed from the wild to be reared in ranches for leather production, have so far proved to be an effective means of crocodile conservation. A proportion of the stock of crocodiles is returned to the wild once it is past the vulnerable hatchling stage and a portion of the profits from the sale of skins is donated to the relevant conservation authority. In this way both the target species and its habitat may be maintained indefinitely.

DIPPER

Well-oiled waterbirds

Dippers flit about waterside rocks and boulders and walk and fly in and out of the water. Under their plumage is a thick layer of down that helps to insulate them and to repel water. Such is the effectiveness of their thick body feathers that dippers can withstand extremely low water temperatures in the winter. They can even feed under ice if necessary.

Dippers have large preen glands that supply all the oil needed to keep their plumage waterproof. The birds also have movable flaps over their nostrils and well-developed third eyelids, known as nictitating membranes, to keep out spray. Unlike other waterbirds however, dippers do not have webbed feet. Their feet are like those of most perching birds. As a result they have to paddle rapidly to make headway on the water's surface.

When a dipper is underwater, it uses its wings to swim through the water and its feet to walk along the bottom. Unlike other diving birds, such as cormorants, grebes and loons, dippers are very buoyant, although this does not seem to impair their ability to stay on the bottom of fast-flowing streams and rivers. At one time it was believed that the flow of water over a dipper's back pressed it against the bottom. It is currently accepted that the dipper prevents itself from rising though the water by powerful wingbeats.

Apart from running in and out of water, a dipper can also dive in and surface and take off without pausing. The usual duration of a dive is about 10 seconds in 1–2 feet (30–60 cm) of water. Dippers can stay underwater for up to half a minute and have been known to go down to a depth of 20 feet (6 m).

Chase prey underwater

Dippers are hard hit by severe winters, but where the ice is thin and there are plenty of holes, or where there is an air space between the water and the ice, they are able to continue feeding. The bulk of their food is insect larvae, including caddis flies, dragonflies and stoneflies. They also take water beetles, crustaceans, worms and mollusks, and catch small fish, such as minnows, and newts, searching either among boulders or along the streambed. Often a dipper

The white-throated dipper lives along fast-flowing streams in Europe and western Asia. Dippers are the only passerines, or perching birds, to lead a truly aquatic life.

THE DIPPERS, OF WHICH THERE ARE five very similar species, are wrenlike birds with short wings and tails. They grow to a length of up to 8 inches (20 cm), roughly the size of the starling, *Sturnus vulgaris*, or a small thrush. Dippers dwell along clear, fast-flowing rivers and streams, and lead a life quite unlike that of any other bird. They are the only truly aquatic members of the large order Passeriformes, or perching birds.

Dippers are nonmigratory birds, though they may descend to lower elevations or fly to the south of their range during severe winters. The white-throated dipper, *Cinclus cinclus*, with brown plumage and a white bib, is found over most of Europe and in some parts of western Asia. In Asia its range overlaps with that of the brown dipper, *C. pallasii*, but the latter species keeps to streams on the lower slopes of mountains. The American dipper, *C. mexicanus*, with a slate gray body and brown head, lives in the west of North and Central America from Alaska south to Panama. The white-capped dipper, *C. leucocephalus*, inhabits the Andes Mountains, while northwest Argentina and southwest Bolivia are home to the threatened rufous-throated dipper, *C. shulzi*.

AMERICAN DIPPER

CLASS **Aves**

ORDER **Passeriformes**

FAMILY **Cinclidae**

GENUS AND SPECIES *Cinclus mexicanus*

ALTERNATIVE NAME
American water ouzel (archaic)

WEIGHT
1¾–2½ oz. (50–72 g)

LENGTH
**Head to tail: about 7½ in. (19 cm);
wingspan: 12–13¾ in. (30–35 cm)**

DISTINCTIVE FEATURES
**Stocky, compact body; short wings and tail;
sooty gray plumage with brownish head**

DIET
**Mainly aquatic invertebrates, especially
insect larvae; some small fish**

BREEDING
**Age at first breeding: 1 year; breeding
season: March–June; number of eggs:
4 or 5; incubation period: 15–17 days;
fledging period: 24–25 days; breeding
interval: 1 year**

LIFE SPAN
Up to 8 years

HABITAT
**Fast-flowing mountain streams up to
tree line at 11,500 ft. (3,500 m); also on
slow-moving rivers with artificial rapids,
such as near water mills**

DISTRIBUTION
**Pacific coastline of North America from
Alaska south to California and east as far
as Rocky Mountains; northwestern Mexico
south to Panama**

STATUS
Locally common

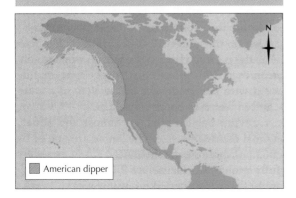

■ American dipper

will stand on a submerged boulder and catch small animals as they float past in the water. At fish farms dippers can become a pest by eating fish eggs and very young trout.

Bankside nests

A pair of dippers establishes and guards a territory that consists of a stretch of stream or river about ¼–½ mile (0.4–0.8 km) long. Neighboring pairs are usually well spread out with some distance between territories. Nests are made in banks and cliffs overlooking the water and in stone walls, under bridges and among tree roots. Only occasionally are they found at any distance from the water. The nests are cup-shaped and 8–12 inches (20–30 cm) in diameter. They are made chiefly of moss and intertwined grasses, lined with grasses and leaves and covered with a roof of moss. There are usually four or five eggs, brooded by the female alone. She leaves the nest only rarely, to feed. The eggs hatch in 15–17 days and the chicks stay in the nest for 3½–4 weeks, depending on the species.

Nests vulnerable to flooding

In 1962 James Alder, an ornithologist from the north of England, was studying dippers. After a period of heavy rain, the stream that he was observing became so swollen that Alder believed all dipper nests there would be destroyed. However, two of the nests were built in the bank under an overhanging flap of turf, which had been left behind as the bank underneath had been washed away. The parent dippers were able to continue feeding their chicks, diving into the water with billfulls of food and reappearing seconds later with bills empty. Later inspection of the nests showed that the water had lapped them, but that air had been trapped inside under the overhangs, saving the chicks.

Dippers can swim and walk underwater. They are capable of staying submerged for about 30 seconds, and of descending to depths of up to 20 feet (6 m).

DRAGONFLY

Nearly all dragonflies lay their eggs in water. The female inserts her eggs into water plants or (above) releases them so that they sink to the bottom.

DRAGONFLIES ARE COLORFUL, POWERFUL fliers and are among the fastest of all insects in the air. Most dragonflies are large and hold their wings stiffly extended on each side when at rest, whereas other insects generally fold them over the back. The wings are capable of only simple up-and-down movement. There is no coupling device joining the front and back wings, as in butterflies and advanced moths, and there is a fine network of "veins" supporting the wing membrane. These characteristics suggest that dragonflies are primitive insects that have existed with little change for a very long time. The earliest known fossil dragonflies are from the late Carboniferous period, and were deposited about 300 million years ago. Dragonflies similar to those living today were alive in the Jurassic period, 150 million years ago, when dinosaurs were on the earth.

The name dragonfly is frequently used to stand as an equivalent of the insect order Odonata. However, the members of the suborder Zygoptera (the damselflies) are very distinct in appearance and are discussed elsewhere.

Living dragonflies consist of two suborders, the Anisoptera, which contains all the familiar species, and the Anisozygoptera. Scientists are aware of only two species in this latter suborder; one is native to Japan and the other is native to the Himalayas Mountains.

As in their relatives the damselflies, dragonflies usually have transparent, colorless wings but these may be tinted or patterned, and the body is often brightly colored. Males are generally more dramatically colored than females. They differ markedly from damselflies in having a swift, powerful flight. Estimates of their actual speed are difficult to obtain and vary from 35 miles per hour (56 km/h) up to 60 miles per hour (96 km/h). Dragonflies' antennae are minute but the eyes are enormous in comparison, occupying the greater part of the head. Each compound eye may contain as many as 30,000 facets.

Aerial patrols

Dragonflies fly patrols over a fixed area. They are most often seen near water, which is where they breed, although their powerful flight carries them far away from their breeding places, and they may frequently be seen resting in trees and on bushes. Dragonflies often fly back and forth over a specific area, landing on one of a small number of resting places. The area that the dragonflies patrol may have been selected as suitable for hunting prey or, especially if the area is over water, it may be the territory chosen by a male dragonfly, which will then mate with any female of its own species that flies into this area. These males defend their territories strenuously against other males of the same species. After a while they begin to show evidence of the confrontations they have experienced, in the shape of torn wings and mutilated legs. Whether hunting or fighting, the sense employed most often by dragonflies is that of sight. A dragonfly can detect movement up to 40 feet (12 m) away.

Some species of dragonflies are migratory and may fly great distances over land and sea. Two of these species, *Sympetrum flaveolum* and *S. fonscolombei*, sometimes visit Britain from Europe. The British population of another species, *Aeshna mixta*, is probably regularly reinforced by newcomers from continental Europe.

Unlike damselflies, dragonflies have large, powerful wings and are among the fastest of all flying insects.

DRAGONFLIES

PHYLUM **Arthropoda**

CLASS **Insecta**

ORDER **Odonata**

SUBORDER **Anisoptera and Anisozygoptera**

FAMILY **Aeshnidae; Gomphidae; others**

GENUS AND SPECIES **Many**

ALTERNATIVE NAME
Horse-stinger

LENGTH
Body: up to 6 in. (15 cm); wingspan: up to 7½ in. (19 cm)

DISTINCTIVE FEATURES
Long, slender body; 2 pairs of wings, rear pair more broadly based than front pair; intricate network of veins on wings; at rest wings held flat and at right angles to body; very large eyes that meet in middle

DIET
Adult: small insects, especially gnats and mosquitoes. Larva: midge larvae and other small, aquatic invertebrates; small fish.

BREEDING
Larval period: 2–5 years (temperate regions), usually several months (Tropics)

LIFE SPAN
Adult: up to 10 years in Tropics, elsewhere usually several years

HABITAT
Many aquatic habitats, including ponds, lakes, marshes, rivers, ditches and streams

DISTRIBUTION
Virtually worldwide

STATUS
Many species common; at least 110 species threatened

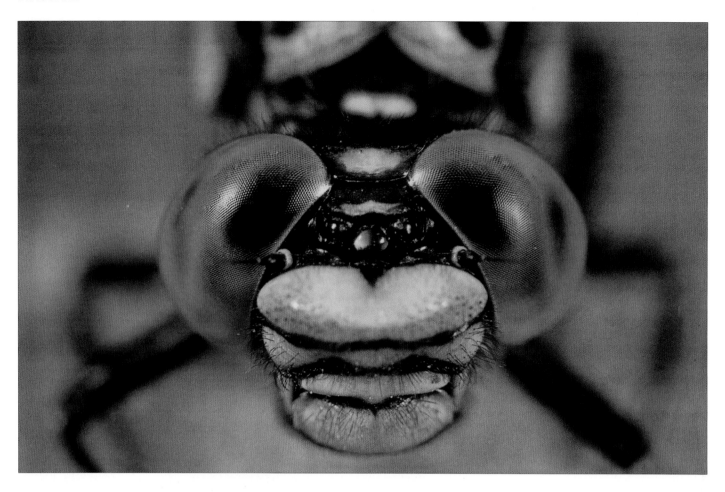

One dragonfly species, *Libellula quadrimaculata*, sometimes migrates in spectacular swarms. In 1862 a swarm of this species was observed in Germany, estimated at nearly 2.5 thousand million strong, and in June 1900 a huge swarm appeared in the sky over Antwerp, Belgium. In 1947 a large migration of another species, *Sympetrum striolatum*, was observed on the southern coast of Ireland.

Masked nymphs

Dragonflies are predatory in all stages of development. The adults catch other insects on the wing, seizing them with their forwardly directed legs and chewing them with their powerful jaws. In the southeastern United States two large species, *Anax junius* and *Coryphaeshna ingens*, are leading predators of honeybees.

The larvae, or nymphs, capture their prey using what is known as a mask, a mechanism that is shared with the damselflies but is otherwise unique among insects. The enlarged labium or lower lip is armed with a pair of hooks. At rest it is folded under the head, but it is extensible and can be shot out in front of the head, the hooks being used to seize the prey like a pair of pincers. The victim is then drawn back within reach of the jaws. Dragonfly larvae also prey on other insects, tadpoles and small fish, and those

of the larger species can considerably reduce the numbers of young fish in a rearing pond. However, young dragonfly larvae also perform a useful ecological service by destroying great numbers of the aquatic larvae of mosquitoes.

The flying tandem

The mating procedure for dragonflies and damselflies is very similar. The male transfers his sperm from the primary sexual organ near the tip of his abdomen to an accessory organ farther forward, at the base of the abdomen. He then alights on the back of a female and curls his abdomen under his own body in order to seize her head, not the thorax as in damselflies, with a pair of claspers at the end of his abdomen. He releases the hold with his legs but continues to grasp his mate with the claspers. The female then curls her abdomen around in such a way that the tip of it makes contact with the male accessory organ. Both before and after mating the two may fly together, with the female held by the male claspers, in what is known as the tandem position. They may even maintain this position while the eggs are being laid.

Dragonflies almost always lay their eggs in water, using one of two methods. Some, including the large hawker dragonflies of the genus *Aeshna*, insert their eggs into the stems of water plants, as damselflies do. Others, such as the golden-ringed dragonfly, *Cordulegaster boltoni*, force their eggs into the sand or gravel at the margins of shallow streams. This second method is seen in most British species. They fly close over the water's surface and repeatedly dip the tip of the body into the water, extruding eggs at the same time, which then sink to the bottom.

Jet-propelled insects

Nearly all dragonflies, and all British species, spend their early life underwater. The nymphs vary in shape. Those that live in mud are short, thick-set and covered with a dense coat of hairs to which the mud clings. When these larvae are at rest, only the eyes and the tip of the abdomen are exposed, the rest being buried. Golden-ringed dragonflies have larvae of this type. Those species that live among waterweed are more slender and active, though no dragonfly larvae are as delicate as those of damselflies.

Dragonfly larvae have gills inside the intestine a short distance from their hind opening, and they breathe by drawing water into the rectum and then driving it out again. This mechanism is also used for another purpose: if it is disturbed, a drag-onfly larva drives the water out forcibly, thereby propelling itself rapidly forward, in a simple form of jet propulsion.

When the larva is fully grown, a period of 2 years or more in most European species, it crawls up a plant growing in the water. It climbs until it is above the water's surface where it under-goes its final molt to metamorphose into an adult dragonfly.

Dragonfly predators

The increasing worldwide destruction of their habitat by pollution, drainage, dredging and infilling of ponds is the most serious threat to dragonflies. As larvae, their chief natural enemies are fish, the young of which are themselves preyed upon by well-grown dragonfly larvae. In fact, dragonfly larvae probably form an important source of food for freshwater fish. When the larvae are small, they are also eaten by other predatory insects, including larger dragonfly larvae, often of their own species. The adults are so swift and active that they have few natural enemies, but several small birds of prey, including the hobby, *Falco subbuteo*, feed extensively on them. In the tropical coun-tries of East Asia dragonflies were at one time caught with sticks smeared with a form of bird lime and eaten fried in oil.

Prehistoric giants

The present-day Odonata are among the largest living insects. In tropical America there are damselflies with bodies 5 inches (12.5 cm) long and wings spanning 7 inches (18 cm). These are slender, fragile creatures and are greatly exceeded in bulk by the Borneo dragonfly, *Tetracanthagyna plagiata*, which also has a wingspan of 7 inches and a body measuring about 5 inches in length. No modern dragonflies, however, compare in size with some that lived in forests 300 million years ago. At Commentry, France, fossil remains of these species have been found, including impressions of wings, which show that the wingspan of the largest prehistoric species, *Meganeuramonyi*, was as much as 27 inches (69 cm), similar to that of a crow. They are by far the largest insects known to have lived on the earth, although no larval remains have been uncovered so far.

Many male dragonflies (A. cyanea, below) are brightly colored. Females generally have less striking colors.

EGRET

THE EGRETS FORM A GROUP of herons found
in many parts of the world. Many egrets
are distinguished by the fine, lacelike
plumes or "aigrettes" that the males sport in the
breeding season and that have given rise to
the species' common name. Most egrets are
primarily or entirely white.

The cosmopolitan great egret or great white
egret, *Egretta alba*, is pure white and, at 33½–40
inches (85–100 cm), is a little smaller than the
great blue heron, *Ardea herodias*. It ranges from
the central United States to Argentina, across
parts of Europe and Asia and south through
Africa and Australia. The little egret, *E. garzetta*,
which is also pure white but half the size of the
great egret, is found in most of the warmer parts
of the Old World, from southern England to
South Africa, and in Australia. The snowy egret,
E. thula, is white in color with plumes on the
head, breast and back and has a similar range in
the New World as the great egret. The range of
the eastern reef egret or blue reef heron, *E. sacra*,
extends from Myanmar (Burma) south to New
Zealand. Its plumage is usually dark slate but
may also be white or a mixture of the two.

The best-known egret is the cattle egret,
Ardeola ibis. At 20 inches (50 cm) it is smaller
than even a little egret. Its plumage is white with
buff on the back and on the plumes covering the
rump and with buff plumes on the crown. The
cattle egret is known both for its close association
with grazing mammals such as cattle, and for its
rapid spread worldwide.

Waterside wanderers

Like other herons, egrets frequent pools, streams
and marshes, where they feed or roost in flocks.
They also breed together, often joining colonies
in which several species of heron may be nesting
together. Different species prefer to nest at
different heights but there is still some competition for nest sites. When nesting, a colony of
egrets crowds together in one tree. Studies of
other birds that nest in colonies, such as penguins or gulls, have revealed that nesting close
together stimulates courtship activities and can
give protection from predators.

Some egrets are migratory. Much of the
European population of the little egret migrates
to tropical Africa in the winter. Of two little

GREAT EGRET

CLASS	**Aves**
ORDER	**Ciconiiformes**
FAMILY	**Ardeidae**
GENUS AND SPECIES	***Egretta alba***

ALTERNATIVE NAMES
Great white egret; great white heron; great American heron; white heron; large heron

LENGTH
Head to tail: 33½–40 in. (85–100 cm); wingspan: 55–67 in. (1.4–1.7 m)

DISTINCTIVE FEATURES
Large size; long bill, neck and legs; neck rather snakelike, with double kink; all-white plumage; yellowish iris. Nonbreeding adult: yellowish bill; black legs. Breeding adult: black tip to bill; brownish legs.

DIET
Mainly fish; also small mammals, amphibians and insects

BREEDING
Age at first breeding: 2 years; breeding season: egg-laying mainly April; number of eggs: 3 to 5; incubation period: 25–26 days; fledging period: about 42 days; breeding interval: 1 year

LIFE SPAN
Up to 23 years

HABITAT
Extensive wetlands, freshwater margins and irrigated land; nests in reed beds or other aquatic vegetation

DISTRIBUTION
Tropical and temperate zones worldwide; absent from Canada and northern U.S., western and northern Europe, northern Asia, North Africa and Middle East

STATUS
Locally common

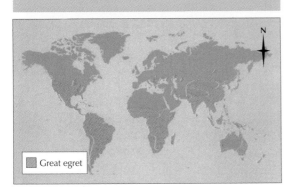

Great egret

egrets tagged in Camargue, southern France, one was later found in Gambia and another in Timbuktu, West Africa. More notable, however, are the random movements of egrets, when they have been swept well away from their normal ranges by winds. A little egret tagged as a July nestling in southern Spain was found in January of the following year in Trinidad, and a great egret was found on the subantarctic island of South Georgia nearly 1,500 miles (2,400 km) from the mainland of South America. Weather records for the few days before the bird was spotted show that winds had probably blown the egret from South America. The most prolific traveler among the egrets is the cattle egret, which must have crossed the Atlantic in some numbers and has become firmly established in America. It has also colonized Australia and now occasionally crosses to New Zealand.

The snowy egret (above) is about 10 inches (25 cm) smaller than the great egret. Both species share the same range in the New World.

Following cattle to feed

Most egrets feed in shallow water, capturing invertebrates, frogs and fish in their long, pointed bills. However, the cattle egret is an exception in this respect. It feeds on dry land, apparently preferring not to enter the water, although it has been seen to catch fish.

Cattle egrets usually feed on insects in grassland. They forage in flocks, the birds at the rear leapfrogging over their companions in front so that the flock is slowly moving forward. As the birds move out in front to seize a grasshopper or other insect, they disturb other insect prey, which fly up and are promptly seized by the egrets following behind. The leapfrogging forward of the trailing egrets ensures that all the birds get a fair share of the food.

Apart from following their companions for the food they stir up, cattle egrets will also follow large animals. In the cattle egrets' original home in Africa, they can often be seen walking alongside buffalo or domestic cattle catching the insects disturbed by their hooves. Cattle egrets also follow antelopes, zebras and elephants and occasionally they may be observed following cranes and spoonbills, or even tractors.

In America in the 20th century a group of ornithologists set up a watch on a flock of cattle egrets that habitually followed one herd of cattle.

During the heat of the day the cattle retired to the shade of trees and the egrets abandoned them to feed on their own. A count of the insects caught and the amount of walking involved in catching them showed that when following the cattle, the egrets did a third less work, and took 1½ times the number of insects that they caught when they fed on their own.

Chicks live on insects

Egrets nest when there is an abundance of insects to feed their chicks. In warm countries this period occurs after the onset of the rainy season. The birds make nests from sticks piled up in the branches of trees and here the males display to attract females. Both sexes incubate the three to five eggs. The young, which have plumage that is considerably less ornate than that of the adults, feed by taking their parents' bills crosswise in their own bills to receive food.

Hunted for their plumage

In nature, egret nests suffer from the depredations of egg-stealing mammals that can climb trees and from hawks that swoop to take eggs and chicks. However, the main threat to egrets in the past, and to a certain extent in the present, was the high value of their feathers to humans as fashion accessories. Demand for the plumes of

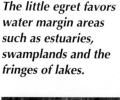

The little egret favors water margin areas such as estuaries, swamplands and the fringes of lakes.

the breeding egrets in the 19th century was met by an enormous supply. In 1898 the plumes of 1,538,000 egrets were exported from Venezuela alone, and if the demand for their plumage had continued at this level, some egret species might well have become extinct. About this time, national and international bird protection bodies such as the International Council for Bird Preservation and the Royal Society for the Protection of Birds, a British charity, were formed. These organizations began to highlight the issue of the exploitation of birds for their plumage and to arouse public concern about the fate of the egrets. The use of bird plumes became outlawed, although even today the continued occasional demand for plumes results in the resurgence of egret hunting.

Cattle egret colonists

The spread of the nine-banded armadillo, *Dasypus novemcinctus*, through the United States and of the collared dove, *Streptopelia decaocto*, through Europe is well-known to biologists. However, such spreads do not come close to matching the global expansion of the cattle egret.

Cattle egrets reached Australia some time after the arrival of European settlers in the late 18th century, and probably reached northern South America about a hundred years later. The first official record of an egret, which had been shot and preserved in a museum collection, was in Guyana in 1937. Equally vague is the date at which the cattle egrets began breeding in America. The first record is in 1950, though it is likely that the birds bred earlier than this. Once established, the cattle egrets spread rapidly. In 1941 or 1942 they had reached Florida and they have now colonized much of the southern and eastern United States and spread as far north as Ontario in Canada, where they now breed.

The spread of the cattle egret has been closely studied by zoologists as it is of scientific interest to see how an animal is able to colonize new territory. Forest clearance and swamp drainage in America have opened up grasslands where the cattle egret may feed without conflicting with the fish-eating native herons. Where the different species do compete for nesting sites, the cattle egret breeds a little earlier and so can pick the most promising nest sites.

The great egret has a characteristic double kink in its neck. It is by far the tallest species of egret.

71

FLAMINGO

Pictured here are lesser flamingos engaged in a group courtship display. Flamingos' necks and legs are proportionately longer than those of any other bird.

THERE ARE FIVE SPECIES OF flamingos, and they can be found in America, Africa, Europe and Asia. The greater flamingo, *Phoenicopterus ruber*, standing up to 5 feet (1.5 m) high, is found in the Caribbean region and the Galapagos Islands and from southern Europe south to South Africa and east to India. Scientists divide the greater flamingo into two subspecies. Caribbean and Galapagos Islands birds belong to the subspecies *P. r. ruber* and are known as Caribbean flamingos. They have an orange-pink bill and brighter pink plumage than do birds of the subspecies *P. r. roseus*, which includes greater flamingos from the rest of the species' range.

The lesser flamingo, *P. minor*, is the most common flamingo and occurs in Africa south of the Sahara, and in Madagascar, parts of the Middle East and India. Half of the global population of this flamingo lives on the Rift Valley lakes of Ethiopia, Kenya and Tanzania. The lesser flamingo is two-thirds the size of the greater flamingo and is brighter pink, with a crimson bill and red legs. It prefers permanent, warmer waters in which there is rapid production of blue-green algae, on which it feeds. The lesser flamingo also requires freshwater springs for drinking and bathing. Greater and lesser flamingos are both gregarious species and breed, feed and travel in

flocks, some of which can be vast. One lesser flamingo flock in East Africa numbered at least 1 million pairs.

The remaining three species of flamingos are found exclusively in South America. The range of the Chilean flamingo, *P. chilensis*, extends from Peru south to Tierra del Fuego and east to southern Brazil and Paraguay. This species numbers about 500,000 birds. The Andean flamingo, *P. andinus*, is confined to the Andes Mountains, as is James flamingo, *P. jamesi*, the former usually at altitudes of more than 8,200 feet (2,500 m) and the latter mainly at more than 11,500 feet (3,500 m). The I.U.C.N. (World Conservation Union) lists both species as vulnerable. Scientists estimate the Andean flamingo population to be about 150,000 birds, while there are thought to be no more than 50,000 James flamingos left in the wild.

Nomadic filter-feeders

Flamingos are highly nomadic and many populations migrate. For example, ornithologists have discovered that many of the greater flamingos that spend summer in the Camargue marshes in southern France fly south across the Mediterranean to pass the winter in Africa on the same lakes as lesser flamingos.

GREATER FLAMINGO

CLASS	**Aves**
ORDER	**Phoenicopteriformes**
FAMILY	**Phoenicopteridae**
GENUS AND SPECIES	***Phoenicopterus ruber***

ALTERNATIVE NAME
Caribbean flamingo (*P. ruber ruber* only)

WEIGHT
**Male: 6½–9 lb. (3–4 kg).
Female: 4½–7¼ lb. (2.1–3.3 kg).**

LENGTH
**Head to tail: 4–5 ft. (1.2–1.5 m);
wingspan: 4½–5½ ft. (1.4–1.7 m)**

DISTINCTIVE FEATURES
**Extremely long neck and legs; huge, sharply
decurved bill; webbed feet. Adult: pale pink
to whitish overall; crimson and black wing
feathers; pink and black bill; reddish pink
legs and feet. Juvenile: brownish overall;
grayish bill; dark gray to black legs and feet.**

DIET
**Mainly aquatic insects, crustaceans and
mollusks; also diatoms and blue-green algae**

BREEDING
**Age at first breeding: 2–3 years; breeding
season: irregular and non-seasonal; number
of eggs: usually 1; incubation period: about
28 days; fledging period: about 75 days**

LIFE SPAN
Up to 15 years

HABITAT
**Shallow waters, including coastal lagoons,
estuaries, salt pans and brackish inland lakes**

DISTRIBUTION
**Parts of Caribbean, South America, Mediter-
ranean, Africa, Middle East and southern
and Central Asia; also Galapagos Islands**

STATUS
Populations fluctuate from year to year

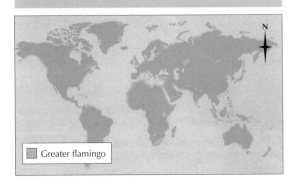

Greater flamingo

Flamingos are always found on lakes or
lagoons of brackish water, where the minute
plants and animals that they eat exist in the vast
concentrations needed to feed a flock. Flamingos
extract their food from the water by a filtering
mechanism. They wade through the water with
their necks lowered and their heads upside
down, sweeping their bills from side to side and
sieving food from the water. The upper and
lower mandibles of a flamingo's bill are fringed
with lamellae, or bristles, that trap particles as
the bird sucks in water. An outer layer of coarse
bristles keeps out large particles, while minute
algae such as diatoms are collected on an array of
bristles inside the bill. The collected algae are
then worked off onto the tongue (which is thick
and fleshy with spines) and swallowed after the
water has been expelled.

*Flamingos' plumage is
tinged with pink,
except for their black
flight feathers. The
pinkish wash is partly
synthesized from the
foods the birds eat,
which contain
carotenoid pigments
similar to those found
in carrots. Pictured is
the greater flamingo.*

Differences in diet

The greater flamingo has a more varied diet than
most of the other species, and feeds at a range of
water depths. Its bill has fewer lamellae than do
those of other flamingos and it also has a flatter
upper mandible. The greater flamingo uses this

shallow-keeled mandible to sweep up snails and shrimps, as well as quantities of mud from which it extracts the organic matter, rejecting the inedible silt. The greater flamingo sometimes paddles around in the mud to disturb the sediment and stir up any potential food within it.

The Chilean flamingo's bill is also shallow keeled and the bird feeds in a similar way to the greater flamingo. The lesser flamingo, though, like the Andean and James flamingos, has a deep-keeled bill that it uses to sweep shallow surface waters for algae. The fact that the lesser flamingo is a more specialized feeder than the greater and Chilean flamingos accounts for the huge gatherings of lesser flamingos that occur when feeding conditions are ideal. These birds feed almost exclusively on a single food—algae—and so must take advantage of an abundance of that food when it is available.

Greater and lesser flamingos often feed together in mixed flocks on the lakes of East Africa. The slight difference in their feeding grounds, diets and feeding techniques is sufficient to prevent the two species from competing for food resources.

Irregular breeders

Flamingos breed in large groups. In East Africa, where flamingos are most abundant, the crowds of nesting birds may be enormous, numbering more than 900,000, perhaps even 1 million, pairs. Sometimes a nest site may remain deserted for several consecutive years. Then the flamingos may rear two broods in quick succession.

The erratic nature of flamingo breeding is most likely due to changes in the water level of the breeding lake. Flamingo nests are towers of mud 6–14 inches (15–36 cm) high with a depression in the top for the eggs. The water level has only to rise 12 inches (30 cm) or so for the nest site to be inundated. On the other hand, if the water level of an alkaline lake drops, thick deposits of soda may form and become caked on the legs of flamingo chicks when they fledge. In 1962 Lake Natron, on the Tanzania-Kenya border, was flooded and the flamingos moved to Lake Magadi in Kenya to breed. Here the water level was low and thousands of chicks died, their legs caked with soda. The periodic mass mortality of chicks and the failure of adults to breed in successive seasons are the prices flamingos pay for the lack of diversity in their nest sites.

Hundreds display together

Flamingos perform spectacular courtship rituals made up of numerous displays, including standing stiffly with the head and neck erect, (head-flagging), flicking the wings (wing-saluting) and ritualized preening. The males initiate courtship, but both sexes take part.

Andean flamingos are confined to lakes high in the Andes Mountains of South America. Like all flamingos, they nest in very large groups, or colonies.

During displays a guttural uproar reigns, and the flock appears to be shimmering as the birds jerk their heads sideways, fitfully and never in unison, or bend their necks, sweeping their bills across their backs. From time to time the males run back and forth in tightly bunched flocks, with their necks held straight up and bills pointed skyward. Within the colony of thousands of flamingos these flocks of males flow and eddy, their long legs twinkling as they rush to and fro.

Straight-billed chicks

Flamingos lay a single egg in the saucer-shaped depression in the nest, and both parents take turns to incubate the egg for about a month. After the chicks hatch, they stay on the nest for up to 5 days, then, about 2 weeks after hatching, they join the other chicks in large groups, or crèches, supervised by several adults. By this time the chicks can run and swim.

Flamingo chicks look very much like goslings (young geese). They are covered in gray down and their bills are straight, not sickle-shaped like those of their parents. Because of the resemblance of young flamingos to goslings and the gooselike flight of the adults, scientists thought flamingos were related to geese, but most ornithologists now think that flamingos are related to storks and ibises.

Until its bill has developed the characteristic adult shape, a young flamingo is unable to feed itself and has to rely on its parents. To feed its chick, the parent stands behind it and lowers its head so the chick may take the tip of its bill in its own. The adult secretes a milky red fluid that runs down into the chick's mouth. Both male and female flamingos can produce this "milk." When the chick is 4 weeks old, its parents begin to feed it regurgitated food. Parents are able to recognize their own chick's voice even when the birds are in a crowd.

The main predators of lesser flamingos are fish eagles, which can pick up young birds and carry them off. Hyenas, cheetahs and jackals also kill stragglers. In Roman times flamingo tongues were a delicacy, and flamingos are still eaten by local hunters. Flamingos were also once prized for their plumage, but now the main human threat to these birds is water pollution and the disturbance of their breeding colonies, particularly by low-flying aircraft.

How do they sit down?

How does a heron or a flamingo sit down on its nest? This question was long disputed. In 1697 William Dampier thought that the flamingo leaned back on its nest as if sitting on a shooting stick. Even a century ago there were still some strange ideas on this point. One was that the flamingo sat astride its nest, another that it sat with its legs sticking straight out behind. The correct answer is that it sits like any other bird. The legs are doubled up beneath it, the "knees" (actually the ankles; the knees are hidden beneath the body feathers) hinge backward, so the folded legs stick out behind the sitting bird.

Flamingos are graceful in flight, but have a laborious take-off routine. They must run over the surface of the water until they have sufficient flow of air over their wings to get airborne.

FLYING FISH

THERE ARE TWO MAJOR GROUPS of flying fish: the two-winged and the four-winged varieties. In the first only the pectoral fins are enlarged. In the second the pelvic (paired) fins also are enlarged, making two pairs of wings. It is this type that is noted for its colorful fins. Flying fish are mainly tropical, but venture into temperate seas during the summer.

There are 52 species, the commonest being the two-winged flying fish, *Exocoetus volitans*. It is around 10 inches (25 cm) long and is found in all tropical seas. The commonest of the four-winged flying fish is *Cypselurus heterurus*. It is normally around 1 foot (30 cm) in total length and is found on both sides of the tropical Atlantic. The largest four-winged type is *C. californicus*, which reaches around 18 inches (46 cm). In summer this species provides an attraction for visitors to California's beaches. In spring and summer it is fished commercially, most of the catch used as bait for swordfish and tuna fishing.

Dangers above and below

When swimming, flying fish fold their long fins against their bodies. They feed on zooplankton and other small fish near the water's surface. In turn, flying fish are the prey of larger, predatory fish, and also of marine mammals. Among the predatory fish, their main enemy seems to be the dolphinfish of the family Coryphaenidae. They are also eaten by sharks, tunas, bluefin, mackerels, squids, dolphins and porpoises.

The flying habit probably evolved largely in response to this heavy predation. Whenever a flying fish leaves the water for the air, seabirds, such as frigate birds, albatrosses and gulls, may also attack, but this threat is by no means as great as that from beneath the waves.

Seaweed nests

In the Tropics, flying fish breed all year round. They spawn on floating seaweed and on other floating objects such as wood, plants and even plastic bottles. Some species seem to use sargassum weed entirely for this purpose. On it they make nests by drawing the weeds together with white elastic strings, and the eggs are fastened to one another and to the nest by similar but thinner threads or filaments.

Once they spawn, the young flying fish are so unlike the adults that in the past they have been described as different species. Besides being patterned in many colors, the young of many flying fish species have a pair of large, flaplike barbels, or whiskers, which hang down from the

tip of the lower jaw. They may also have these whiskers around their mouths. For example, in the young Californian flying fish the barbels form a red, many-fingered outgrowth. In the young 2-inch (5-cm) long Caribbean flying fish, barbels extend back beyond the tail, like streamers. The whiskers resemble the stamens of a poisonous plant called *Barringtonia*, which other fish avoid, and so are thought to protect the young fish from predators.

Gliding or true flight?

For many years it was hotly debated whether or not flying fish flapped their wings while airborne. The reason this doubt continued for so long was largely because the fish were so hard to photograph. Also, there is an illusion of wing-flapping when the fish are preparing for takeoff and are washed by wavelets. At this time the rapidly moving tail vibrates the body, making it quiver, so that the fins appear to be beating the air.

Studies of flying fish anatomy, however, suggest that the fish did not have the right muscles to be able to beat their wings. Experiments in wind tunnels pointed to the same conclusion. Finally, stroboscopic photography was used (that is, photography that makes repeated exposures at short intervals of fractions of a second). The pictures showed the successive positions of the moving wings and proved conclusively that flying fish do not really fly in the true sense of the word, but rather glide.

A four-winged flying fish with one set of wings extended. The wings are really fins modified to allow the fish to glide above the ocean surface.

When a flying fish leaves the water to escape a predator it spreads its fins and can glide for a considerable distance. It enters the water again in one of several ways, including headfirst (above), tail first or by a belly flop.

FLYING FISH

CLASS	**Osteichthyes**
ORDER	**Beloniformes**
FAMILY	**Exocoetidae**

GENUS **Exocoetus, Cheilopogon, Cypselurus, Fondiator, Hirundichthys, Oxyporhamphus, Prognichthys** and **Paraexocoetus**

SPECIES **52, including Atlantic flying fish, Cheilopogon heterurus (detailed below)**

LENGTH
Up to 18 in. (46 cm)

DISTINCTIVE FEATURES
Streamlined body; 2 pairs of enlarged winglike fins: large, stiff pectoral fins that may be as long as the body and smaller pelvic (paired) fins. Young: flaplike barbels on chin and around mouth; bright and varied coloration.

DIET
Small surface-living organisms such as plankton and small fish

BREEDING
Breeding season: May–June (Atlantic); eggs attached to floating objects with filaments

LIFE SPAN
Not known

HABITAT
Open waters, near surface

DISTRIBUTION
Subtropical and temperate seas: western Atlantic from Nova Scotia south to South Carolina; eastern Atlantic from southern Norway and Denmark south to Canary Islands; western Mediterranean

STATUS
Less common than many tropical species, but not under threat

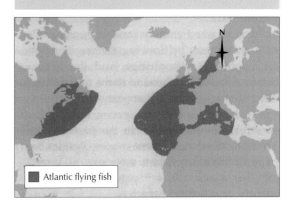

Atlantic flying fish

Taking flight

If it is being chased by a predator, a flying fish increases its swimming speed and heads upward to the surface of the water. To increase speed it makes itself more streamlined by keeping its pectoral fins folded against the body. As its body lifts above the water, it spreads its fins and taxis along the surface with the lower lobe of its tail fin moving in a sculling action. The lower lobe is longer than the upper lobe and is vibrated at a rate of up to 50 beats a second. Then the pelvic fins are spread like wings and this gives enough lift to raise the tail fin clear of the surface and get the fish fully airborne.

Gliding out of trouble

The average speed in the air is about 35 miles per hour (56 km/h). At the start it is about 40 miles per hour (64 km/h) and this falls off to about 20 miles per hour (32 km/h) at the end as momentum is lost. The fish may land on its belly with a splash, or it may dive headfirst, drop back into the water tail first, or even land on its back. It may then resume the sculling action and taxi once more for another flight.

Usually only one or two flights are made, but there are records of up to 11 flights in succession, covering a distance of 1,000 feet (300 m) or more. Each flight, or leap, lasts 2 to 15 seconds and may cover between 45 and 200 yards (40–185 m). Most flights are made just above the water, but flying fish have been known to land on the decks of ships up to 36 feet (11 m) above sea level. These higher flights may occur when a fish strikes an up-current of air if the takeoff is into the wind. Because of their anatomy, four-winged flying fish are better fliers than the two-winged variety.

GANNET

GANNETS ARE GOOSE-SIZED seabirds related to boobies and live in temperate regions of the world. The three forms are considered by most ornithologists to be separate species, but some believe them to be varieties of a single species. There is little difference among the three.

The gannet, *Morus bassana*, sometimes called the northern gannet, breeds on both sides of the North Atlantic. In North America there are a few colonies around Newfoundland and the Gulf of St. Lawrence. The gannet also breeds off the coasts of Iceland, the Faeroes Islands and the British Isles, with small colonies in Norway, northwestern France and the English Channel. The Cape gannet, *M. capensis*, breeds off the coasts of South Africa. The Australian or Pacific, gannet, *M. serrator*, breeds in the Bass Strait, between Australia and Tasmania, and in the Tasman Sea, between Australia and North Island, New Zealand.

Ocean wanderers

Gannets are oceanic birds, coming ashore only for the breeding season. They are strong fliers and cover vast distances, especially during the first year of life. Banding studies have shown that birds from the New Zealand population of the Australian gannet migrate to Australian waters, setting out shortly after they have left the nest and crossing the intervening sea at an average of up to 240 miles (385 km) a day. The northern gannet migrates southward outside the breeding season, reaching the Gulf of Mexico and West Africa.

Gannets live by feeding on fish and squid, plunging in from a height or diving from the surface. Fish are caught as the birds surface rather than being impaled on the bills of the gannets as they penetrate the water. The gannets do not dive deep and chase their prey, propelling themselves with both feet and wings.

The main prey species of the northern gannet are haddock, herring, mackerel, saithe, sprat and whiting. These fish are important commercially but it is very unlikely that the gannets affect the numbers caught by fishers. In fact, commercial catches of herring and many other fish in the North Atlantic are falling, probably because of overfishing, yet the gannet population there is steadily rising. The Australian gannet feeds mainly on anchovies, although it will take a variety of fish.

Gannet colonies are usually perched on small offshore islands and rocks, often no more than steep-sided towers rearing out of the sea.

Familiar colonies include Bass Rock, in the Firth of Forth on the east coast of Scotland, and Bird Rock, in the Gulf of St. Lawrence. The nests are closely packed together, perhaps 2–2½ feet (60–75 cm) between each, so that the cliff ledges and the tops of the rocks or islands are often white with birds.

Frequent fights when nesting

In February, when the rocks are still being lashed by winter gales, male northern gannets appear in the colonies to reestablish ownership of last year's nest or, if breeding for the first time, they fly low over the colonies looking for abandoned nests. Fights are frequent as gannets defend their nests or seek to oust interlopers. These are not

At the nest male and female gannets greet one another with head-shaking and bill-clattering displays.

sham fights, as usually is the case among birds that nest in dense colonies. The gannets grapple each other's bills or grab their opponent's head or neck, shaking, twisting and lunging.

One theory is that gannets may originally have nested on cliff ledges and that nesting on the flat spaces on top of rocks and islands is relatively recent. This would explain the species' tendency to engage in long fights. If cliff-nesting birds fight, one of them is sure to be pushed over the edge within a short time, automatically cutting short the fight. Gannets, on the other hand, grapple with their bills and wrestle to and fro, neither bird appearing to be able to disengage. The fierceness of the gannets' behavior is continued in their courtship. The females are pecked during mating and whenever the males return to the nests after feeding.

The nests are large, compacted piles of seaweed, grasses, earth and all sorts of rubbish, including fishnets and tin cans. One list of materials included a gold watch and a set of false teeth. The pile is cemented by droppings and proves useful as a jumping-off point for takeoff, as gannets have considerable difficulty taking off from flat ground.

Feet make an incubator

The single egg, about 3 inches (7.5 cm) long, is translucent pale blue at first, later turning to a chalky white. As the egg is being laid, the female gannet bends its tail under its body, directing the egg into the nest. Gannets have no brood patch where the egg is held to keep it warm. Instead the egg is held between the webbed feet. The parent holds the egg lengthwise under its body

Gannets nest in large, crowded colonies atop small islands and rocks. Pictured are northern gannets at Bass Rock, Scotland.

GANNET

CLASS	**Aves**
ORDER	**Pelecaniformes**
FAMILY	**Sulidae**
GENUS AND SPECIES	***Morus bassana***

ALTERNATIVE NAME
Northern gannet

WEIGHT
5⅓–8 lb. (2.4–3.6 kg)

LENGTH
Head to tail: 3–3⅓ ft. (0.9–1 m); wingspan 5¼–6 ft. (1.6–1.8 m)

DISTINCTIVE FEATURES
Strong, spear-shaped bill; streamlined, elongated body; very long wings; webbed feet; long, pointed tail. Adult: snow white with black wingtips and pale yellow head; bluish gray bill. Young: blackish brown with variable white markings; black bill.

DIET
Almost entirely fish; some squid

BREEDING
Age at first breeding: 5 or 6 years; breeding season: April–September; number of eggs: 1; incubation period: 42–46 days; fledging period: 84–97 days; breeding interval: 1 year

LIFE SPAN
Probably up to 40 years

HABITAT
Seas and oceans, mainly in coastal waters; nests on sea cliffs, especially on small islands

DISTRIBUTION
Breeds in North Atlantic, from eastern Canada east to northwestern Europe. Nonbreeding birds wander, reaching as far south as Gulf of Mexico and West Africa.

STATUS
Locally common

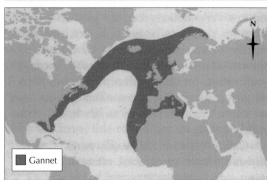

Gannet

and wraps a web around each side of the egg, overlapping underneath. Both parents incubate, working in shifts of 1–2 days apiece.

Incubation lasts about 44 days on average. The chick hatches naked but quickly acquires a coat of down. At first it is brooded on top of the parents' feet and then later it sits by itself in the nest while both parents collect food for it. The chicks take fish by thrusting their heads into the parents' mouths.

When the young gannets have fledged, at the age of about 3 months, they are abandoned by their parents and left to fend for themselves. They leap out of their nests and if they are lucky immediately become airborne. Otherwise each has to struggle through the colony to the cliff edge, being attacked on the way and perhaps killed by the other gannets. Once airborne, the young gannets can fly quite well, but after they have settled on the sea they cannot rise again. On leaving the nest they are very fat, and must spend time losing weight until they can become airborne again and learn to catch their own food.

Safe sanctuaries?

On their inaccessible offshore stacks and rocks gannets are immune to mammalian predators. At a few breeding grounds, however, humans have harvested the sitting birds or their young. For instance, on Bird Rock the building of a light-house gave access to the gannet colony, which was nearly wiped out because the birds were killed for use as fish bait.

The main enemies of northern gannets are herring gulls, *Larus argentatus*, and great black-backed gulls, *L. marinus*, which steal the gannets' eggs. Jaegers also chase the adults, forcing them to disgorge the semidigested food that they are carrying back to their chicks.

Dive-bombing technique

A flock of gannets feeding is a most spectacular sight. Like boobies, they plunge vertically into the sea, with wings half closed, from a height of 100 feet (30 m) or more. There is a continual "rain" of gannets diving down and disappearing with a spurt of spray. Later they emerge and climb again to rejoin their companions, before repeating the descent.

Hitting the water at perhaps 100 miles per hour (160 km/h) could result in severe injury. However, gannets and boobies have strengthened skulls that protect the brain. An intricate system of air sacs in the head cushions the impact, and the nostrils open inside the bill, preventing water from entering the air passages.

Cape gannets (above) of the seas around southern Africa have more black in their wings than the gannets of the North Atlantic. All three species have very long wings and streamlined bodies, an ideal shape for gliding over the sea and plunge-diving for fish.

GARTER SNAKE

ARTER SNAKES, WHICH BELONG TO the genus *Thamnophis*, are the most common and often the most familiar snakes of the United States and Canada. They also occur in Central America south to Costa Rica. There are 13 species in the United States, although two of these are more frequently called ribbon snakes. The range of six of these species extends northward into Canada. The common garter snake is found further north than any other reptile in the Western Hemisphere.

Garter snakes are nonvenomous, comparatively small and rather slender. They are nearly always marked with stripes running along the length of the body. Garter snakes are usually about 2 feet (60 cm) in total length, but specimens that measure 3 feet (90 cm) are not uncommon and the record length is 5 feet (1.5 m).

The common garter snake has a distribution that extends from the Yukon south to just over the Mexican border, and from the West Coast right across North America to the East Coast, although it is not found in the deserts of the Southwest. Other species with widespread distributions include the wandering garter snake, sometimes called the western terrestrial garter snake, which is found from British Columbia

south to New Mexico, and the plains garter snake, found from Alberta to Texas and Indiana. At the other extreme, the narrow-headed garter snake and the Mexican garter snake are found only in Arizona, a small part of New Mexico and small areas in Mexico. The short-headed garter snake is even more restricted and is found only in a small part of Pennsylvania and a tiny fragment of adjacent New York State.

A variable appearance

Since a number of species of garter snakes have such widespread distributions, it is not surprising that even members of the same species are immensely variable in appearance. Common garter snakes, for example, may be black, brown or olive green with three yellowish, orange or red stripes. These red stripes are particularly prominent in a rare subspecies, the San Francisco garter snake, which occurs only at a few sites in San Mateo County, California. The belly is usually yellow, greenish brown or bluish brown in color. Occasionally all-black individuals are also seen.

Garter snakes live in a variety of habitats, from sea level to high up in the Rockies. The mountain garter snake is the only species of reptile in the Rocky Mountain National Park, and

Garter snakes, such as this wandering garter snake, nearly always have a series of stripes running along their bodies, but the number and color of stripes varies greatly.

the Mexican garter snake occurs at up to 13,000 feet (4,000 m). Garter snakes are often restricted to the neighborhood of streams and lakes in the western half of the United States, but are found almost everywhere. Plains garter snakes live in the suburbs of Chicago, where they hibernate in cracks in the ground near the bases of buildings.

Group hibernation

In the northern regions of their range, garter snakes are the last reptiles to go into winter quarters and the first to emerge, as early as March. They hibernate in a burrow, or hibernaculum, which may be as deep as 3 feet (90 cm) underground. Often the snakes hibernate together in vast numbers, and in places their simultaneous emergence in the spring has become a tourist attraction. A traditional saying of Native Americans is that the first clap of thunder brings garter snakes out of hibernation.

Young garter snakes of most of the species feed almost entirely on earthworms in their first year. After that, although worms are the chief item in their diet, the snakes also eat frogs, toads and salamanders, sometimes fish and occasionally birds' eggs. Large garter snakes may hunt mice and other small mammals.

Large litters

Mating takes place near the winter quarters, soon after the snakes come out in early spring. The male garter snake has tiny barbels on his chin, which he passes along the female's back as he prepares to mate with her. Once mating is over,

Although garter snakes prefer to be near water or marshy places, they can be found in almost any habitat. Pictured is a red-sided form of the common garter snake.

GARTER SNAKES

CLASS	**Reptilia**
ORDER	**Squamata**
SUBORDER	**Serpentes**
FAMILY	**Colubridae**
GENUS	***Thamnophis***
SPECIES	**About 20, including common garter snake, *T. sirtalis*; wandering garter snake, *T. elegans*; and plains garter snake, *T. radix***

ALTERNATIVE NAMES
Ribbon snake (certain species only); western terrestrial garter snake (*T. elegans* only)

LENGTH
Usually about 2 ft. (60 cm); sometimes up to 3 ft. (90 cm)

DISTINCTIVE FEATURES
Rather small overall; slender body; 3 or more pale stripes run along length of body in most species

DIET
Adult: mainly earthworms, frogs and salamanders; also small mammals, birds, fish, slugs and leeches. Young: almost entirely earthworms.

BREEDING
Age at first breeding: 2 years; breeding season: summer; number of young: up to 80; breeding interval: 1 year

LIFE SPAN
Usually up to 5 years

HABITAT
Wide variety of habitats; often near water or marshes

DISTRIBUTION
Central Canada south to Costa Rica

STATUS
Generally common. San Francisco garter snake, *T. sirtalis tetrataenia*: endangered.

Garter snakes

the snakes disperse to their summer ranges. The young are born live in summer in litters of usually 50 to 60, but the number of young varies from as few as 12 to as many as 80. The newly born garter snake is 6 inches (15 cm) in total length. It grows about 1 foot (30 cm) per year for the first 2 or 3 years. It is mature at 2 years old, and is ready to mate in its third spring.

Killed in error

There is a very heavy death rate among garter snakes, particularly during the first few months. Even after adulthood, garter snakes suffer heavy predation from a wide variety of animals and on average do not live for more than 3–5 years.

Garter snakes are preyed upon by hawks, owls, skunks, cats and some other snakes. All-black individuals, or those with indistinct stripes, are sometimes killed by people who mistake them for venomous snakes. Inevitably, they are also killed in large numbers on roads. A garter snake's defense is to give out an obnoxious fluid from a pore on either side of the vent. It may bite, but this has little effect on humans.

Live young

Some snakes lay eggs and are said to be oviparous (egg-producing), while others, such as garter snakes, bear live young. In this the garter snake is said to be ovoviviparous. The eggs remain inside the mother until they hatch. All snakes' eggs contain yolk for feeding the developing embryos. In ovoviviparous snake species, however, oxygen for breathing and moisture must be supplied by the maternal tissues. As a result, the shells must be very thin and are little more than a transparent membrane in most cases. In garter snakes, as well as in the European adder, *Vipera berus*, and in the sea snakes and Australian copperheads of the subfamily Hydropheinae, a sort of placenta is formed to carry nourishment from the mother to her developing young. It is a very simple affair, nothing like as efficient as the placenta of mammals, but it is enough to supplement the yolk supply already present in the egg.

The main advantages of this form of reproduction are that there is no chance of the eggs drying up, their temperature remains fairly constant and the eggs are protected from predators until hatching. The mother chooses basking areas with suitable temperatures. This is important in latitudes where summers are short and where even midday temperatures are low.

The disadvantage of ovovivipary in snakes is that the female is encumbered when she is with young. She is less agile and therefore handicapped in hunting and avoiding enemies. In most ovoviviparous species this is minimized by the broods carried being in small numbers. It is remarkable, therefore, that garter snakes should commonly have such large broods of young.

Garter snakes (checkered garter snake, Thamnophis marcianus, *above) are notable for giving birth to large broods of live young.*

GILA MONSTER

ONLY TWO OF THE APPROXIMATELY 3,000 known species of lizards are venomous. These are the Gila monster (pronounced "heela"), *Heloderma suspectum*, and the beaded lizard, *H. horridum*. The two species are very similar in general appearance. Gila monsters are found in the deserts of the southwestern United States and adjacent parts of Mexico. The name is derived from the Gila Basin in Arizona. In the United States their range extends north to south from the southwest corner of Utah to most of the border of Arizona and just into New Mexico. The range continues into Mexico and southward to the coast. There are isolated records of sightings in southern Nevada and southeastern California.

Gila monsters can grow to 23 inches (58 cm) in total length. They are heavy bodied, rather stocky lizards weighing up to 3¼ pounds (150 g). The eyes are small and the legs relatively short. The tail is also short and of variable thickness, because it is used as a fat store. The general body color is black, but this is overlaid with a complex pattern of yellow and pink patches. These become bands of color on the tail. Gila monsters usually have 4 or 5 such bands.

The bright colors and bold patterns of Gila monsters and beaded lizards are an example of warning coloration, where the animal advertises to potential predators that it is venomous. Surprising though it may seem, at dusk or after dark the same colors and patterns are quite effective camouflage for the lizard as they help it to merge into the variegated, monochrome background.

Alternate gluttony and fasting

These lizards normally move about very slowly, although when trying to evade capture they can move much more swiftly and struggle actively, hissing all the while. They spend long periods of time in their burrows in sand or sandy soil. They are particularly active in the rainy season, and are mostly seen at dusk or at night during the summer. However, during the cooler spring weather, they come out by day into the sunshine.

Being slow movers, Gila monsters must eat things that cannot run away. These are mainly eggs of birds and other reptiles, baby birds, baby mice and rats. Like most reptiles, they track their prey partly by smell but more especially by taste, using the tongue to pick up scent particles on the

Gila monster raiding a bird's nest. The tongue is snakelike and longer than that of most other lizards.

GILA MONSTER

CLASS **Reptilia**

ORDER **Squamata**

SUBORDER **Sauria**

FAMILY **Helodermatidae**

GENUS AND SPECIES *Heloderma suspectum*

WEIGHT
Up to 3¼ lb. (150 g)

LENGTH
Average 20 in. (51 cm)

DISTINCTIVE FEATURES
Heavy bodied, with short legs and small eyes; body color black with complex pattern of yellow and pink patches; venomous

DIET
Bird and reptile eggs; small mammals and birds (especially fledglings)

BREEDING
Little known. Breeding season: April–July; number of eggs: usually 4 to 7; hatching period: about 30 days, or hatch in the following spring.

LIFE SPAN
Up to 20 years in captivity

HABITAT
Semiarid habitats; abundant at bottom of small canyons and streams with eroded deep beds and desert soils; also in oak woods, sandy beaches and sand dunes

DISTRIBUTION
Arizona and adjacent areas; Sonoran Desert and surrounding areas of Mexico

STATUS
Increasingly scarce; protected in Arizona

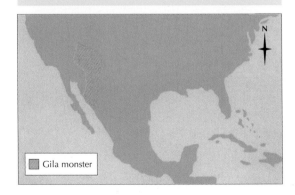

Gila monster

ground. These are conveyed by the tongue to Jacobson's organ, a sort of taste-smell organ in the roof of the mouth. Gila monsters eat insects and earthworms in captivity, and from the behavior of these captive animals it seems unlikely that venom is used to kill prey. They either seize an egg, crushing the shell and raising their head so the contents flow into the mouth, or bite the egg in two, using their tongue to lap up the contents. The Gila monster drinks liquid food by lapping it up and holding its head back to let the liquid run down its tongue.

While active, these lizards eat all they can find and store the surplus as fat in the body, especially in the tail. When food is less available, and during drought, they can survive long periods of fasting. The fat tail might then shrink to one-fifth its former girth and the rest of the body can become extremely emaciated. Nonetheless, the Gila monster will quickly recover once it can find food, even after perhaps 3 years of fasting.

One of only two venomous lizards, the Gila monster is not thought to use its venom to kill prey.

Inefficient venom apparatus

The venom glands are in the lower jaw, although teeth in both jaws are grooved. Each gland has several ducts that open into a groove between the lower lip and the gum, and the poison finds its way from this to the grooves in the teeth. Neither the Gila monster nor the beaded lizard can strike as a snake does but must hold on with the teeth using a viselike grip, sometimes chewing to help conduct the venom. If bitten by a monster, the main problem is to free the tight-gripping jaws.

Nests in the sand

Mating takes place between April and July, and the eggs are laid in July or August. These are laid in a hole dug by the female with her front feet and covered with sand. There are 3 to 15 in a clutch, but 4 to 7 is the usual range. Each egg is oval, measuring 1½ by 2½ inches (6.5–7.75 cm), and has a tough, leathery shell. They hatch in about a month, or they may overwinter and hatch the following spring. Remarkably little is known abut the details of the reproductive cycle. Each newly hatched lizard is 3½–4¾ inches (9–12 cm) in length, with colors that are more vivid than those of the parents.

Legally protected

Little is known of the natural enemies of the two venomous lizards, but by 1952 the Gila monster was becoming so rare it had to be protected by law to save it from extinction. This was mainly because it was being caught and sold in large numbers as a pet. Those who caught them were paid 25–50 cents an inch, and the lizards were then sold at 1–2 dollars an inch.

Lizard with a bad name

Many erronous beliefs have gathered around the Gila monster in the past. One is that it cannot eliminate body wastes, which is why it is so venomous. For the same reason its breath was believed to be evil-smelling. Another is that it can spit venom, whereas at most, when hissing, it may spray a little venom. The lizard also has been credited with leaping on its victims, largely the result of the way it will lash out from side to side when held in the hand. Its tongue has been said to be venomous, the lizard itself impossible to kill and possessed of magical powers. Lastly, the Gila monster has been said to be a cross between a lizard and a crocodile.

The first scientists to study the Gila monster were not sure whether it was venomous. They therefore named it *Heloderma suspectum*. Zoologists were more certain about the beaded lizard, which they named *H. horridum*. Now we know that the Gila monster produces a neurotoxin that causes swelling, loss of consciousness, vomiting, palpitations, labored breathing, dizziness, a swollen tongue and swollen glands. Not all these symptoms appear in all victims, however. The swelling and the initial pain are due to the way the poison is injected, as the lizard holds on and chews with a sideways action of the teeth. A single bite is unlikely to be fatal for a human being.

The bold patterns of the venomous Gila monster are an example of warning coloration. Many potential predators leave it well alone.

GRAY FOX

SOMETIMES CALLED THE TREE FOX, the short-legged gray fox is noted for its ability to climb and it uses trees much more than other foxes do. Up to 27 inches (68 cm) in head and body length and 4–15½ pounds (2–7 kg) in weight, the gray fox has a bushy tail that may be up to 17 inches (44 cm) long. The general color of its fur, or pelage, is gray with white underparts, but there is a rusty tinge along the sides of its neck, lower flanks and the underside of its tail. The gray fox has a black line running along the middle of its back, continuing along the tail, and black lines on its face. There is also a noticeable ridge of stiff hairs along the top of the tail. The size and color of the gray fox vary from one region to another. In the northeast of the fox's range its coat is a dark gray, while in the southwest it is paler and slightly redder.

Two species

There are in fact two species of gray foxes. Most common, the gray fox, *Urocyon cineroargenteus*, ranges from southern Canada through the United States to Mexico, Central America and northern South America. A second species, the island or beach fox, *U. littoralis,* is a smaller animal with shorter ears. It lives only on certain islands off southern California, each island having its own subspecies. It scavenges the beaches and makes its den among the cacti.

Tree-climbing dogs

Gray foxes live in forests, especially of southern pines, and in brush country in the dry areas of the southwestern United States and Mexico. It is difficult to assess numbers because the species is not only mainly nocturnal but is also quite shy and adept at keeping out of sight. It is therefore relatively seldom seen. Even its yapping bark often passes unrecognized, partly because it is rather like the call of the coyote, *Canis latrans*.

During the day, the gray fox rests in thick vegetation, among rocks or in a tree hollow. Much of its diet of small vertebrates and insects is caught on the ground. Nonetheless, the fox sometimes climbs into trees in search of food, especially to find fruits in season, eggs, or to catch birds. More commonly, it will go up into trees when disturbed or under threat.

To get into a tree the fox will run up a leaning trunk, or climb a straight trunk by gripping it with its forelimbs and pushing upward with the hind feet. The long claws on the toes of its hind feet act as climbing irons. Once in the tree the fox is able to leap from one branch to

another and can traverse branches that may be less than 1 inch (2.5 cm) in diameter. When descending, the fox backs down the tree. Once on the ground, it is not a fast runner and cannot run over long distances.

A varied diet

The gray fox's diet is wide and includes mice, squirrels, small birds and eggs, as well as insects. It also eats more plant food and vegetable matter than is usual in the dog family. Grain and fruits, especially wild grapes and wild cherries, form the bulk of its food at certain seasons and in particular areas. With such a wide diet the gray fox readily takes to farmland and can be a nuisance, especially where there is poultry.

The gray fox is also established in some built-up areas, such as the outskirts of New York City. Its actual dietary requirements were worked out by Richard F. Dyson, Curator of Large

A gray fox in the southern United States. Its fur is a paler gray with redder coloring on its neck, flanks and tail compared to gray foxes in the north.

A nocturnal species, the gray fox survives on a varied diet that includes mice, lizards, small birds, insects, fruits and grain.

Mammals at the Arizona-Sonora Desert Museum at Tucson. Because some of the mammals were overweight and had shaggy coats he tested gray foxes for 6 months and found they kept in excellent health on 3.8 percent of their own body weight of food each day, this diet including flesh and fruit. Later it was shown that this held true for some other carnivores.

United families

The breeding season for gray foxes depends on where they live. Foxes breed from December to March in the southeastern United States, but from January to May in New York. The cubs are born after a gestation period of between 50 and 63 days. Litters normally average 3 or 4 cubs, but the range may be from 1 to 10. At birth the cubs are black, blind and helpless, about 3½ ounces (100 g) in weight. They are weaned at 6 weeks. The male helps in bringing up the family, the cubs finally leaving the parents at the age of 5 months. The cubs reach sexual maturity at around 8 months. Gray foxes have been known to live up to 13½ years in captivity.

In terms of predators, the gray fox may be killed by gray wolves, coyotes, bobcats and lynx but today its main enemies are humans. Because of the gray fox's habit of going quickly to ground or up into trees, it is not hunted but trapped. In this the trapper takes advantage of the regularity with which a gray fox uses a run through the vegetation and sets his or her traps accordingly. The pelts make only second-rate furs. The survival of the island fox, partly because of its specific range, is now considered to be entirely dependent upon conservation measures.

GRAY FOX

CLASS **Mammalia**

ORDER **Carnivora**

FAMILY **Canidae**

GENUS AND SPECIES **Gray fox, *Urocyon cineroargenteus*; island fox, *U. littoralis***

ALTERNATIVE NAMES
Gray fox: tree fox. Island fox: beach fox.

WEIGHT
Gray fox: 4–15½ lb. (2–7 kg).
Island fox: 4–13¼ lb. (2–6 kg).

LENGTH
Gray fox. Head and body: 19–27 in. (48–68 cm); tail: 10½–17 in. (27–44 cm)
Island fox. Head and body: 19–20 in. (48–50 cm); tail: 4⅓–11½ in. (11–29 cm).

DISTINCTIVE FEATURES
Gray fur with rusty to reddish tinge; white underbelly; dark stripe along back

DIET
Mice, squirrels, small birds and reptiles, eggs, insects, grain and fruits

BREEDING
Age at first breeding: about 8 months; breeding season: December–March (southeast U.S.), January–May (north); gestation period: 50–63 days; number of young: usually 4; breeding interval: 1 year

LIFE SPAN
Up to 13½ years in captivity

HABITAT
Forests, woods, brushland and rocky terrain

DISTRIBUTION
Gray fox: southern Canada south through U.S. to northern South America.
Island fox: islands off southern California.

STATUS
Gray fox: common. Island fox: dependent on conservation programs.

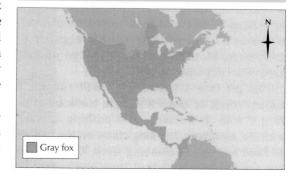

Gray fox

GRAY WOLF

A female gray wolf and her cub at the den entrance. There is usually only one breeding pair in a pack of wolves.

THOUGHT BY MANY TO be at least one of the possible ancestors of the domestic dog, the wolf was once widespread over Europe, most of Asia and North America. During this time it had a range probably greater than that of any other land mammal. Today two distinct species of large wolf remain, the gray wolf, *Canis lupus*, the largest member of the Canidae family, and the red wolf, *C. rufus*. The gray wolf is still found in the wilder parts of Europe, Asia and North America, while the red wolf is now restricted to the south-central United States. There are numerous local races or subspecies of these two species, however, that differ widely in size and color.

The gray wolf is the larger of the two, with a head and body length ranging from 3¼ to 5¼ feet (1–1.6 m) and a tail of 14–22 inches (35–56 cm). Its height at the shoulders can be up to 38 inches (97 cm) and it weighs from 65 to 130 pounds (30–60 kg). In general these measurements will differ between subspecies and geographical locations, with the gray wolf tending to be heavier in the more northern parts of its range. One shot in east-central Alaska is said to have weighed 175 pounds (80 kg). The red wolf is more slender, weighing on average 33 pounds (15 kg), occasionally up to 70–80 pounds (32–36 kg).

Dark and light phases

Both the gray and red wolves are doglike in appearance. They have large heads with erect, rounded ears. Their long muzzles have strong jaws that contain six or seven cheek teeth on each side, including a well-developed carnassial. Their limbs are long and slender with four toes on the hind foot and five on the forefoot, each bearing nonretractile claws. When angry, wolves

GRAY WOLF

CLASS	**Mammalia**
ORDER	**Carnivora**
FAMILY	**Canidae**
GENUS AND SPECIES	***Canis lupus***

ALTERNATIVE NAMES
Timber wolf; tundra wolf; plains wolf

WEIGHT
65–130 lb. (30–60 kg)

LENGTH
Head and body: 3¼–5¼ ft. (1–1.6 m); shoulder height: up to 38 in. (97 cm); tail: 14–22 in. (35–56 cm)

DISTINCTIVE FEATURES
Large head with long muzzle and erect ears; much longer legs and larger paws than domestic dog; coloration variable but usually light brown or gray, sprinkled with black and with white underparts and legs

DIET
Mainly large mammals and carrion; also smaller mammals, fish, crabs and garbage

BREEDING
Age at first breeding: 22 months; breeding season: January–March; gestation period: 60–63 days; number of young: usually 4 to 7; breeding interval: 1 year

LIFE SPAN
Up to 16 years in captivity

HABITAT
All land habitats and topography except deserts and high mountain tops

DISTRIBUTION
Wild parts of North America, Greenland, Europe, the Middle East and Asia

STATUS
Endangered in parts of the U.S. except where recovered or in experimental populations

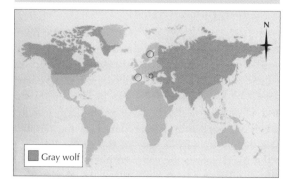

Gray wolf

erect the long hair on the nape of their necks so that it looks like a mane. There is a scent gland used for recognition on the upper side of the tail near its base.

The color of the gray wolf varies considerably over its range but it is usually gray sprinkled with black, apart from the legs and underparts, which are white or yellowish white. Black or dark and white or light-colored phases occur quite commonly. On the Arctic coast of Alaska and in western Canada, wolves are sometimes white throughout the year, but more usually they are a mixture of white and gray tinged with brown. The red wolf is more tawny and small ones sometimes look like coyotes.

Gray wolves sometimes exhibit dark and light phases. They are also lighter in color, even white, in the winter.

Great endurance

The gray wolf is a highly efficient carnivore. It also has great fighting ability, intelligence and endurance. It can adapt to most habitats other than deserts and high mountains, but mainly lives in wild, open country and forests. It hunts by day and hides at night among rocks, under fallen trees or in holes dug in the ground.

Wolves sometimes hunt singly or in pairs, but more often they move in a family party or pack consisting of five to 15 or more individuals. These packs are usually based around a single, dominant breeding pair. A single, large wolf can bring down and kill a large deer, but a pack is

A pack of gray wolves in the Bavarian forest, Germany. Gray wolves now inhabit a fraction of their former range in Europe, Asia and North America.

able to tackle even larger animals, such as moose or elk. A wolf runs at an average speed of only 22–24 miles per hour (35–39 km/h) and reaches a maximum of 28 miles per hour (45 km/h) for short distances. Nonetheless, it has remarkable powers of endurance and can keep up a loping run for mile after mile. Wolves' powers of endurance are greater than most large game animals, so they can usually outrun their prey. They travel widely and there is a record of a red wolf in Oklahoma that covered almost 125 miles (200 km) in 2 weeks, crossing four mountain ranges. They are also good swimmers, and sometimes pursue deer and other prey into the water.

Wolves make use of pathways through their territory, often incorporating game trails and cattle tracks in these hunting routes. Such routes might cover more than 100 miles (160 km) and have numerous "latrines" that also function as scent posts, along with vantage points on high ground for observation.

Large eaters

A wolf can eat an enormous amount of food at one sitting. For example, it might eat one-fifth of its body weight at one meal and then go without food for a considerable time. The size of prey taken depends on geographical location and pack size. Primarily the gray wolf is a predator of mammals larger than itself. It will kill large animals such as caribou, reindeer, musk oxen, deer, elk, moose, mountain sheep and horses. At times and in places where these animals are not available, wolves will eat smaller prey such as mice, rabbits and squirrels. Fish and crabs are sometimes taken, as well as carrion and household garbage. When natural food is short, the wolf will take to killing any domestic livestock and poultry within its range. However, stories of attacks on humans have not been authenticated.

A large family

Wolf packs are governed by strict domestic hierarchies for both males and females. Usually only one female per pack reproduces. The breeding season is from January to March, with a gestation period of 60–63 days. There can be between three and 11 cubs in a litter, but more usually four to seven are born in a den prepared by the female. The den is usually a hole in the ground and is often used year after year. At birth the cubs are blind, with a sooty brown fur. In the Arctic, where the white color phase predominates, the cubs' fur will be light blue or dull slate in color. Their eyes open 5–9 days after birth. Both parents teach the cubs to hunt and kill prey. The cubs tend to leave their natal pack, the pack in which they were born, before 20 months of age. Alternatively they might join the pack to attempt to reach alpha (breeding or dominant) status.

Slaughtered by humans

Over many centuries humans have been the chief enemies of wolves. Constant efforts have been made to exterminate both the gray and red wolf because of their destructiveness to domestic stock. Numerous methods have been used to kill them, including poison, steel traps, shooting and hunting by dogs.

In the lower 48 states of the United States, the gray wolf was deliberately exterminated from 99 percent of its former range. In addition, human settlement has deprived it of much territory. Today populations of gray wolves that survive in the lower 48 states are classified as endangered in several states or as threatened (in Minnesota), or have been delisted (northern Rocky Mountain region) by the U.S. Fish and Wildlife Service based on substantial recovery. The Mexican subspecies of gray wolf is extinct in the wild, while Italy's population is vulnerable. Wolves in Spain and Portugal are conservation dependent. In 1995 the gray wolf was reintroduced to Yellowstone National Park from which it had been exterminated in 1923. By 2009 the regional population had increased to well over one thousand wolves, prompting renewed efforts to reduce the population.

The red wolf once roamed throughout the southeastern and south-central United States. It was effectively extinct in the wild by 1980, but captive-bred wolves have since been reintroduced to a few sites in Texas, Louisiana, Mississippi, South Carolina and North Carolina.

The wolf in legend

From earliest times the wolf has been depicted in literature and legend as a symbol of savagery, courage and endurance. Beowulf, the legendary Teutonic hero, and many Anglo-Saxon kings and nobles incorporated "wolf" into their names as an indication of their fighting prowess. In North America the Native Americans also used the name for their most powerful warriors. Yet there have also been many stories, from way back in history, of wolves that have raised human children from infancy, lovingly looking after them and protecting them from other predators. The most famous story is that of Romulus, the legendary founder of Rome, and his twin brother, Remus. In more recent times there is a story from India of a child raised by a wolf until she was about 9 years old. However, such stories are almost certainly untrue.

Wolves hunt in packs, normally preying upon mammals much larger than themselves.

GROUNDHOG

THE GROUNDHOG OR WOODCHUCK is also known as the whistle-pig and is popularly called a "chuck." It is a common rodent in most of Canada and the eastern United States and is well known for its reputation for forecasting the weather.

The groundhog's body is thickset and 12–24 inches (30–60 cm) in length with a 4–10-inch (10–25-cm) hairy tail. Its weight varies from about 6⅔ pounds (3 kg) when the animal emerges from hibernation in the spring to 12 pounds (5.5 kg) before it goes to sleep again in September. A large groundhog may weigh as much as 15½ pounds (7 kg) at this time. The groundhog has a flat head with large teeth and small ears. Its four toes have long claws used for digging. The color of its pale fur varies from yellow to reddish brown.

The groundhog's range in the east extends from Labrador and Nova Scotia in Canada, south to Virginia and Alabama in the United States. It then ranges west as far as Kansas and north through Minnesota and central Canada to the northern Rockies and Alaska.

True hibernation

The groundhog prefers open grassland habitats but also frequents woods and farmland. It digs its burrow in well-drained soil, on rocky hillsides, for example, or in gullies but often in bushy woods at the edge of meadowland. The burrow has several exits and the entrance has a large pile of freshly removed earth around it. Burrows vary in depth according to the soil. In soft earth a tunnel may be as much as 6½ feet (2 m) below the surface. The burrow consists of several compartments for sleeping and hibernating and for latrines. The groundhog is a very clean animal and regularly cleans its latrines, taking the waste up above ground to be buried at the entrance.

The groundhog is solitary and diurnal (day-active), feeding in the morning and again in late afternoon or evening. It never wanders far from its burrow, its home range being only about 100 yards (90 m). Groundhogs can swim well and, unlike most large rodents, will climb for food.

In autumn the groundhog hibernates, starting its sleep earlier in the northern parts of its range. It settles down in one of the chambers in its burrow, sealing it off with earth, rolls up in a ball and goes into a deep sleep. Its breathing slows down until it almost stops: 14 breaths per minute compared to the normal of 262 breaths per minute. In addition, its temperature will

Groundhogs, common across much of Canada and the eastern United States, are also called woodchucks, "chucks" and whistle-pigs.

Groundhogs eat voraciously during spring and summer, building up their weight before they go into hibernation in September.

GROUNDHOG

CLASS	**Mammalia**
ORDER	**Rodentia**
FAMILY	**Sciuridae**
GENUS AND SPECIES	***Marmota monax***

ALTERNATIVE NAMES
Woodchuck; whistle-pig

WEIGHT
6⅔–15½ lb. (3–7 kg)

LENGTH
**Head and body: 12–24 in. (30–60 cm);
tail: 4–10 in. (10–25 cm)**

DISTINCTIVE FEATURES
**Large, thickset body; flattened head; large
teeth; small ears; long claws on toes; pale,
yellowish to reddish brown fur; erect
posture when vigilant**

DIET
**Grasses, roots, shoots, leaves, flowers, fruits,
bark and tree seeds; occasionally acorns,
snails, insects, small birds and crops**

BREEDING
**Age at first breeding: about 2 years;
breeding season: March–April; gestation
period: 28–32 days; number of young:
usually four or five; breeding interval: 1 year**

LIFE SPAN
Up to 12–15 years in captivity

HABITAT
**Mainly open grassland and farmland; also
woods; digs burrow in well-drained soil**

DISTRIBUTION
**Easternmost Alaska and western Canada,
east toward Newfoundland and eastern
U.S., south to Virginia and Alabama**

STATUS
Locally common

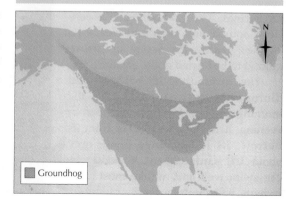

Groundhog

gradually drop to between 40 and 57° F (4–14° C). This compares to its normal temperature of 95–104° F (37–40° C). When the groundhog emerges in the spring it looks very thin and hungry and has lost as much as half of its weight.

A pest to farm crops
The groundhog is mainly vegetarian, feeding on grasses, shoots, leaves and flowers, particularly clover, and sometimes acorns. It will eat bark from trees and also takes fruits such as blackberries, raspberries, cherries and windfall apples. It occasionally eats snails, insects and small birds.

In some farmland areas the groundhog has become a pest, eating all kinds of farm produce and cereal crops. In addition to feeding voraciously, it spoils the crops by trampling. In some parts of the United States the groundhog's numbers have been controlled by gassing the animal in its burrows.

Looking for a mate
As soon as the male groundhog comes out of hibernation in the spring, it goes to look for a mate. Fights often break out between two males

and considerable damage may be inflicted before the weaker animal retreats, leaving the victor in possession of the female. Mating takes place in March and April.

After a gestation period of 28–32 days, between one and eight, although more normally four or five, babies are born in the burrow. The young "chuck" is pink, naked and blind at birth, less than 4 inches (10 cm) long and weighing only 1–1½ ounces (28–43 g). The female feeds her babies sitting on her haunches or standing on all fours. After a month the youngsters' eyes open and they make their first trip out of the burrow. They are weaned in 35 days and by midsummer, when they are 2 or 3 months old, they have been driven out of the home burrow by the mother. However, they continue to live in a nearby burrow. The mother watches over the youngsters during this time and at the first sign of danger warns them with an alarm whistle. The young groundhogs are sexually mature and able to breed after 1 or 2 years.

Many enemies

In captivity groundhogs have been known to live for 12–15 years. For most animals in the wild, however, their life span is considerably less, a result of the groundhog's many natural predators. For example, the species is preyed on by bears, coyotes, gray wolves and pumas, as well as by eagles and hawks. It is also often attacked by farm dogs. In addition, the groundhog is an important game animal in some areas. Humans hunt it for sport and for its flesh which, except when old, makes very good eating. The hunters and predators have to be very quick and sharp-eyed, as "chucks" are wary and bolt for cover at the slightest hint of danger.

Weather forecaster

The groundhog is a legendary weather forecaster in North America. It is said that if it emerges from hibernation on February 2nd and sees its own shadow, it will return to sleep for another 6 weeks. If this is the case, there will be a further 6 weeks of winter. If, however, it does not see its own shadow, winter is over and spring has come. According to Will Barker, in "*Familiar Animals of America*," this legend dates back to early Colonial times. He states that in European folklore it was the Eurasian badger, *Meles meles*, that was supposed to look for its shadow on February 2nd, and early European settlers in America transferred the myth to the groundhog.

The groundhog is one of the few large rodents that often climbs bushes and trees. However, it is perhaps best-known in North America for its legendary ability to forecast if the winter is over.

HARE

THE BROWN OR COMMON HARE and the common or European rabbit are similar, but the hare has softer fur, longer and more profuse whiskers and black tips to its ears. Its ears are also much longer, usually longer than its head, and its tail is black above and white on the sides and underside. The hare's hind legs are much longer and better developed than those of a rabbit. When running it is the stiltlike action of the hare's hind legs, especially when seen from behind, that distinguishes it from a rabbit.

Hare or rabbit?

The most important biological distinction between true rabbits and true hares, however, is that when young hares, or leverets, are born they are already well developed. Their eyes are open, they have a fur coat and they have the ability to hop and use their legs soon after birth. Young rabbits are naked, blind and helpless at birth.

In the past, rabbits and hares were classified as a subdivision of the rodents. This classification has since been changed from the order Rodentia to a new order, Lagomorpha, which also includes the pikas. The use of the words "rabbit" and "hare" has been somewhat mixed and misapplied to particular species. The Belgian hare, for example, is actually one of many domestic breeds of the European rabbit.

The brown or common hare, *Lepus europaeus*, is one of the best-known species, not only because it was the first to be described scientifically, but also because it is so widespread. It ranges across central and southern Europe, the Middle East and Africa. The brown hare is about 2 feet (60 cm) long with a 3½-inch (9-cm) tail. It weighs on average 8 pounds (3.6 kg). Its fur is tawny and slightly more reddish on the neck, shoulders and flanks. The sides of its face and the outer surfaces of its legs are rather yellowish.

The brown or common hare is widespread in much of Europe, the Middle East and Africa.

Compared to rabbits, hares have longer ears and longer, better developed hind legs. They are also more likely to be solitary and rarely burrow.

HARES

CLASS	Mammalia
ORDER	Lagomorpha
FAMILY	Leporidae
GENUS	*Lepus*
SPECIES	About 30, including brown hare, *L. europaeus*; northern hare, *L. timidus*; and snowshoe hare, *L. americanus*

ALTERNATIVE NAMES
Brown hare: common hare. Northern hare: mountain hare; blue hare; varying hare.

WEIGHT
3–15½ lb. (1.3–7 kg)

LENGTH
Head and body: 16–27½ in. (40–70 cm); tail: 1⅓–4 in. (3.5–10 cm)

DISTINCTIVE FEATURES
Large ears; long legs, especially hind legs; long vibrissae (whiskers); usually brown fur on upperparts, paler fur on belly; some species turn white in winter in snowy regions

DIET
Grasses, herbs, shoots and leaves

BREEDING
Age at first breeding: less than 1 year; breeding season: varies according to species; gestation period: 40–50 days; number of young: 2 to 4; breeding interval: 3–4 months

LIFE SPAN
Up to 7 years in captivity

HABITAT
From tundra and alpine habitats to temperate farmland, African savanna and scrub

DISTRIBUTION
Almost worldwide

STATUS
Most species common

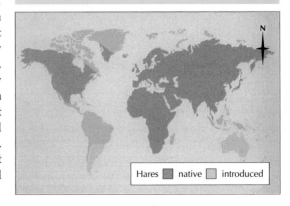

Hares ■ native ■ introduced

The underparts are white except on the breast and legs. The jack, or male, is slightly smaller in the body than the doe, or female, has a shorter head, and has more red on the shoulders.

The brown hare's diet is wholly vegetarian. It mainly feeds on grasses and browses on low herbs and shrubs. Hares sometimes do serious damage to commercial crops.

Alert and agile

Hares are mainly solitary except in the breeding season. Sometimes several can be seen together. At other times up to a dozen or more will come out in the evening to feed, but they soon disperse. During the day a hare lies in a form, a hollow in coarse grass or other herbage that retains the shape of the animal. Hares rarely burrow. Their tactics are to lie low and keep still, but their senses are always alert, as illustrated by the constantly twitching nostrils and whiskers. In the open a hare will rise on its haunches, or it might momentarily rise right up onto its hind legs, to survey its surroundings with ears erect. When chased a hare can run at great speed. It also relies on jinking, suddenly twisting and turning to elude its pursuer.

Madly in love

The most famous feature of the brown hare's breeding season is the courtship behavior of the jacks and does. Their antics have led to the saying "Mad as a March hare." The courtship and premating antics of both males and females include bucking, bounding, kicking and standing on the hind legs to box with one another. This boxing is usually an action of the female repelling the unwanted attentions of a male.

Mating is said to be promiscuous and reaches a peak in spring, but hares will mate at any time of the year. Females might give birth to up to six young, but this number depends to some degree on location and season. Normally litters of between two and four leverets are born from February to September, but in the Northern Hemisphere this occurs mainly in April.

Well-developed young

Baby hares are very well developed when they are born. They can hop and move about using their legs just a few minutes after they are born. Each leveret soon makes its own form and is visited by the doe to be suckled. The young are independent at around 1 month old. Hares may live up to around 7 years in captivity, but most hares will only live a year or so in the wild.

They form the staple food for many small and medium-sized predators, including the larger birds of prey.

All shapes and sizes

The brown hare's range extends across Europe and Asia. There are many local forms throughout this range. Local races of the brown hare are also found in Africa, on grassland or savanna with scattered trees and shrubs. The northern or mountain hare, *Lepus timidus*, is another typical species but it occurs farther north, in the Alps, Scandinavia and Greenland. A subspecies, *L. timidus scoticus*, is found in Scotland. Here and elsewhere it is also known as the blue hare. The northern hare's coat goes white in winter except for the tips of its ears, which remain black. In spring and autumn the coat appears almost blue when the brown hairs of the summer coat are mingled with the white hairs of the winter coat. The species gets a fourth name of "varying hare" because of this change in the color of its coat between summer and winter.

The northern hare lives on high ground, usually among rocks. It is smaller in the body than the brown hare and has a larger head, longer legs and ears and a shorter tail. Its main enemy is the golden eagle, *Aquila chrysaetos*.

The snowshoe hare is one of several species that change color, from brown to pure white in winter, although the tips of its ears remain black.

snowshoe hare. It is only 16 inches (40 cm) long from head to tail, with a 2-inch (5-cm) tail. This small species weighs up to 4½ pounds (2 kg). It does not burrow and behaves in other ways like the brown hare except that it feeds mainly on bark and twigs. In summer its coat is reddish brown with black on the back, its legs are light brown and its underparts are white. Its winter coat, on the other hand, is white except for the black ear tips.

This change is governed by the shortening length of day rather than any seasonal change in temperature. This has been shown in laboratory conditions where the normal change from brown to white has been prevented in hares by extending the "daylight" to a regular 18 hours using artificial light. Similarly, the white coat will change to brown even at the low temperatures of winter if the animal is exposed for long periods to artificial light. Another outstanding feature of the snowshoe hare, and the one from which it gets its name, is the hairy mats on the soles of its feet. These "snowshoes" help it to move over soft snow without sinking.

Breeding for this species takes place between March and August. Both sexes are promiscuous and the males indulge in much fighting, using their teeth. After a gestation period of 30–38 days, litters of three to four young, or even as many as ten, are born. They show an advanced development at birth, similar to that of other species of hares.

A baby snowshoe hare. Just days after birth, the young hares are separated by their mother and left in different hiding places.

Altogether there are 30 or so species of hares that occur naturally on all principal land masses except Australia. These include species in the United States, Africa and Asia. Others have been introduced to Australia, New Zealand and South America. The brown hare, for example, was introduced to Australia during the 19th century, where it has since become a pest. Many of the different species look fairly alike but differ in small details of the bone structure of their skulls.

Snowshoes on their feet

In the United States the term jack rabbit is used to describe species such as *L. townsendii, L. californicus* and others. The so-called jack rabbits are discussed elsewhere. Another North American species, *L. americanus*, is popularly called the

The ecology of trapping

Hares are popular animals with hunters, providing both meat and fur. A phenomenon observed and documented in the Hudson Bay Company's records of furs brought in by trappers is that snowshoe hares are subject to 10-year cycles of abundance and scarcity. Their populations build up to a peak and then fall to a minimum. As the numbers of hares increase, so do the numbers of foxes, lynx and martens that prey on them. Similarly, a population slump is followed by a steep fall in the numbers of fur-bearing predators.

HARVESTING ANT

Harvesting ants exhibit a strict division of labor within a colony. Small workers gather and transport seeds to the nest. Here the seeds are husked and crushed by larger workers, later to be fed to developing larvae.

HARVESTING ANTS ARE named for their habit of collecting seeds and grains and storing them in large quantities in their underground nests. These ants are found in the drier regions of the subtropics and some of them live in deserts. In southern Europe, Africa and Asia they are represented by *Messor*, *Pheidole* and other genera, while in subtropical North America ants of the genera *Pogonomyrmex* and *Ischnomyrmex* have adopted a similar mode of life.

Harvesting ants are polymorphic social insects, that is, they are divided into specialized forms or castes, each of which carries out a particular function within the colony. The ordinary workers are quite small and normally proportioned, but there are also larger workers and certain individuals, the largest ants of all, in which the jaws are enlarged and the heads are proportionally enormous to accommodate huge jaw muscles. Each caste has its own role in the colony.

Villagelike colonies
The nests of colonies of harvesting ants are large, sometimes forming a mound 20 or 30 feet (6–9 m) across and penetrating 6 feet (1.8 m) or more into the ground. The entrance is often surrounded by a craterlike wall of coarse soil particles. The ants forage in large groups and the tracks leading to the nest look like well-marked roads. Within the nest there are special chambers, or granaries, in which the grain is stored.

The seeds are collected from living grasses and from standing crops of grain, or from the ground where they might have scattered during harvesting. In the Mediterranean and the Near East harvesting ants collect wheat, in Asia they take millet. In some regions these ants take so much of a cultivated crop that they have become serious grain pests.

The division of labor
The small workers gather the seeds and bring them home, where the husk or chaff is removed by the larger workers using their powerful jaws. These large individuals also crush the seeds when they are needed for food. Crushed and masticated grain is given to the growing larvae, and the adult ants also live on the store during times of drought when the foragers can find nothing edible outside the nest. The discarded

HARVESTING ANTS

PHYLUM	**Arthropoda**
CLASS	**Insecta**
ORDER	**Hymenoptera**
FAMILY	**Formicidae**
GENUS	***Messor; Monomorium; Pheidole; Pogonomyrmex; Ischnomyrmex;* others**
SPECIES	**Many**

ALTERNATIVE NAME
Harvester ant

LENGTH
***Messor* worker: up to ⅖ in. (1 cm)**

DISTINCTIVE FEATURES
Highly polymorphic (appearing in various forms). Larger workers: proportionately huge heads; powerful mandibles.

DIET
Harvested seeds and grains

BREEDING
After mating, new queen feeds first batch of young with saliva; these workers tend subsequent eggs; females come from fertilized eggs; males from unfertilized eggs

LIFE SPAN
Queen: several years. Worker: less than this.

HABITAT
Deserts and dry grasslands

DISTRIBUTION
Warm regions of Mediterranean, Africa, Asia, North and South America and Australia

STATUS
Common

Harvesting ants (genus Messor, above) take grass seeds to the nest. These ants also harvest millet and grain, and in some regions have become a serious pest to cultivated crops.

Accidental crops

When the ants fail to prevent germination, they bring the sprouting grain to the surface and throw it on the rubbish heap, where some of the seeds may germinate successfully and produce plants. It was once thought that these ants deliberately cultivated such crops around their nests.

Some plants are specially adapted to be dispersed by harvesting ants. The seeds have food bodies called elaiosomes and special chemical attractants that stimulate the ants to collect them. When the ants grip the elaiosome they take the whole seed. The elaiosome is removed, fed to the developing larvae in the nest and the hard seed is discarded, intact and viable. This phenomenon is termed myrmecochory and is found worldwide.

New colonies

The life cycle of the harvesters is similar to that of other ants. Winged females mate with winged males. After mating, the males die and the females shed their wings. Each female or queen then starts a new colony, seeking out a crevice in which to lay her eggs and raise a small brood. The queen feeds this first batch of young with saliva and these become workers. Eggs continue to be laid by the queen or queens and further larvae are tended and fed by the workers. The young pass through a pupal stage before reaching maturity. Females are raised from fertilized eggs, males from unfertilized eggs. Whether a female becomes a worker or a reproducing female depends on diet.

chaff is thrown outside on a rubbish heap, which comes to form a ring around the nest and is a clearly visible feature of a flourishing colony.

Well-kept granaries

Within the nest the storage chambers are kept well drained so the seed remains dry and does not germinate. If the seeds begin to germinate the ants bite off the embryonic root or radicle, preventing further growth. When heavy rain does penetrate to the storage chambers, the damp seed is brought to the surface and spread out around the nest to dry. The quality of the seed as food is improved by this treatment, as the starch in the seeds is partly converted to sugar.

HERMIT CRAB

walking, but the next two pairs are small and are used to grip the shell. The last pair of limbs on the abdomen, which in a lobster form part of the tail fan, are sickle-shaped and used for holding on to the central column of the shell. The hermit crab has swimmerets (small, unspecialized appendages under the abdomen) only on the left side.

Shore-dwelling young

The common hermit crab, *Pagurus bernhardus,* is found in European and North American coastal waters. Normally only the young are found on the shore, their red and yellow front ends projecting from shells such as winkles, top shells and dog whelks. They are nimble in spite of their burdens and are well protected from the pounding of waves, and from drying up when the tide is out. Nevertheless, the young prefer to live in pools in most situations, and are often found under seaweed and large stones. The older ones of this species reach a length of 4 inches (10 cm), although some individuals grow to as much as 6 inches (15 cm). They live in deeper water and occupy the larger shells of common and hard whelks.

Creative shelter

Semiterrestrial hermit crabs of the genus *Coenobita* live on tropical coasts. They usually occupy ordinary snail shells, but Indonesian coenobites have been seen wearing such odd substitutes as joints of bamboo, coconut shells and even a broken oil lamp chimney. *C. diogenes,* of Bermuda, lives in shells that are in fact fossil or subfossil since they belonged to a snail, *Livona pica,* now extinct in Bermuda. The shell of another hermit crab, *Pylopagurus,* becomes encrusted with a bryozoan (moss animal). It is thought that the actual shell is dissolved, leaving only the moss animal's chalky skeleton. It is this skeleton that cloaks the crab and grows with it.

Hermit crabs (Pagurus megistas, above) are well adapted to their shell-dwelling habit, their abdomens often being soft and twisted to fit the shells in which they live.

HERMIT CRABS LIVE IN abandoned sea snail shells. In all species the form of their bodies is modified accordingly. The banana-shaped abdomen, protected in its "hermitage," is soft and curves to the right to fit the inside of the snail shell. The front end of the hermit crab's body has the hard covering typical of crabs and lobsters, and the right claw is larger than the left in most cases. There are a few exceptions where the claws are equal, or the left is larger than the right. The crab uses its larger claw to close the entrance of the shell. It has two pairs of legs behind the claws, which are used in

The hermit crab, *Pylocheles,* found in deep water in the Indian Ocean, lives in pieces of bamboo. Its abdomen is straight. *Xylopargus* of the Caribbean is also adapted to its living quarters. It is found at depths of 600–1,200 feet (183–366 m) in hollow cylinders of wood. The rear end of its body is shaped to make a kind of stopper.

COMMON HERMIT CRAB

PHYLUM **Arthropoda**

CLASS **Crustacea**

ORDER **Decapoda**

FAMILY **Paguridae**

GENUS AND SPECIES **Pagurus bernhardus**

LENGTH
Usually less than 4 in. (10 cm); occasionally up to 6 in. (15 cm)

DISTINCTIVE FEATURES
Crab that lives in empty gastropod (sea snail) shells; soft, banana-shaped abdomen, twisted to right to fit shell; right claw usually much longer than left; 2 pairs of walking legs; 2 pairs of smaller legs for gripping shell. Adult: often found in whelk shells. Juvenile: in variety of small shells.

DIET
Tiny scraps of dead animals and plants

BREEDING
Age at first breeding: 1 year or more; breeding season: all year; number of eggs: 10,000 to 15,000; larva undergoes 4 molts; juvenile then emerges to seek suitable empty shell for a home

LIFE SPAN
Up to 4 years

HABITAT
Adult: coastal waters down to about 260 ft. (80 m), occasionally to 1,640 ft. (500 m); most seabed types except soft mud. Young: between tidemarks; especially in pools, under seaweed or large stones.

DISTRIBUTION
North Atlantic coasts including North America, western Baltic and Mediterranean

STATUS
Common

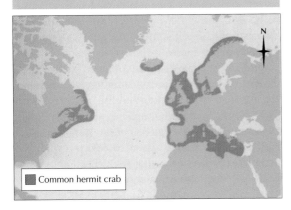

Common hermit crab

Some marine hermit crabs have less mobile homes. They live in holes in coral or sponge. This is a habit to some extent shared by lobsters and perhaps indicates the origin of the hermit crab's way of life. The robber or coconut crab, *Birgus latro*, of the South Sea Islands, is a land-living hermit crab several pounds in weight and 6 inches (15 cm) across. The adult of this species has lost the shell-dwelling habit, and although the abdomen is still twisted it has a hard covering and is kept tucked under the thorax. The robber crab makes burrows at the bases of coconut trees and lines them with coconut husks.

Hermit scavengers

Hermit crabs are mainly omnivorous scavengers, tearing up food with their smaller left claws and transferring it to their mouths. The common hermit crab feeds on tiny animals and plants, tossed with sand and debris between its mouthparts using its left claw. Some other hermit crabs can filter particles from the water with bristles on the antennae. Every so often they wipe the antennae across the mouth to take the food collected. The land-living coenobites, meanwhile,

Here a young common hermit crab can be seen moving into the empty shell of an edible periwinkle.

Here three anemones have attached themselves to the shell of a large hermit crab. The anemones benefit from being able to feed on the crab's leftover food.

The semiterrestrial hermit crabs, *Coenobita,* and the robber crab, *Birgus,* must still visit the sea to hatch their eggs because their larvae are marine. Although the adult robber crab does not carry a shell, its young will do so as they come ashore, only shedding their shells later on.

Moving house

Periodically, the growing hermit crab sheds its external skeleton. A split appears on the abdomen and the crab wriggles out of its old skin. As the hermit crab outgrows its home, this must be replaced with a larger one. The crab examines the new shell with its claws for several minutes, and then, if it seems good enough, hurriedly transfers its abdomen from the old shell to the new one. Sometimes one hermit crab may try to drive another crab from its shell.

Fascinating partnerships

Like any hard object lying on the seabed, the shell of a hermit crab tends to become encrusted with weeds, sponges, barnacles and hydroids (marine invertebrates including simple jellyfish and hydras). Certain sea anemones also associate with hermit crabs and form close partnerships with them. Known as symbiotic relationships, these are of mutual benefit to the animals. Large specimens of the common hermit crab, for example, often carry one species of anemone, *Calliactis parasitica,* on their shells. As the hermit feeds, the anemone sweeps the seabed with its outstretched tentacles and gathers fragments left by the crab. The hermit crab may sometimes benefit from bits of food caught by the anemone.

Another hermit crab, Prideaux's hermit crab, *Pagurus prideauxi,* which is light reddish brown in color and 2 inches (5 cm) long, regularly carries the anemone, *Adamsia palliata.* This species, unlike *Calliactis,* is found only on hermit crab shells. The basal disc of the anemone wraps tightly around the shell, completely enclosing it. As the crustacean grows, so does the anemone, adding to the effective capacity of the shell. As a result the shell does not have to be replaced. In this case, the mouth of the anemone lies just behind that of the hermit crab. Anemones are armed with stinging cells, and these help protect the hermit crab, discouraging, for instance, the attacks of predatory octopuses and squid.

Paguropsis typica goes a stage further than Prideaux's hermit crab by carrying the anemone, *Anemonia mammilifera,* without the need for a snail shell as well. Another species of hermit crab, *Parapagurus pilosimanus,* has large eyes in spite of the fact that it lives in water too deep for light to penetrate. It has been suggested that *Parapagurus* finds its way about by light emitted from the phosphorescent anemone that cloaks it.

often climb bushes for plant food and may even attack young birds. The robber crab feeds on coconuts that have cracked open falling from trees, along with carrion, fruits and sago pith. It, too, is a climber and can scale the trunks of sago palms and other trees.

Breeding and growth

The common hermit crab breeds through much of the year and females with between 10,000 to 15,000 dark violet eggs attached to the swimmerets on their abdomen are to be found at most times. Such crabs come partially out of their shell from time to time and fan their swimmerets to aerate the eggs.

As the larvae hatch, molting at the same time to become zoea larvae, the mother sits partly out of her shell and gently wipes the swimmerets with a brush of bristles on her small fourth pair of legs. The tiny, shrimplike zoea larvae shed their skins four times, growing each time. At the fourth molt the young hermit crab is ready to seek its first shell home. This stage lasts 4 to 5 days. Sexual maturity is not reached for a year or more. The sexes differ externally only in the form of the swimmerets, which have differing functions. However, in many species the male hermit crab is larger than the female.

HONEYBEE

Honeybee workers on a honey and pollen storage comb. The female workers maintain the colony: they feed the larvae, build and repair the comb and forage for nectar, pollen, water and resin.

In the colonies of social bees there are two kinds of females. The fertile females are called queens and the sterile females are the workers. The workers do all the work of maintaining the economy of the colony. The male honeybees are called drones.

Giant relatives

Only four species of the genus *Apis* are known, and one of them, the eastern honeybee, *A. indica*, is so similar to the European honeybee that it is sometimes regarded as a subspecies. The eastern honeybee is domesticated in tropical Asia. Both the other species inhabit the eastern Tropics. The giant honeybee, *A. dorsata*, is a large bee that makes enormous hanging combs in the open. Large branches overhanging cliffs and buildings, especially water towers, are favorite sites for colonies. These bees may be dangerous if disturbed. Despite this, a tribe called the Dyaks of Borneo climb by night, throw down the combs and gather the honey. The small honeybee, *A. florea*, is by contrast a fairly docile insect. A colony consists of a single comb that contains only 1 or 2 ounces (28–56 g) of honey.

Household chores

The great majority of European honeybees are now living in hives, although wild colonies may be found, almost always in hollow trees. In midsummer a strong colony normally contains one queen, 50,000 to 60,000 workers and a few hundred males or drones.

ANY OF THE FOUR SPECIES of social bees belonging to the genus *Apis* can be called honeybees. However, the name is most usually associated with the European domestic bee, *A. mellifera*, sometimes called the western honeybee. This species differs from all other social bees and social wasps of temperate climates in that it forms colonies that survive the winter by living on reserve stores of food. As a result, European honeybees may occupy a particular dwelling site or nest for an indefinite length of time. In social wasps and bumblebees, on the other hand, all the members of the colony die at the end of the summer with the exception of the fertilized females or queens. These hibernate and found new colonies the following spring.

Worker bees are short lived, surviving perhaps 4 to 6 weeks. For the first 3 weeks after emerging from the pupa the worker's duties lie within the hive. Her first spell of work is as nursemaid to the developing larvae, and she passes on a great deal of the food she eats to these, partly by direct regurgitation and partly by giving them a jellylike secretion from certain salivary glands on her head. By the time she is around 12 days old her wax glands have developed and she turns to building and repairing the comb of geometrically arranged cells in which the larvae are reared and food is stored. At this time she also starts to take the nectar and pollen brought in by returning foragers, converting the nectar to honey and storing it away. At the same time she helps to keep the hive tidy, carrying dead bees and other debris outside. At 3 weeks old the worker bee is ready to go out foraging for nectar, pollen, water and resin, which are the four substances needed for the hive's economy.

HONEYBEES

PHYLUM	**Arthropoda**
CLASS	**Insecta**
ORDER	**Hymenoptera**
SUBORDER	**Apocrita**
FAMILY	**Apidae**

GENUS AND SPECIES **European honeybee,** *Apis mellifera*; **eastern honeybee,** *A. indica*; **giant honeybee,** *A. dorsata*; **small honeybee,** *A. florea*

ALTERNATIVE NAMES
A. mellifera: **hive bee; western honeybee**

LENGTH
**Queen (fertile female): ⅗ in. (1.5 cm).
Worker (sterile female): ⅖ in. (1 cm).
Drone (male): slightly larger.**

DISTINCTIVE FEATURES
Social bees that build complex nests

DIET
**Adult bees: flower pollen and nectar.
Worker and drone larvae: nectar, honey and pollen; some royal jelly (secretion produced by workers' special glands).
Queen larva: royal jelly alone.**

BREEDING
Breeding season: all summer; number of eggs: up to 1,500 each day; hatching period: 3 days; larval period: 6 days (worker), 8 days (drone); pupal period: 12 days

LIFE SPAN
Queen: several years. Worker: usually 4–6 weeks; ones that develop later in year will survive winter. Drone: 4–5 weeks.

HABITAT
**Domesticated bees (majority): nest in hives.
Wild bees: nest in hollow trees.**

DISTRIBUTION
Probably originated in warmer regions, such as Southeast Asia. *A. mellifera*: reared domestically in most western countries. Other species: eastern Tropics.

STATUS
Common

Resin is used to make a sort of varnishlike cement called "propolis" with which any small openings or crevices in the hive are sealed.

Searching for nectar

In searching for nectar-yielding flowers, the worker bee is guided by her senses of smell and sight. Honeybees cannot see red at all but can see ultraviolet light, which is invisible to humans. Bees guide themselves to and from the hive by reference to the angle of the sun, or to the angle of polarized light from the sky. They have a sense of time that enables them to compensate for the continuous change in the sun's position.

After 2 or 3 weeks of foraging the worker is worn out and dies. Workers hatched in the autumn have a longer life before them, as they build up food reserves in their bodies and survive through the winter. During this time their activity is greatly reduced. The bees keep warm by huddling together in a mass and feeding on the honey that they have stored.

The queen rules the great horde of female workers by secreting a substance from her body, the presence or absence of which controls their behavior. Her chief role, however, is egg-laying, and at midsummer she may be laying 1,500 eggs a day. This enormous fecundity is needed to compensate for the shortness of the workers' lives.

Mating with and fertilizing the queens is the only useful part played in honeybee economy by the male drones. Males that do mate with the queen die immediately after. During summer

Foraging for nectar and pollen is hard work. After just 2 or 3 weeks of foraging, worker bees become worn out and die.

Fertilized and unfertilized eggs

Queens may be produced in a hive in response to the urge to swarm or because of the aging of the mother queen. In either case the queens fly out to seek mates immediately on becoming adult. The sperm is stored by the queen in an internal sac called the spermatheca, and sperm is released to fertilize the eggs as she lays them. All eggs that are fertilized produce females, either workers or queens. Drones are only produced from eggs that develop without being fertilized.

The larval and pupal stages of honeybees (collectively known as the brood) are passed in the wax cells into which the eggs are laid, one in each cell. The larvae are entirely helpless and are fed by the workers. The development of a worker bee takes around 3 weeks: 3 days as an egg, 6 as a larva and 12 as a pupa. The natural mating behavior of queen and drone bees makes any control of pairing and breeding impossible, but in recent years a technique for artificially inseminating chosen queens with sperm from chosen drones has been developed.

Common and royal food

The natural food of bees consists of nectar and pollen. The bees also make honey from nectar and store it for food. The larvae are fed partly on a mixture of nectar or honey and pollen, and partly on a secretion from various glands of the workers, the substance that is often called royal jelly. When a fertilized egg is laid in a normal-sized cell, the larva is fed at first on jelly and later on pollen and honey, and it develops into a worker. When production of queens is needed, the workers make larger cells into which the queen lays ordinary fertilized eggs. The larvae from these, however, are fed on royal jelly alone and they develop into queens. Drone larvae are fed similarly to those of workers but for a few more days and in slightly larger cells.

Predators and disease

In spite of their stings, bees are preyed on by birds, dragonflies and some kinds of wasps. Wax moths lay their eggs in the hives and the larvae live on wax, pollen and general comb debris, sometimes doing serious damage. The large death's head hawkmoth, *Acherontia atropos*, invades colonies and steals the honey, piercing the wax comb with its short, stiff proboscis. The greatest threat to honeybees, however, is disease and starvation.

Cells cut away to show pupae. Females are produced from fertilized eggs, while the male drones are produced by unfertilized eggs. To produce queens, the female larvae are fed on royal jelly alone.

they usually live for 4 or 5 weeks and are fed by the workers. In autumn any drones remaining in the colony are driven outside to die.

Swarming

New colonies are founded by what is known as swarming. At this time extra queens are produced in the hive and then large numbers of workers, accompanied by some drones and usually one queen, leave the hive and fly together for some distance. They then settle in a large cluster and search for a suitable site for the colony. Once one is found, the new colony is made by some of the workers. At this stage they can easily be persuaded to settle down in artificial quarters of any kind merely by shaking the swarm, with its attendant queen, into a suitable receptacle.

Honeybees have been kept by humans for their honey for many hundreds of years. This has been mainly a matter of inducing the bees to make colonies in hollow receptacles of various kinds, such as earthenware pots, logs and straw baskets, and then taking the honey they produce.

HUMMINGBIRD

HERE ARE OVER 320 SPECIES of these minute, brightly colored birds living in the Americas. The largest is the giant hummingbird, *Patagona gigas*. At 8½ inches (21 cm) it is huge compared with the bee hummingbird, *Mellisuga helenae*, of Cuba, which is little more than 2 inches (5 cm) long. Half of the bee hummingbird's length is bill and tail, the body being the same size as a bumblebee. It is the world's smallest living bird.

Hummingbirds are very diverse in form, although all of them are small and have the characteristic rapid wingbeats producing the hum that gives them their name. They have brilliant, often iridescent, plumage, which has led to their being given exotic names such as ruby and topaz, and also to their being killed in their thousands and their skins exported to Europe for use in ornaments. A feature of many hummingbirds is the long, narrow bill, often straight but sometimes curved, as in the two species of sicklebills in the genus *Eutoxeres*. The sword-billed hummingbird, *Ensifera ensifera*, has a straight bill as long as its head, body and tail put together. Hummingbirds are most common in the forests of South America, but they range from southern Alaska to Tierra del Fuego, the southernmost tip of South America. Some species are so rare that they are known only from museum collections.

Hummingbird stamina

Considering the diversity of habitats and food in the South American forests, it is not surprising that there should be so many kinds of hummingbirds living there. It is rather surprising, however, to learn that hummingbirds breed as far north as southeastern Alaska or in such high altitudes as the heights of the Andes. The rufous hummingbird, *Selasphorus rufus*, breeds from Alaska south to California, migrating to Mexico for the winter, a very long journey for so small a bird.

The ruby-throated hummingbird, *Archilochus colubris*, also migrates to and from North America, where it is found from Nova Scotia south to Florida. It crosses the Gulf of Mexico or passes through Mexico overland on each trip. Unlike nonmigratory hummingbirds, it stores a layer of fat equal to half its body weight before setting off. This store amounts to less than 1 ounce (28 g), and the distance a bird can fly is propor-

Rufous hummingbirds (male, below) are the northernmost species, breeding as far north as southeastern Alaska.

A hummingbird's wings are connected only at the shoulder joint and thus can move in all directions, allowing the bird to hover while feeding. A male ruby-throated hummingbird is shown.

RUBY-THROATED HUMMINGBIRD

CLASS	**Aves**
ORDER	**Apodiformes**
FAMILY	**Trochilidae**
GENUS AND SPECIES	***Archilochus colubris***

WEIGHT
Up to 2 oz. (56 g)

LENGTH
Head to tail: 3½ in. (9 cm)

DISTINCTIVE FEATURES
Tiny size; compact, strongly muscled body; long, extremely thin bill; forked tail. Male: metallic green upperparts; iridescent red throat, appears black in poor light; whitish underparts. Female: dusky white chin and throat; buff flanks.

DIET
Flower nectar, small arthropods and flies

BREEDING
Age at first breeding: 1 year; breeding season: April–June; number of eggs: 2; incubation period: 16 days; fledging period: 15–20 days; breeding interval: 2 or 3 broods per year

LIFE SPAN
Up to 9 years

HABITAT
Breeding: deciduous and mixed forest; also parkland and gardens. Winter: tropical forest and scrub.

DISTRIBUTION
Breeds in eastern North America from Florida and Louisiana north to Alberta and Nova Scotia. Winters in Central America from central Mexico south to Costa Rica.

STATUS
Common in southern half of breeding range, becoming uncommon farther north

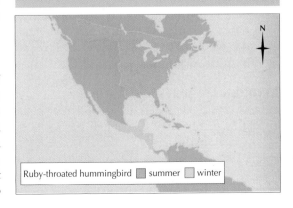

Ruby-throated hummingbird ■ summer ☐ winter

tional to the ratio of fuel and body weight. Small birds can carry a large store of fat for their size and so are capable of great feats of stamina. Research suggests that ruby-throated hummingbirds carrying at least ¼ ounce (2 g) of fat should be able to fly more than 590 miles (950 km), far enough for a nonstop flight across the Gulf of Mexico. Hummingbirds also have, relatively, the largest pectoral (breast) muscles of any birds, up to 30 percent of their total weight.

Hummingbird speed

Even ignoring these migratory feats, the flight of hummingbirds is truly remarkable. Their wings beat so fast they appear as a blur. Small species have wingbeats of at least 80 per second and in courtship displays even higher rates have been recorded. There are reports, as yet unconfirmed, of wingbeats of up to 200 per second. The fast wingbeats enable the hummingbirds to dart to and fro, jerking to a halt to hover steadily. They are also extremely fast in straight flight and speeds of 70 miles per hour (112 km/h) have been recorded. In dives they can reach 60 miles per hour (95 km/h). Specialized filming has shown that hummingbirds do not take off by leaping into the air like other birds, but instead lift off using their rapid wingbeats.

Nightly hibernation

Flying in this manner requires a large amount of energy, so hummingbirds must either feed constantly or have plentiful energy reserves. Even at rest their metabolism (the rate at which they produce energy) is 25 times faster than that of a chicken and their heart rate might reach 1,260 beats per minute. At night, when they are unable to feed, hummingbirds conserve their food reserves by becoming torpid (going into a form of nightly hibernation). In the Andes Mountains a hummingbird's temperature drops from 100° F (38° C) to 66° F (19° C), about the temperature of the surrounding air, and their metabolism is reduced six times.

Nectar-seekers

Hummingbirds feed on nectar and small soft-bodied animals. To sip nectar they hover in front of flowers and insert their pointed bills down the corolla (the petals' base) or, if that is too long, pierce it near the bottom. The nectar is sucked through a tubular tongue that resembles those of flowerpeckers. Pollen is often brushed onto the hummingbirds' heads and transferred to other flowers, so pollinating them. For the flowers of the South American jungle, hummingbirds have an extremely important role as pollinators.

Small insects are caught on the wing and spiders are taken from their webs. Most species of hummingbirds are unable to manipulate insects in their bills and have to rush at them, forcing the prey into their bills. Some pick insects and spiders from flowers. Individual hummingbirds often consume more than half their total weight in food, and may drink twice their weight in water, every day.

Aerobatic displays

In most species the males defend a territory and during courtship they display to the females, flying about in arcs, swoops and dashes, singing songs that are almost too high-pitched for humans to hear. Most hummingbirds have twittering or squeaky songs. The males are usually

promiscuous, mating in the air with several females, but in a few species, such as the violet-eared hummingbirds (*Colibri* spp.) pair bonds are formed and the male helps rear the family.

In most hummingbirds the nest is a delicate cup of moss, lichen and spiderwebs placed on a twig or among foliage. The two eggs are incubated for 2 or 3 weeks and minute, naked chicks hatch out. They are fed by the parent hovering alongside, putting its bill into theirs and pumping out nectar. The chicks grow very rapidly and leave the nest by about 3 weeks old.

Hovering skill

When feeding, hummingbirds can be seen hovering steadily and even flying backward. They can do this because their wings are connected to the body only from the shoulder joint, and therefore can swivel in all directions. When hovering, the body hangs at an angle of about 45° so the wings are beating backward and forward instead of up and down.

In each complete beat the wing describes a figure eight. As it moves forward (the downstroke), the wings are tilted so they force air downward and the bird upward. At the end of the stroke the wings flip over so that the back is facing downward and on the upstroke air is again forced downward. To fly backward, the wings are tilted slightly so air is forced forward as well, and the hummingbird is driven back.

A hummingbird is able to consume more than half its total body weight in nectar and insects each day.

HUMPBACK WHALE

Mother with her calf. Individual humpbacks can be told apart by the distinctive white markings or patches on their bellies and flippers and beneath their tail flukes.

THE HUMPBACK WHALE belongs to the same family as the better-known baleen whales, but has a number of distinct features that place it in a genus of its own. Its name probably comes from its appearance as it dives, when it arches its back just before disappearing below the water's surface. This whale's most character-istic feature is an extremely long set of flippers. Far longer in proportion than in any other whale, they may be as much as one-third of its total body length. The body, far from being stream-lined, is quite barrel-shaped and stocky.

Individual markings

Humpbacks migrate to colder climates to feed in summer. They tend to hug the coastlines as they pass the Tropics to waters of high latitudes. Keeping close to the coasts in this way has made their migrations well-known but has also made the whales an easy prey for hunters in the past.

Humpbacks grow 38 to 50 feet (11.5–15 m) in length, the females being slightly longer than the males. Their color is normally black above and white below, but there are a number of variations on this. The back is generally all black or a very dark, slate gray, but the underside varies consid-erably from almost totally white to nearly all black. Some scientists have tried to divide hump-backs into subspecies on the basis of their color, but this method has been found to be unreliable.

However, it is probable that there is some sort of division, as before humpbacks were protected, whalers would notice they caught all-dark whales, then all-light whales as they worked through various schools passing along the coast. There are also sufficient color variations for these to be used in recognizing individual animals.

Long, distinctive flippers

The humpback's long flippers are usually dark on the upper or outer surface and white on the lower or inner surfaces. In the same way the tail flukes are dark above and pale below. The flippers also have a distinctive outline. The lower margins are scalloped, and they have a number of irregular humps or tubercles along this edge. These tuber-cles also occur on the upper part of the head and along the jawline, and each usually has one or two short coarse hairs growing from it.

On its underside, the humpback has a number of grooves running as far back as the navel. These number 2 to 36 compared with an average of 85 to 90 in the fin and blue whales. Each groove is separated from its neighbor by as much as 8 inches (20 cm), and sometimes the concave part of the groove contrasts with the body color around it. The whale's short dorsal fin is set rather far back and is stubby with a broad base. There may be as many as 400 baleen (whalebone) plates on each side of the whale's

HUMPBACK WHALE

CLASS	**Mammalia**
ORDER	**Cetacea**
FAMILY	**Balaenopteridae**
GENUS AND SPECIES	***Megaptera novaeangliae***

ALTERNATIVE NAME
Humpbacked whale

WEIGHT
Up to 53 tons (48 tonnes)

LENGTH
38–50 ft. (11.5–15 m)

DISTINCTIVE FEATURES
Stocky, barrel-shaped body; extremely long flippers; low, stubby dorsal fin; tubercles (humps or knobbles) on head, lower jaw and lower edge of flippers; black or dark gray overall, with white patches of varying size on belly and beneath tail flukes

DIET
Southern humpback: mainly krill. Northern humpback: krill; small fish such as mackerel, anchovies, sardines and capelin.

BREEDING
Age at first breeding: 4 or 5 years; breeding season: primarily late winter; gestation period: 330–345 days; number of young: 1; breeding interval: 2 years

LIFE SPAN
Up to 70–80 years

HABITAT
Seas and oceans; mainly in coastal waters, including small bays and estuaries

DISTRIBUTION
Summer: high-latitude polar waters. Winter: warmer waters near equator.

STATUS
Uncommon; endangered in the U.S.

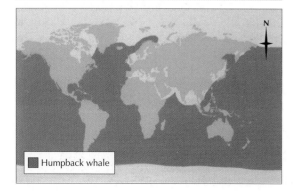

Humpback whale

mouth, but the average is around 300. Each plate is 2 feet (60 cm) in length and grayish black in color. Sometimes there are a few white baleen plates. When present, these are usually at the front of the mouth and they are often associated with blotchy white markings on the skin in about the same position as the plates themselves.

Summer and winter migrations

Humpbacks are found in all oceans but are typically whales of the coasts, often coming close inshore, even into small bays and estuaries. In spite of this, they are very rarely found stranded as some other whale species often are.

Humpback whales migrate every summer to polar waters at high latitudes to feed. They then migrate back to warmer, tropical waters in winter. It is at this time that the young are born and mating takes place. Although there are separate populations of humpbacks in both Arctic and Antarctic waters, by moving toward the equator in the winter months there is possibly some interchange between the two.

The humpbacks sometimes seen off the British coasts spend the summer months feeding with their calves to the north and east of Norway. They then move westward and then south in February and March, migrating as far as the western coast of North Africa. Here another generation of calves is born, and further mating takes place during April and May. After this the whales migrate north again, passing the Outer Hebrides and the Faeroes, to the north of Scotland, and finally reaching northern Norway around July or August.

It has been suggested that humpbacks leap from the water so as to rid themselves of barnacles. This whale was photographed off Admiralty Island, Chatham Strait, Alaska.

The migrations of the southern populations of humpbacks have been studied in considerable detail, and these follow the same pattern as those in northern waters. The whales spend the summer in the Antarctic feeding on the abundant krill and some small fish. As the winter approaches they move gradually northward.

Orderly migrations

The first southern humpbacks to go north are the females that have just finished suckling their calves. The newly weaned calves go with them. Next are the immature animals, then the mature males and finally the pregnant females. They all go as far as the warm equatorial waters, where the pregnant females give birth and then mate once more. In the return migration the pregnant females go first, followed by immature animals, then the mature males and finally the adult females with their newborn calves. By the time they reach the Antarctic feeding grounds the herds have all mixed together and they stay this way until it is time to travel north again.

Krill is the main food

The food of humpback whales, particularly those that are found in the Southern Ocean, consists mainly of krill. Whales in the Northern Hemisphere are more likely to supplement this diet of planktonic crustaceans with a variety of small fish such as mackerel, sardines, anchovy and capelin. When the humpbacks are in tropical waters to breed, they actually feed very little. Most of the feeding is done in colder waters, where enough reserves of blubber are built up to last through the rest of the year.

Mating antics

Humpbacks are well known for their amorous antics. They roll over and over in the water, slapping the surface or each other with their long flippers. This causes considerable commotion and the noise is said to be audible several miles away. Sometimes the whales leap completely clear of the water in their play, although it has been suggested that this is more often done to rid themselves of encrusting barnacles.

Killed on the coast

As is the case with many whale species, the humpback's greatest enemies used to be commercial whalers. Killer whales or orcas take their usual toll, but the humpback, with its coast-hugging habits and fixed migratory routes, was an easy prey for humans. It used to be that when a whale fishery started up, it was usually the humpback species that was killed first. Today there is total protection of humpbacks apart from a few subsistence whaling operations in Greenland, Tonga and the Caribbean. Their numbers have now risen to about 12,000 to 15,000 whales.

Barnacle trouble

Humpback whales are usually heavily infested with barnacles and whale lice. It was long ago noted that humpbacks passing the South African coast on their way north were heavily barnacled but those returning from tropical waters were only lightly infested. It was believed that when the whales got to where the Congo River emptied into the sea they moved inshore into much less salty water, where the barnacles died and dropped off.

A humpback whale dives off the coast of southeastern Alaska. Humpbacks migrate to high latitudes in summer to feed.

KILLER WHALE

THE KILLER WHALE HAS A doubly unsuitable name. It is, strictly speaking, a dolphin, the largest of the family Delphinidae, whose 30 or so species include the closely related false killer whale, *Pseudorca crassidens*, and pilot whales, as well as the much more familiar beak-snouted species. Moreover, despite its wide reputation for great ferocity, the "killer" is no more murderous than any other large, strong predator. The orca, as it is also known, is a powerful, highly intelligent mammal adapted to living in close-knit family groups called pods. It hunts collectively.

The female grows to a maximum length of about 28 feet (8.5 m), but usually stops at around 15 feet (4.5 m). A mature male may be as long as 32 feet (10 m), but again is typically shorter. This marked sexual dimorphism (difference between the sexes) is rare among whales, though it is seen also in the sperm whale, *Physeter catodon*.

In addition to its impressive size, the killer whale's coloration is distinctive. Both sexes are black above and white below. Occasionally the white is yellowish. The chin is white, and there is a white oval streak just above and behind the eye. There is a small, pale patch just behind the dorsal fin that varies in shape and hue from one animal to the next. The white on the underside sweeps up toward the tail, and the flanks are white between the dorsal fin and tail. The flippers, which are broad and rounded, are black all over, whereas the tail flukes are white below.

The dorsal fin is conspicuously straight and tall in the male, usually about 2 feet (60 cm) high but growing to 6 feet (1.8 m) in a mature individual. Breaking the water in a graceful arc when killer whale pods are breathing at the surface, the tall fin is a useful guide to identification. The female has the sickle-shaped dorsal fin more expected of a dolphin. An old male may also have very long flippers, up to one-fifth the animal's total length; that proportion in young males or adult females reduces to only one-ninth.

Killer whales are found in all seas but are specially numerous in the Arctic and Antarctic, where there is abundant food to satisfy their large appetite. They favor coastal waters, where prey stocks are greatest, and can often be seen in estuaries and bays. Some populations are migratory, perhaps following the movements of prey. One such is the North Atlantic population, which heads farther north during the warmer months into food-rich polar waters.

Living in groups

The pods in which killer whales live number from two to several dozen animals of either sex and any age group. A typical pod comprises four or five females and calves led by a large, mature alpha male and his mate. The composition of larger pods is such that calves are always the most numerous individuals, followed by young females, young males, and breeding adults. Pod

A female killer whale at full breach. Also known as orcas, killer whales are the largest species of dolphin.

KILLER WHALE

CLASS **Mammalia**

ORDER **Cetacea**

FAMILY **Delphinidae**

GENUS AND SPECIES *Orcinus orca*

ALTERNATIVE NAMES
Orca; grampus; great killer whale; blackfish; sea wolf

WEIGHT
2⅓–2½ tons (2.5–2.9 tonnes)

LENGTH
Male: up to 32 ft. (10 m); female smaller

DISTINCTIVE FEATURES
Black upper body; white or cream chin, belly and underside of tail flukes; white flash behind eye; grayish patch behind dorsal fin. Male: stocky; steeple-like dorsal fin. Female: less stocky; sickle-shaped fin.

DIET
Mainly fish and squid; also seabirds, other dolphins, turtles, seals and sea lions; very occasionally large baleen whales

BREEDING
Age at first breeding: 15 years (male), 12 years (female); breeding season: all year; gestation period: average 515 days; number of young: 1; breeding interval: 3–8 years

LIFE SPAN
Up to 50–90 years

HABITAT
Usually coastal waters where prey is abundant, but known to dive to depths as great as 1,100 yd. (1,000 m)

DISTRIBUTION
Oceans worldwide, especially in cooler waters toward poles

STATUS
Generally uncommon, but not threatened

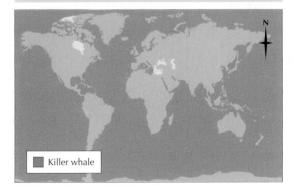

Killer whale

members keep in touch constantly, using an apparently complex language of clicks, whistles, screams and pulsed calls. They not only collaborate when hunting, but also come to the aid of sick or injured family members. Highly inquisitive, they take a close interest in anything likely to be edible. In the Antarctic they loiter around whaling vessels, an easy source of food. When on the move, the pod cruises at around 7 knots (13 km/h), the speed soaring easily to 29–33 knots (33–45 km/h) when required.

Warm-blooded prey

The killer whale probably earned its name from the fact that it is the oceans' largest predator of mammals, but this greatly understates its broad diet. Its staple is fish, although the killer whale may also prey on squid, penguins, seals, other dolphins and whales—even the blue whale.

Several pods may join up to form hunting packs of 40 or more. When attacking a large whale, they work as a team. First, one or two seize the tail flukes to slow the whale down and stop it from thrashing about. Others then go for the head and try to bite the lips. As the whale gradually becomes exhausted, its tongue lolls from its mouth, a rich delicacy to be seized and removed by the killers. It is now all over for the whale, and the hunters take their fill, usually from around the head region. Adding to their

Killer whales live in family groups called pods. A typical pod is made up of four or five females and calves led by a large, mature male and his mate.

occasional attacks on full-grown whales, killer whales have earned the hate of whalers because they often take the tongues from whales that have been harpooned and are lying alongside the factory vessel awaiting processing.

Seal killers

More usually, killer whales prey on seals and porpoises, and there are a number of records of complete seals found in a killer's stomach. A total of 13 porpoises and 14 seals were once found in the stomach of a killer whale, while another held 32 full-grown seals. Off the Pribilof Islands in the Bering Sea, killer whales are often seen lying in ambush for fur seal pups swimming out into the open sea for the first time. Along the coast of Argentina killer whales have been filmed rushing up into the surf zone of a beach to snatch sea lions from the shore.

In the Antarctic, penguins form an important part of the diet, tempting pods to head south into the pack ice, often taking easy routes in the wake of ice-breakers. Here, too, seals are a rich food source, specially when pups or nursing mothers are confined to ice floes. Scientists based on the Antarctic Peninsula have witnessed killer whales swimming beneath ice floes and then surging up under the floe to tip it over or smash it, toppling the seals into the water and into the waiting jaws of the killers. Another technique used by a pod was to breach in unison and send a wave washing over the floe to unseat the seals.

A single calf

Breeding can occur at any time of the year, although mating peaks in May–July in the Northern Hemisphere. The female gives birth to a single calf after 15–16 months. The newborn is about 6½–13 feet (2–4 m) long and weighs about 400 pounds (180 kg). A calf is weaned at about 14–18 months old and is not likely to breed successfully until 12–18 years old.

Humans the only enemy

Killer whales face no natural predators. Despite a few reports of attacks on divers, there is no substantiated evidence that the killers themselves are a menace to humans unless provoked. Human activities have always posed a far greater threat to killer whales. During the 20th century until the mid-1980s Norway, Greenland and Japan hunted small quotas commercially for meat and oil. A more insidious danger comes from marine pollution. Mercury, PCBs and other toxic substances are passed through the food chain and rapidly build up in the bodies of cetaceans, particularly those, like killer whales, that hunt in pollution-prone coastal waters.

Tamed killer whales are crowd-pleasers at oceanaria, where they perform tricks, but there is mounting opposition to such spectacles, with even Hollywood taking a conservationist stance in the *Free Willy* movies. Eco-friendly tourism now caters to people who are prepared to watch this magnificent marine mammal in the wild.

Killer whales favor coastal waters such as bays and estuaries, where most prey is to be found. Their tall dorsal fins are a useful guide to identification.

LADYBUG

SMALL, BRIGHTLY COLORED beetles, oval or almost circular in outline, ladybugs were regarded with affection long before it was realized that they are useful as well as pretty. The name ladybug (sometimes ladybird or lady beetle) dates from the Middle Ages, when the beetles were associated with the Virgin Mary and called "beetles of Our Lady." Their coloration is generally red or yellow with black spots, and the pattern tends to be variable, extremely so in some species. A few, like that known as *Coccidula rufa*, are brown without conspicuous markings and are not usually recognized as ladybugs. The colorful species have a strong and bad smell, and they taste equally bad. Their bright colors doubtless serve as a warning to predators not to try to eat them. Both ladybug adults and their larvae prey on aphids, killing them in great numbers.

Easy to spot

Other than color, ladybugs are most easily identified by their spots. In Britain, for example, the four most common species are the 2-spot, 10-spot, 7-spot and 22-spot ladybugs (or ladybirds, as they are exclusively known there). The first four of these have been given the scientific names *Adalia bipunctata, A. decempunctata, Coccinella septempunctata* and *Thea vigintiduopunctata* respectively. In each the second name is a Latin translation of the number of spots on the two elytra (wing cases). Even scientists balk at long names, so these four ladybugs are usually referred to as *2-punctata, 10-punctata, 7-punctata* and *22-punctata.*

The first species is red with a single black spot on each elytron (wing case), but black specimens with four red spots are common, and the beetle is sometimes yellow with black spots. The underside and legs are black. The second species is reddish or yellow, usually with five black spots on each elytron, but the ground color may be black as in the previous species. The underside is brown and the legs yellowish. The 7-spot is larger than the first two species and its colors hardly vary at all. It is orange red with a black spot on the line dividing the elytra and three others farther back on each side. The last species is much smaller with 11 black spots on each side on a bright yellow ground.

The eyed ladybug, *Anatis ocellata*, is a large British species. It has black spots on a red ground, each spot being surrounded by a halo

A mating pair of 7-spot ladybugs. The strong coloration of adult ladybugs warns birds and other predators that the beetles smell foul and taste bad.

LADYBUGS

CLASS	**Insecta**
ORDER	**Coleoptera**
FAMILY	**Coccinellidae**
SUBFAMILY	**Epilachinae, Coccinellinae and Chilocorinae**
GENUS AND SPECIES	**4,500 species worldwide, including about 400 in U.S.**

ALTERNATIVE NAMES
Ladybird (Britain only); lady beetle

LENGTH
Adult: ⅟₂₅–⅖ in. (1–10 mm)

DISTINCTIVE FEATURES
Adult: small or medium-sized; body usually round or oval; upperside of elytra (wing cases) brightly colored in most species and usually patterned with spots, bands or stripes; short, clubbed antennae; short legs. Larva: covered with bristles; colored black, orange, blue or red, depending on species.

DIET
Most species: aphids, or nectar and pollen when aphids are scarce; other species: plants and mildew

BREEDING
Breeding season: spring–early summer; number of eggs: usually 100 to 200; hatching period: 5–8 days; larval period: about 21 days; breeding interval: 1 year

LIFE SPAN
Usually up to 1 year

HABITAT
Almost any terrestrial habitat

DISTRIBUTION
Virtually worldwide

STATUS
Generally common

A group of ladybugs (Adalia conglomerata) hibernating on the trunk of an ash tree. Adult ladybugs emerge in summer and breed the following spring.

of yellow. The eyed ladybug is generally ⅖ inch (9 mm) in length, and it lives among the foliage of various pine trees.

Crowded winter resorts

In summer ladybugs fly actively about among foliage. In winter they hibernate as adults, often in large groups. Sometimes 50 or 100 of them can be found crowded together under a piece of loose bark, on a post or in a porch. They often congregate in houses and usually go unnoticed until they come out in spring. In California crevices and caves on certain hilltops are well known as hibernation resorts where ladybugs gather in the thousands.

Hordes and hordes of ladybugs

Ladybugs usually lay their orange-colored eggs on the undersides of leaves, in batches of 3 to 50. Several batches are laid by one female, totaling 100 to 200 eggs, sometimes more. Because the beetles themselves feed on aphids or greenflies, they tend to choose places where these are abundant in which to lay, so the larvae find food handy from the start. The eggs hatch after 5 to 8 days, turning gray shortly before they do so. The larvae are active, bristly and variously colored in patterns of black, orange, blue and red. Like the adult beetles, they feed on aphids, but since they are growing rapidly they are far more voracious. The larval stage lasts 3 weeks or so, during which time several hundreds of aphids are eaten.

When thousands of aphid-eating ladybugs are each laying hundreds of eggs, and every larva is consuming hundreds of aphids, it is evident that very large numbers of greenflies are destroyed, and the benefit to plants, both wild and cultivated, is enormous. The pupa is usually attached to a leaf. The whole life cycle takes from 4 to 7 weeks, so several generations of ladybugs may be produced in a summer, although there is usually only one generation in a year. One small group of ladybugs are not predatory but feed as larvae on plant food. A single species occurs in Britain, the 24-spot ladybug, *Subcoccinella viginti-quatuorpunctata*. It feeds mainly on plants such as campions, chickweed, trefoils, vetches and plantains. Elswhere in Europe it is occasionally a minor pest of alfalfa.

Ladybug farms

The principle of using one species of insect to control the numbers of another is now well known and is often favored over the use of poisonous insecticides. An early example of an operation of this kind concerns the use of a ladybug. Toward the end of the 19th century the California citrus orchards were devastated by the cottony-cushion scale insect, which was accidentally introduced from Australia. A brightly colored ladybug, *Rhodalia cardinalis*, was found to be a natural enemy of the scale insect in Aus-

Ladybugs usually lay their orange eggs on the undersides of leaves, in batches of 3 to 50. A few batches are laid by one female, totaling 100 to 200 eggs, sometimes more.

tralia, and in 1889 some of these ladybugs were brought to California and released in the orchards. They effectively controlled the scale insect there, and they have since been introduced into South Africa. The California citrus growers were also troubled by aphids and other plant bugs, and use was made of a native ladybug, a species of *Hippodamia*, that hibernates, as mentioned earlier, in caves in the hills. The *Hippodamia* beetles were collected and sold to the citrus farmers by the liter (8,000 to 10,000 beetles in each liter) and later by the gallon. This control was started in 1910, neglected, then revived during World War II.

Even this is not the end of the story of useful ladybugs in California. In the 1920s the orchards were attacked by another scale insect, genus *Pseudococcus*. Again a ladybug, by the name of *Cryptolaemus montrouzieri*, was brought from Australia. This failed to breed under the natural conditions in western North America, so huge ladybug factories were maintained where they were bred, with careful temperature control. In 1928 alone 48 million ladybugs of this species were set free in the California orange orchards.

LEATHERBACK TURTLE

THE LEATHERBACK OR leathery turtle, sometimes known as the luth, is the largest sea turtle. It differs from other turtles in the structure of its shell. The upper shell, or carapace, is made up of hundreds of irregular bony plates covered with a leathery skin instead of the characteristic plates. There are seven ridges, which may be notched, extending down the back, and five on the lower shell or plastron. Leatherbacks are dark brown or black with spots of yellow or white on the throat and flippers of young specimens. They grow to a maximum length of 9 feet (2.7 m), of which the shell constitutes up to 7⅞ feet (2.4 m), and may weigh up to 1,800 pounds (835 kg). The foreflippers are enormous; leatherbacks 7 feet (2.1 m) long may have flippers spanning 9 feet (2.7 m).

Tropical wanderers
Leatherback turtles are found mostly in tropical seas; they spend more time in deep waters than do the other six species of marine turtles. During the summer months they may wander considerable distances away from the Tropics; they have been found as far north as Alaska, Labrador, Iceland, Scotland, Norway and Japan in the Northern Hemisphere, and as far south as Argentina, Chile, most of Australia (excluding Tasmania) and the Cape of Good Hope. They enter the Mediterranean Sea from time to time,

but do not breed there. It is thought that these movements reflect the migration of jellyfish, which are the mainstay of their diet.

Survival in cool water is aided by "countercurrent heat exchangers" in the flippers. The blood vessels are arranged in such a way that some of the heat that has been produced in the powerful muscles used for swimming is transferred from arterial blood being carried from the body to the flippers to venous blood that is returning to the body. Furthermore, leatherback turtles have very oily flesh, and this may help to insulate them.

A soft diet
The stomach contents of leatherbacks show that they feed on jellyfish, pteropods (planktonic sea snails), salps and other soft-bodied, slow-moving animals, including the amphipods and other creatures that live inside the bodies of jellyfish and salps. Leatherbacks have been seen congregating in shoals of jellyfish, snapping with their horny beaks at the prey. The horny spines in the mouth and throat, 2–3 inches (5–7.5 cm) long, are probably a great help in holding slippery food. In recent years marine pollution has caused problems for leatherback turtles, which sometimes mistake floating polythene bags and other plastic garbage for jellyfish and try to eat them. The plastic is indigestible and may kill the turtles.

A female leatherback turtle coming ashore to lay her eggs. The upper shells of leatherbacks are made of hundreds of bony plates covered with extremely tough, leathery skin.

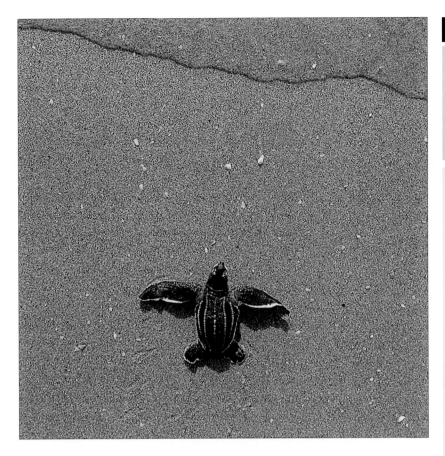

Most hatchlings perish. On beaches they fall prey to crabs, monitor lizards, vultures, small cats, raccoons, gulls and frigate birds. If they manage to reach the sea, the babies must then face predatory fish and squid.

LEATHERBACK TURTLE

CLASS	**Reptilia**
ORDER	**Testudines**
FAMILY	**Dermochelyidae**
GENUS AND SPECIES	***Dermochelys coriacea***

ALTERNATIVE NAMES
Leathery turtle; luth

WEIGHT
Up to 1,800 lb. (835 kg); usually less than 1,200 lb. (545 kg)

LENGTH
Largest on record had a shell 7⅚ ft. (2.4 m) long; shell usually up to 6 ft. (1.8 m)

DISTINCTIVE FEATURES
Largest marine turtle in world; outer part of carapace (shell) made of tough, leathery skin rather than hard scales

DIET
Mainly jellyfish; also salps and pteropods (planktonic sea snails)

BREEDING
Age at first breeding: probably 8–15 years; breeding season: April–October (Caribbean), December–April (Indian Ocean); October–March (Eastern Pacific); number of eggs: 60 to 150, laid in 4 or 5 batches; hatching period: usually about 50 days; breeding interval: 2–3 years

LIFE SPAN
Probably at least 30 years

HABITAT
Tropical oceans; wanders into subtropical and temperate waters in summer

DISTRIBUTION
Worldwide except Arctic and Antarctic

STATUS
Endangered; estimated total population: 150,000 to 400,000 adults

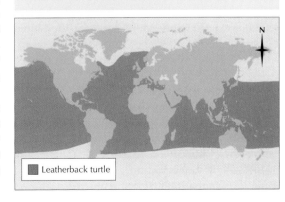

Leatherback turtle

Life is a beach

Breeding takes place on beaches in many parts of the world, including the east Florida coast and at several sites around the Gulf of Mexico. Other nesting beaches are found in Central and South America, the Caribbean, the Atlantic coast of Africa, and at many sites in the Pacific. In total, there are more than 70 nesting beaches for leatherback turtles, many of them shared with other sea turtle species.

Females come ashore in small bands to lay their eggs, usually late at night. They come straight up the shore to dry sand, stop, and then start to dig the nest. They do not select the nest site by digging exploratory pits and testing the sand, as do green turtles. Each female digs with all four flippers, working rhythmically, until she is hidden in the sand. She then digs the egg pit, scooping with her hind flippers until she has dug as deep as she can reach. About 60 to 150 eggs, 2–2¼ inches (5–5.7 cm) across, are laid; then she fills the nest with sand and packs it down. Finally she masks the position of the nest by plowing about and scattering sand, and then makes her way back to the sea.

Each female lays about about four times in one season. The eggs hatch in 7 weeks, and the babies hatch together and rush down the sandy shore to the water. Atlantic leatherback turtles usually breed between April and November; the timing is more variable in the Pacific Ocean.

LOON

THE LOONS, OR DIVERS, are water birds with streamlined bodies, very short tails and straight, pointed bills. Their legs are set well back, like other powerful swimmers such as grebes, darters and cormorants. In common with grebes, but unlike darters and cormorants, loons have not developed an upright stance on land. Furthermore, their legs are enclosed in the body down to the ankle joint, so loons can only shuffle clumsily, a few paces at a time.

"Loon" is a North American name derived from the Old Norse *lómr*, or awkward person, in allusion to the birds' shuffling gait on land. In Iceland they are still known as lomr.

Northern breeders

When breeding, loons are distributed around the higher latitudes in the Northern Hemisphere. The common loon or great northern diver, *Gavia immer*, has a black and white spotted body and collar in summer. It breeds in most of Canada, extending south into the northern parts of the United States, as well as in Greenland, Iceland and Bear Island. In the winter, it flies to rocky coasts and generally moves southward. The yellow-billed loon, *G. adamsii*, known as the white-billed diver in Britain, closely resembles the common loon except for its pale, whitish yellow bill.

The Arctic loon or black-throated diver, *G. arctica*, and the red-throated loon or red-throated diver, *G. stellata*, have similar plumage patterns and distributions. In summer the former has black and white barrings on its back, dark gray on the head and neck and a black patch on the throat. In the red-throated loon the throat patch is reddish chestnut and the head and neck are dove gray. Both species breed in northern Canada, Siberia and northern Europe, including Scandinavia and Scotland. The red-throated loon is also found on Greenland, Iceland, the Faeroes, Spitzbergen and other Arctic islands.

Powerful swimmers

Loons are strong swimmers, and by expelling air from their bodies and plumage, they can swim with only head and neck showing. They may submerge gradually, so quietly that hardly a ripple is left, but at other times they plunge straight downward. During the breeding season,

loons are found on ponds, lakes and slow-moving rivers. Common loons favor remote, large or medium-sized lakes with plenty of undisturbed deep water. Red-throated loons, on the other hand, prefer much smaller, shallower pools and can therefore occur at greater densities than the other species.

Diving for fish

While feeding, loons stay under for a minute at the most, most dives lasting only 10–20 seconds. If alarmed, however, they can stay under longer and dive to great depths. One was caught in a fishing net below 200 feet (60 m). Loons swim with their partially webbed feet, using their wings only as stabilizers.

Loons eat mainly fish, both freshwater and marine, including species such as sand eels, gudgeon and gobies and the young of larger fish such as flounders, trout and perch. Some fish eggs, crustaceans, mollusks, aquatic insects and frogs are also eaten.

Sometimes fishers complain that loons spoil the fishing, but even when the birds gather in loose flocks in winter, they are very unlikely to have any serious effect on fish populations. It is true that loons do on occasion become tangled in lines and nets, damaging them.

Loons (Arctic loon, above) are superbly adapted for swimming fast and chasing fish underwater. They make strange wailing or whistling calls in the breeding season.

A common loon on its simple waterside nest. Loons find moving on land so difficult that they nest right at the water's edge.

COMMON LOON

CLASS	**Aves**
ORDER	**Gaviiformes**
FAMILY	**Gaviidae**
GENUS AND SPECIES	***Gavia immer***

ALTERNATIVE NAME
Great northern diver (Britain only)

WEIGHT
8–10 lb. (3.6–4.5 kg)

LENGTH
Head to tail: 28–36 in. (70–90 cm); wingspan: 4¼–5 ft. (1.3–1.5 m)

DISTINCTIVE FEATURES
Streamlined body; long, spearlike bill; partially webbed feet set far back on body. Summer: black bill; bright red eye; glossy black head and upperparts checkered with white. Winter: grayish bill; grayish brown head and upperparts; white throat and neck.

DIET
Mainly fish; also crustaceans and mollusks

BREEDING
Age at first breeding: 2 years; breeding season: eggs laid late May–June; number of eggs: 2; incubation period: 24–25 days; fledging period: probably 70–77 days; breeding interval: 1 year

LIFE SPAN
Up to 20 years or more

HABITAT
Summer: pools and lakes of subarctic zone. Winter: mainly rocky coastlines.

DISTRIBUTION
Summer: Canada and northernmost U.S.; parts of Greenland; Iceland. Winter: Pacific and Atlantic coasts of North and Central America; coasts of northwestern Europe.

STATUS
Locally common

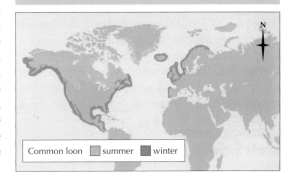

Common loon ▢ summer ▢ winter

Loons can take off only from the water, and then only after a long run across the surface. The wings are small for the size of the body, but loons fly powerfully once aloft and have been clocked at 60 mph (97 km/h). Landing is spectacular; the loon circles the pool or lake on rapidly beating wings, then glides down at a steep angle. As it skims toward the water it lowers its feet and slides to a halt with spray thrown up on either side.

The cry of the northlands

No one who has heard the eerie call of a loon is likely to forget it; it is a symbol of the bird's wild northern homeland. It is impossible to describe this call except poetically. The red-throated loon has been described as calling like the "wail of a lost spirit, echoing and re-echoing around the hills," while the blood-curdling wails of common loons have been sometimes mistaken for the howls of gray wolves. According to the Norse people, if loons flew overhead calling, they were following souls to heaven.

Waterside nests

Loons form a strong pair-bond and pairs probably stay together for life, returning to the same nest site every year. Courtship takes place on the water, with the pair of loons chasing each other, either splashing, half-flying across the surface or swimming with the body partly submerged and the neck held out stiffly. Mating takes place on the nest or in the water, both birds submerging for part of the time.

The nest is usually no more than a depression in a hummock near the water's edge, but the common loon sometimes builds a heap of decaying vegetation. A slipway may be formed as the loons shuffle to and fro.

Incubation of the two or rarely three eggs is shared by the parents. The black fluffy chicks emerge after about 24–25 days and soon take to the water. At first they cannot dive and can swim only weakly; the ripples from the slightest breeze keep them pinned against the bank. They often ride on their parents' backs or retire to the nest when tired, but soon they are able to dive well, disappearing underwater for 6–7 seconds if danger threatens.

The chicks grow rapidly and their diving ability improves apace. Their parents continue to feed them for up to 6 weeks in the case of the red-throated loon, or up to 10–11 weeks in the common and yellow-billed loons. Young loons do not reach sexual maturity for 2–3 years.

Dangers to the chicks

If a loon is disturbed on the nest it freezes with neck stretched low, and if further disturbed it slips quietly off the nest and into the water, submerging and surfacing some distance away. Unless a predator sees the loon leave the nest it will not know a nest is there. Foxes, mink, otters, crows, jaegers and gulls are the main enemies of loons. Another danger is sudden changes in water levels due to heavy rain, which can flood the waterside nests.

Prophesying weather

In the Shetland Islands, north of Scotland, red-throated loons are traditionally called rain geese. They have long been said to foretell rain when their cry, which sounds rather like "we're all wet, worse weather," rings out over the lakes and barren moorland. There are also various local sayings connecting the movements of loons and the weather. For example, one says that when the loons fly inland to their breeding lakes up in the hills in late spring it is time to put the fishing boats to sea.

Red-throated loons breed on smaller pools than the other three species, some no more than 65 feet (20 m) long. They often commute to larger waters nearby to fish.

LUNGLESS SALAMANDER

T HE NAME LUNGLESS salamander covers about 260 species of salamanders living in tropical and North America. They have neither lungs nor gills but breathe through their skin and the lining of the mouth. There are also seven European species, all of the genus *Speleomantes*, found in France, Italy and Sardinia.

Lungless salamanders range in size depending on species, from 2 to 8½ inches (5 to 22 cm). A few live permanently in water, but most are completely terrestrial. They are mainly somberly colored, black, gray or brown, but some have patches of red. The red-backed salamander, *Plethodon cinereus*, occurs in two color phases: red and gray, each with a black-and-white spotted belly. Varying proportions of red and gray individuals are found in any batch of its larvae.

Most lungless salamanders have the usual salamander shape: a long, rounded body and short legs, the front legs with four toes, the back legs with five. The tail is roughly the same length as the body. Exceptions include the four-toed salamander, *Hemidactylium scutatum*, which has four toes on each foot. The long-tailed salamander, *Eurycea longicauda*, is so called because its 7-inch (18-cm) tail dwarfs its 4-inch (10-cm) body. The California slender salamander, *Batra-*

choseps attenuatus, is snakelike, with vestigial (imperfectly developed) legs. It lies under fallen logs, coiled up tightly.

Some species are widespread. For example, the dusky salamander, *Desmognathus fuscus*, ranges over eastern North America from New Brunswick southward to Georgia and Alabama and westward to Oklahoma and Texas. Other species, such as the Ocoee salamander, *D. ocoee*, are very localized. It lives in damp crevices in rocks in Ocoee Gorge in southeastern Tennessee.

From deep wells to tall trees

Terrestrial lungless salamanders live mostly in damp places, under stones or logs, among moss, under leaf litter, near streams or seepages or even in surface burrows in damp soil. The shovel-nosed salamander, *Leurognathus marmoratus*, lives in mountain streams all its life, hiding under stones by day. Others live on land but go into water to escape predators. The pygmy salamander, *Desmognathus wrighti*, is only 2 inches (5 cm) long and lives in the mountains of Virginia and North Carolina. It can climb the rough bark of trees to a height of several feet. The arboreal salamander, *Aneides lugubris*, is able to climb trees to a height of 65 feet (20 m) and

The long-tailed salamander, so named because its tail is nearly twice the length of its body. Almost all lungless salamanders are found in tropical and North America.

sometimes makes its home in old birds' nests. One species of flat-headed salamander uses its webbed feet to walk over slippery rocks, using the tail for balance.

Several species live in caves or natural wells that go down to depths of up to 230 feet (70 m). All these species are blind. One species retains its larval gills throughout life, and one cave species spends its larval life in mountain streams but migrates to underground waters before metamorphosis, at which point it loses its sight.

Creeping, crawling food

All lungless salamanders eat small invertebrates. Those living in water feed mainly on aquatic insect larvae. Those on land hunt slugs, worms, wood lice and insect larvae. One group of lungless salamanders, genus *Plethodon*, are known as woodland salamanders. They live in rocky crevices or in holes underground and eat worms, beetles and ants. One species of woodland salamander, the slimy salamander, *P. glutinosus*, eats worms, hard-shelled beetles, ants and centipedes as well as shieldbugs, despite their strong odor. One of the European species catches its food with a sticky tongue.

Diverse breeding methods

Among the lungless salamanders there is as much diversity in breeding as in the way they live. Some lay their eggs in water and the larvae are fully aquatic. Others lay them on land, and among this second group are species in which the females curl themselves around their batches of 20 to 40 eggs as if incubating them. In a few species the female stays near her eggs until they hatch, but does not incubate them or give them

The eastern tiger salamander, Ambystoma tigrina, *is a large species that has both spotted and banded varieties.*

LUNGLESS SALAMANDERS

CLASS	**Amphibia**
ORDER	**Caudata**
FAMILY	**Plethodontidae**
GENUS	**About 30, including *Ambystoma, Aneides, Batrachoseps, Desmognathus, Ensatina, Eurycea, Gyrinophilus, Hemidactylium, Plethodon* and *Speleomantes***
SPECIES	**About 270 species**

LENGTH
2–8½ in. (5–22 cm)

DISTINCTIVE FEATURES
Adult (most species): long, rounded body with tail of similar length; short legs; 4 toes on front legs, 5 toes on back legs; mainly black, gray or brown in color with variety of markings. Larva: external gills.

DIET
Terrestrial species: mainly slugs, worms, ants, wood lice and insect larvae. Aquatic species: aquatic insect larvae.

BREEDING
Varies according to species. Breeding season: usually summer; number of eggs: 5 to 5,000; larval period: several weeks to several years.

LIFE SPAN
Not known

HABITAT
Most species: damp woodland, leaf litter, wet meadows, streamsides, seepages, rock piles and caves

DISTRIBUTION
Most species: tropical and North America; 7 species in France, Italy and Sardinia

STATUS
Critically endangered: 3 species; endangered: 4 species; vulnerable: about 25 species; many others locally common

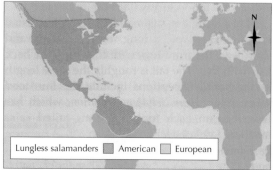

Lungless salamanders ▮ American ▮ European

any special care. The woodland salamanders lay their eggs in patches of moss or under logs, and the larvae metamorphose before leaving the eggs.

Breeding in the dusky salamander

A typical species is the dusky salamander. The male deposits his sperm in a spermatophore, or capsule. He then rubs noses with the female. A gland on his chin gives out a scent that stimulates the female to pick up the spermatophore with her cloaca (a chamber into which the urinary, intestinal and generative canals feed). Her eggs are laid in clusters of about 25 in spring or early summer under logs or stones. Each egg is 1/6 inch (4 mm) in diameter, and the larvae on hatching are about 3/8 inch (9 mm) long. They have external gills and go into water. Here they live until the following spring, when metamorphosis takes place. The adults, 5 inches (13 cm) long, are dark brown or gray in color. When it first metamorphoses, the young salamander is brick red and light cream in patches. Later it takes on the colors of the fully grown adult.

Not so defenseless

Lungless salamanders, like other salamanders and newts, have few means of defence against predators. A possible exception is the arboreal salamander, which has fanglike teeth in the lower jaw. The slimy salamander gives out a sticky, glutinous secretion from its skin when handled, and this also possibly deters predators. Lungless salamanders are preyed upon by small snakes and frogs. Especially vulnerable are the larvae and the young salamanders.

The yellow-blotched salamander, *Ensatina croceator*, of California, has a curious behavior that may be defensive. It raises itself on the tips of its toes, rocks its body backward and forward, arches its tail and swings it from side to side. It also gives out a milky astringent fluid from the tail. More extraordinary, the yellow-blotched salamander is able to squeak like a mouse, which may also deter predators. Because it has neither lungs nor a voice box, it does this by contracting the throat, forcing air through the lips or nose.

Breath through the skin

The most distinctive common feature of these salamanders is that they lose their larval gills as they grow and never develop lungs. Instead, their skin has become the breathing organ, with the skin lining the mouth also acting the part of a lung. It does this by having a network of fine blood vessels in it, like the lining of a lung. The arboreal salamander has a similar network of fine blood vessels in the skin of its toes, and these may provide an additional breathing method.

Many salamanders (Jefferson salamander, Ambystoma jeffersonianum, above) lay their eggs in water. When the larvae hatch they have external gills and are fully aquatic. Later, as adults, they breathe through their skin.

LYNX

There are several forms of lynxes, which are usually separated into three distinct species: the Eurasian lynx (above), Spanish lynx and Canada lynx.

LYNXES ARE BOBTAILED members of the cat family. The bobcat, *Felis rufus*, of North America, stands somewhat apart from the others and is discussed elsewhere, as is the caracal or desert lynx, *F. caracal*.

The original animal to be given the name is now distinguished as the Eurasian lynx, *F. lynx*. It is 2½–4¼ feet (0.8–1.3 m) long, with a 4–10-inch (11–25-cm) tail. It weighs up to 84 pounds (38 kg) but the male averages 48 pounds (22 kg), while the female weighs about 40 pounds (18 kg). The Eurasian lynx has a relatively short body, tufted

ears and cheek ruffs, powerful limbs and very broad feet. Its fur varies from a pale sandy gray to rusty red and white on the underparts. Its summer coat is thinner, often with black spots, while its winter coat is dense and soft, the spots being less prominent. The Eurasian species ranges through the wooded parts of Europe, and in Asia it extends eastward to the Pacific coast of Siberia and southward to the Himalayas.

Closely related and very similar in appearance is the Spanish lynx, *F. pardina*. It is generally smaller, 2½–3½ feet (0.8–1.1 m) in length with a 4½–12-inch (12–30-cm) tail. The male averages about 30 pounds (13 kg) in weight, while the female weighs about 20 pounds (9 kg). It has shorter and more heavily spotted fur than the Eurasian lynx. Also called the pardel, the Spanish lynx is now considered endangered and is found only in remote areas of Spain and Portugal.

The Canada lynx, *F. canadensis*, is similar in size to the Spanish lynx but has a shorter tail and longer hair. This species is often without spots, even in summer. It is widespread throughout North America.

The view of several zoologists is that lynx types all constitute one species, *F. lynx*, but for the moment we are following the accepted pattern.

Nocturnal hunters

Lynxes live in remote, wooded, mountainous areas. They are also found in forests, especially of pine, and in areas of thick scrub. They are solitary animals, hunting by night, using sight and smell. Lynxes are tireless walkers, following scent trails relentlessly for miles in pursuit of prey. They are also good climbers and sometimes lie out on tree branches, dropping onto their victims as they pass. Lynxes swim well, and their broad feet carry them easily over soft ground or snow.

The voice is a caterwauling similar to that of domestic tomcats but louder. Also like domestic cats, lynxes use their claws and teeth in fights. Within its home range a lynx buries its urine and feces, but near the boundary of this range both are deposited on prominent places, such as hillocks. These boundary marks are recognized by both the occupant and neighboring animals.

LYNXES

CLASS	**Mammalia**
ORDER	**Carnivora**
FAMILY	**Felidae**

GENUS AND SPECIES **Canada lynx, *Felis canadensis;* Eurasian lynx, *F. lynx;* Spanish lynx, *F. pardina***

WEIGHT
**Canada lynx: 10–38 lb. (5–17 kg).
Eurasian lynx: 17–84 lb. (8–38 kg).
Spanish lynx: up to 28 lb. (13 kg).**

LENGTH
Head and body: 2½–4¼ ft. (0.8–1.3 m); tail: 2–12 in. (5–30 cm)

DISTINCTIVE FEATURES
Compact body; tufted ears; large, broad feet; short bobtail. Eurasian and Spanish lynxes: coat often spotted, especially in summer. Canada lynx: usually spotless.

DIET
Small mammals such as rabbits, hares, pikas and squirrels; also young deer, wild goats and sheep, ducks, game birds, fish and insects

BREEDING
Age at first breeding: 1 year (female); breeding season: late winter–early spring; number of young: 1 to 4; gestation period: 63–74 days; breeding interval: 1 year

LIFE SPAN
Up to 20 years

HABITAT
Remote, wooded mountains and thick scrub

DISTRIBUTION
Canada lynx: northern North America. Eurasian lynx: Scandinavia; Siberia south to Central Asia; southeastern Europe. Spanish lynx: parts of Spain and Portugal.

STATUS
Canada and Eurasian lynxes: uncommon; rare in places. Spanish lynx: endangered.

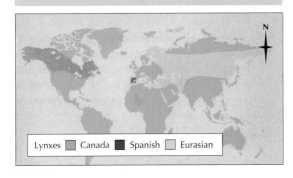

Lynxes ▉ Canada ▉ Spanish ▉ Eurasian

Instant death

Lynxes used to be numerous throughout Europe but are now scarce in most parts. Often they have been hunted and persecuted by humans because of their alleged raids on sheep, goats and other livestock. Some zoologists claim that lynxes are less interested in farmstock than in wild game. The natural food of the Eurasian lynx includes small mammals such as hares, pikas and rabbits, along with ducks and game birds. It will also take young deer and small, wild goats and sheep.

Prey are killed by a bite at the nape of the neck, which severs the spinal cord, or the lynx may use a two-way bite, into the shoulders and then into the nape. Death is instantaneous with both methods. Lynxes will also kill squirrels, foxes, badgers, fish, beetles, especially the wood-boring species, and many small rodents. They tend to kill small game such as rodents in summer, turning to larger game such as deer in

Northern subspecies tend to be larger and grayer than those found farther south. Pictured is a male Siberian lynx, Felis lynx wrangeli, a subspecies of the Eurasian lynx.

winter. The Canada lynx has a similar diet. The snowshoe hare, *Lepus americanus,* is its main prey and the Canada lynx's population regularly increases and decreases in line with that of the snowshoe hare.

Slow developers

Mating takes place in late winter or early spring, the young being born after a gestation period of 67–74 days in the Eurasian lynx and 63–70 days in the Canada lynx. The litter is usually one to four kittens, born well-furred but blind. Their eyes open at 10 days and the kittens are weaned after about 3 months. The young remain with the mother for some time after weaning, until they are between 7 months and 1 year of age.

Although the kittens are somewhat advanced at birth, they are slow in developing. Even at 8 months or more they still have milk teeth and their claws are quite feeble. The young lynx must therefore feed on small rodents or food killed by its mother. Should it become separated from its mother when the first winter snows fall, its chances of survival are slim. The small rodents it needs to survive are able to live under 2 feet (60 cm) or more of snow. The female lynx matures at 1 year old, and the recorded life span is between 13 and 20 years in the wild. Lynxes are reproductively active for 10–14 years.

Lynxes have long been hunted for their fur, but populations are most at risk from destruction of their natural forest habitats.

Driven out of house and home

Humans are the only major threat to the lynxes, but the toll taken by human persecution and by habitat loss to agriculture and forestry has been a heavy one. The dense, soft winter coat has long been valued for garments and trimmings. In Canada, lynx fur was prominent in the transactions of the Hudson Bay Company.

More than hunting, the destruction or commercial management of forests in Europe and Canada has deprived the lynxes of their best and most natural habitat. In Sweden, for example, hunting and changes in the forest drove the Eurasian lynx northward during the 19th century. This meant less food and, more important, less chance of survival for the kittens, due to the longer and more rigorous winters in the higher northern latitudes. Finally, in 1928, the lynx was given legal protection in Sweden. Its numbers have since begun to rise and it is now ranging farther south again.

Although the Canada lynx remains widespread and there are some 100,000 of the Eurasian lynx in Russia and Asia, there are thought to be less than 200 of the latter species remaining in western Europe. It has recently been reintroduced to Austria, Switzerland and Slovenia. Most at risk, however, is the Spanish lynx, with only around 1,200 animals remaining in the wild.

MANATEE

Manatees must rank among the world's most sedate large mammals. Here a West Indian manatee rests just below the water's surface.

WITH THEIR SPLIT LIPS and hairy, creased faces, manatees make bizarre mermaids, yet some people ascribe the legend to them. There are three species. The West African manatee, *Trichechus senegalensis*, is found along the coast and in certain large rivers of West Africa, and the West Indian manatee, *T. manatus*, lives in the Caribbean from the southeastern United States south to northern South America. Finally, the Amazonian manatee, *T. inunguis*, occurs in the Amazon River.

Like the related dugong, *Dugong dugon*, manatees have large, extremely rounded bodies. They are up to 15 feet (4.5) long from head to tail and can weigh up to 1,320 pounds (600 kg). They have hairless skin, paddlelike forelimbs and a horizontal tail that is broadly rounded and shovel-like, not notched into two lobes as in the dugong. The flippers are mobile and can be used as hands. Manatees are dark gray to blackish in color. There are further facial differences between the manatees and the dugong: the manatees have no front teeth and the bristly upper lip is divided and mobile, the two opposing halves being used as a highly versatile grasping organ for plucking underwater vegetation.

A life of ease

Singly, or in groups of 6 to 20, manatees swim sluggishly in the sea, in coastal lagoons and in rivers. Inquisitive creatures, they will investigate any strange objects, such as fishing boats, peering at them myopically, their eyesight being poor. When not feeding, they rest at the surface with only the arched back exposed. In shallow waters they may "stand" with the head and shoulders out of water. Adult manatees swim with the tail, using the flippers to turn, but the babies swim using their flippers. Manatees usually surface every 5–10 minutes and take two or three breaths, but they can remain underwater for 16 minutes so long as they are inactive. Manatees communicate with one another by muzzle-to-muzzle contact. They make high-pitched chirps when alarmed.

Feed on aquatic vegetation

Manatees are active at any hour but feed mainly at night on aquatic plants, especially eelgrass, and they will pluck leaves from land plants overhanging the water. The two lip halves can move independently to grip food, the bristles helping push it in, perhaps with some help from the paddles. Manatees seem to eat any vegetation within reach, provided it is not too tough to be pulled apart with the lips. They occasionally eat invertebrates and fish and there are reports that they may take some fish from nets.

Playful courtship

There is no distinct breeding season, but breeding peaks vary between species and geographical location. When the female is in season she is followed by males for 2–4 weeks, although she is receptive only briefly. The female is promiscuous when in heat. A dozen manatees come together and move as a herd into shallow water. There they pair off. The pairs then drag themselves half out of the water and embrace while lying on their sides. After mating they return to the water and play vigorously as a herd.

MANATEES

CLASS **Mammalia**

ORDER **Sirenia**

FAMILY **Trichechidae**

GENUS AND SPECIES **Amazonian manatee,
Trichechus inunguis; West Indian manatee,
T. manatus; West African manatee,
*T. senegalensis***

WEIGHT
440–1,320 lb. (200–600 kg)

LENGTH
Head to tail: 6½–15 ft. (2–4.5 m)

DISTINCTIVE FEATURES
**Rounded body with small head; square
snout with split upper lip (lip halves can
move independently); small eyes; no
external ear flaps; evenly rounded tail**

DIET
Aquatic vegetation; also invertebrates and fish

BREEDING
**Age at first breeding: 9–10 years (male);
breeding season: all year; number of young:
usually 1; gestation period: around 365
days; breeding interval: 2–3 years**

LIFE SPAN
Up to 44 years in captivity

HABITAT
**Freshwater rivers, lagoons, lakes and
backwaters; also shallow coastal waters and
swampy estuaries (West Indian and West
African manatees only)**

DISTRIBUTION
**Amazonian manatee: Amazon River Basin,
South America. West Indian manatee:
southeastern U.S. south to northern South
America. West African manatee: West Africa.**

STATUS
**West Indian manatee: endangered in the
U.S.**

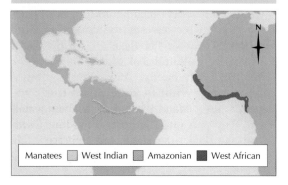

Manatees ☐ West Indian ☐ Amazonian ■ West African

There is usually only one calf at a birth, occasionally twins. Born underwater, the baby is immediately brought to the surface by the mother to take its first breath. The gestation period is about 1 year. The baby is pink, is 3 feet (90 cm) long and weighs up to 60 pounds (27 kg). It becomes mature at 2–3 years old, when about 8 feet (2.4 m) long, but males may not breed until 9 or 10 years old.

*Manatees feed mainly
on aquatic vegetation
and it was once
thought they could be
kept to clear ponds and
rivers of weed.
However, manatees do
not tolerate such a life
of semi-domestication.*

Hunted by humans

Manatees have few natural predators other than alligators. However, they have been killed by local peoples for centuries for their flesh and hides. The Amazonian manatee is now endangered and protected by law in several places in tropical America. Populations of the West African and the West Indian manatees are also declining. Perhaps the biggest menace today is the disturbance of their habitat by the increasing use of outboard motorboats, especially for sport.

Mermaid legend

It is sometimes said that manatees gave rise to the stories of mermaids. The only basis for this is that Christopher Columbus noted in his journal for January 1493 that when off the coast of Haiti he saw three mermaids that rose well out of the water. His opinion of them was that they were not as beautiful as they had been painted, although to some extent they had faces like men. Later Columbus realized they were manatees, animals he had probably encountered before, on the coast of West Africa.

MARMOT

Yellow-bellied marmots, M. flaviventris, sparring. Found in high, rocky parts of the western United States and British Columbia, this species is sometimes an agricultural pest.

THERE ARE 14 SPECIES OF marmots. Among the best-known of these are the alpine marmot, *Marmota marmota*, and the bobak, *M. bobak*, both of Europe, and the hoary marmot, *M. caligata*, of North America. There are various other alpine species in both the Old and the New World. Equally well-known is the groundhog or woodchuck, *M. monax*, of North America. This marmot differs markedly in its habits and is discussed elsewhere.

Marmots are large rodents, ranging in size from 1 to 2 feet (30–60 cm) long with a 4–10-inch (10–25-cm) bushy tail. They weigh 6½–15½ pounds (3–7 kg). Stout-bodied with short legs, the head is wide and short with small, rounded ears, large eyes and large, prominent teeth. The fur is thick, coarse and stiff and varies in color between species and seasons. Marmots live in underground burrows and are well-adapted for digging with their strong feet and claws.

Wide ranging rodents

The alpine marmot is a gregarious animal, living in colonies in and around the forest edges. It is found from about 4,000 to 9,000 feet (1,000–3,000 m) in the Alps and Carpathians and in corresponding alpine districts of central and northeastern Europe. The bobak, also called the Himalayan marmot or steppe marmot, is similar to the alpine species in many respects, but lives more in virgin grasslands. Because agriculture has taken much of its habitat, the bobak has become extinct over large areas of its former range, which used to be throughout Central and southern Asia and extreme eastern Europe. It is still found in parts of Central Asia and eastern Europe. The bobak is golden brown in color, with a black tail tip. The alpine marmot, meanwhile, is pale brown, its back and crown being peppered with black. It has white markings on its face and the outer half of its tail is black.

MARMOTS

CLASS	**Mammalia**
ORDER	**Rodentia**
FAMILY	**Sciuridae**

GENUS AND SPECIES **14 species, including bobak, *Marmota bobak*; alpine marmot, *M. marmota*; and hoary marmot, *M. caligata***

ALTERNATIVE NAMES
Bobak: Himalayan marmot, steppe marmot; hoary marmot: whistler

WEIGHT
6½–15½ lb. (3–7 kg)

LENGTH
Head and body: 1–2 ft. (30–60 cm); tail: 4–10 in. (10–25 cm)

DISTINCTIVE FEATURES
Very large, stocky rodent; thick fur; often gray, beige or orangish in color; long, bushy tail; small ears; large, prominent teeth

DIET
Grasses, sedges, low-growing plants and tubers; also fruits, nuts and invertebrates

BREEDING
Age at first breeding: 2 years; breeding season: spring; number of young: 4 or 5; gestation period: about 30 days; breeding interval: 1 year

LIFE SPAN
Usually up to 15 years

HABITAT
Grassland, steppe and alpine meadows

DISTRIBUTION
Bobak: Central Asia. Alpine marmot: central Europe. Hoary marmot: western North America. Some other species very localized.

STATUS
Several species common; others declining. Endangered: Vancouver Island marmot, *Marmota vancouverensis*.

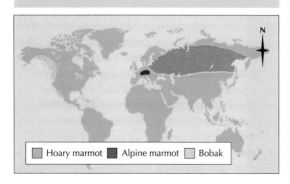

Hoary marmot ◼ Alpine marmot ◻ Bobak

The hoary marmot is silvery gray in color, peppered with black on the back and rump. Its face is black with white cheeks, and the forehead, lower legs and feet are black. This species lives in mountainous parts of western North America, from Alaska south to New Mexico, as well as in the mountains of Siberia. Its habits and life history are similar to those of the alpine marmot.

Other species have a far more localized range, for example the Vancouver Island marmot, *M. vancouverensis*, is found only on Vancouver Island, while the Olympic marmot, *M. olympus*, occurs only in Washington State.

Mountain shelters

Marmots are diurnal (day-active) and leave their burrows on sunny, boulder-strewn slopes, as the first rays of the rising sun fall on them. When an entrance is shaded there may be some delay, and individual marmots differ, some seeming more reluctant than others to leave their burrows. The

Marmots, such as this alpine marmot, are large, stocky rodents with thick fur and large, prominent teeth.

The Olympic marmot (pictured above) is one of those species with an extremely isolated population, being found only in Washington State.

sleeping nests of dry grass are deep in their burrows, which may be several yards long and have several entrances. Late in the fall marmots change the grass in their sleeping chambers before going into hibernation for the winter. The whole family sleeps together, with the burrow entrances blocked.

Marmots spend the first hour after dawn sunning and grooming themselves near the burrow entrances, after which they disperse to the feeding grounds. They feed on grasses, sedges and herbaceous plants as well as roots and tubers. Fruits, nuts and invertebrates are also taken. Unlike many of the related ground squirrels, marmots have no cheek pouches for carrying food. Feeding lasts for about 2 hours in the morning, after which the animals resume their grooming and sunning. There is a further feeding period in the 2 to 3 hours before sundown before the marmots retire for the night.

Slow developers

Marmots mate soon after they emerge from hibernation in the spring. The gestation period is about 30–32 days and there are usually four or five young in a litter, born in the early days of June. The babies first come out of the burrows in mid-July. They stay with the parents until the following spring. The female has one litter each year. Compared with other rodents, the young marmots are slow to develop and are not fully grown until 2 years old. Alpine marmots have been known to live up to 20 years in captivity, although 13–15 years is more common.

Sounding the alert

Marmots are too large to be preyed upon by the smaller predators such as ermines and are mainly taken by foxes and eagles. However, they are alert to danger and extremely wary. Marmots are often seen sitting upright, keeping watch, and are famous for their shrill alarm whistle. Those species that live in colonies have been credited with posting sentinels to stand guard. At the first sign of danger their whistles send the other marmots in the group scurrying to their burrows. The hoary marmot is also known as the whistler because of its sharp call. It is hunted by humans for both its flesh and its fur.

Several marmot species are in decline, but more as a result of agricultural development and isolation of populations. The Vancouver Island marmot is now endangered, while survival of the bobak is dependent on conservation measures.

MILLIPEDE

Fossils of millipedes have been found that date back more than 400 million years, establishing these arthropods as among the first animals to live on land. Some giant fossil millipedes were more than 6 feet (1.8 m) long. Millipedes have changed little since that time, as even their early form was well suited to their native habitats. Today there are about 10,000 known species of millipedes, ranging from soft-bodied species less than 3 millimeters long to armored forms exceeding 8 inches (20 cm). They are usually found in tropical climates. Despite their name, millipedes do not have 1,000 legs. Those species in the genus *Narceus* of North America have 100 to 160 legs, although 200 legs may be typical for most species.

Millipedes were at one time classified alongside centipedes under the name "Myriapoda." One of the obvious ways in which they differ from centipedes is in having two pairs of legs on most of their body segments—the first four segments have only single pairs—and in the variable number of segments. Each body segment contains four spiracles (breathing holes).

In common with other arthropods, millipedes have a shell-like exoskeleton, an external supportive covering, that helps to protect them from attack. The head has short antennae; most species have up to 200 eyes, although a few, such as those that inhabit caves, do not. The general body surface may, however, be light sensitive, as in the species *Oxides gracilis*, which, if illuminated, will move until it finds darkness.

There are some luminous millipede species. The Sierra luminous millipede, *Luminodesmus sequoiae*, sometimes conspicuous at night in the sequoia forests of California, is blind. Its light shines continuously from the time of hatching.

Agricultural boon or pest?

Millipedes are typically light-shy, nocturnal animals living in moist soil, leaf mold and crevices or under logs or stones. They have no defense against sustained dry heat and may die in hot conditions if they cannot find cover.

Millipedes feed on vegetable matter, including fungi and decomposing leaves, and also sometimes on carrion. Although they help to break up plant matter to create soil, some millipede species cause agricultural damage by attacking crops, especially when conditions are favorable and the soil is warm and moist. The spotted snake millipede, *Blaniulus guttulatus*, for instance, eats strawberries, beets, cereals and

A millipede's body is covered with up to 100 segments protected by hard, jointed plates.

potatoes. The potatoes are probably attacked only when the tough skin has already been broken, for the jaws of these and other millipedes are not powerful. Once the potato skin is vulnerable, the snake millipedes burrow inside. The level of damage is variable, although the millipedes may make the vegetables unfit for human consumption. They are also capable of inflicting damage to seedling crops, a fact that has added to their reputation as an agricultural pest.

Chemical warfare

In contrast with the fast-running centipedes, millipedes are built not for speed but for pushing their way powerfully through soil or vegetation. When walking, each leg is a little out of step with the one in front, so waves appear to sweep back along each side of the body. If they are attacked, some species make a rapid escape without using their legs, writhing and wriggling their bodies through the vegetation, while others have a protective reflex of coiling up as soon as they are disturbed. The pill millipedes curl into small balls, and in warmer parts of the world there are millipedes that roll into the size of a golf ball

By rolling into tight balls, thereby reducing their surface area, millipedes reduce the risk of dehydration in hot climates.

Millipedes possess a row of poison glands down each side of the body that are capable of exuding repellant and occasionally caustic compounds, to deter predators. However, such measures are usually only used as a last resort. The secretion may be red, yellow, white or clear, but typically it is brown or yellowish brown. In central Mexico indigenous peoples grind up one millipede species along with various plants for use as an arrow poison. Usually the venom simply oozes from the glands, but a few of the larger tropical millipedes discharge it as a fine

MILLIPEDES

PHYLUM	**Arthropoda**
CLASS	**Diplopoda**
SUBCLASS (1)	**Penicillata**
ORDER	**Polypenida**

SUBCLASS (2)	**Chilognatha**
ORDER	**Sphaerotherriida (Southern Hemisphere); Glomerida (Northern Hemisphere); Siphonophorida and Polyzoniida (sucking millipedes); Spirobolida, Spirostreptida and Julida (snake millipedes); Polydesmida**

FAMILY	**Many**
GENUS AND SPECIES	**About 1,000 species**

LENGTH
Smallest species: less than 1/10 in. (3 mm); largest species: more than 8 in. (20 cm)

DISTINCTIVE FEATURES
Body is cylindrical or flattened and soft or heavily armored; many body segments, with 2 pairs of legs on most; short antennae

DIET
Mainly fresh or decaying vegetable matter; sometimes crops and carrion

BREEDING
Number of eggs: 10 to 300 or more

LIFE SPAN
Up to 2 years or more in ideal conditions

HABITAT
Damp places such as moist soil, under stones and logs, leaf litter and caves

DISTRIBUTION
Throughout tropical and temperate regions

spray. Some species from Southeast Asia are able to squirt chemicals over a distance of up to 18 inches (46 cm). Such millipedes may use these chemical emissions to blind any predators molesting them, at least temporarily. The chemicals may cause human skin to blacken and peel. Some of the large tropical millipedes sport contrasting, bright warning colors. Most predators also find millipedes nauseating to eat.

Tents and mud huts

In mating, which may last for several hours, the male embraces the female, lower surface to lower surface. The genital openings are in pairs on the third body segment, and fertilization takes place inside the female. According to species, 10 to 300 eggs may be laid. Some millipedes simply coat each egg with soil and excrement, so disguising it, and leave it in a crevice in the earth, while the females of other species make elaborate nests and may remain coiled tightly around them for a few days. The nest can take various forms: a hollow sphere of soil and saliva, lined with excrement, or a thin-walled dome of excrement, anchored to the substratum with a narrow tubular chimney, and covered with bits of leaf. The mother will replace these if they are removed. Sometimes the nest is a tent spun from silk. Some millipedes conceal themselves in such silken chambers or tents when they molt, for having cast their skins, they are temporarily very

vulnerable to attack. Usually a millipede eats its cast skin, as well as the silk tent. The young millipede starts life without the full number of legs, perhaps only three pairs, and acquires more at successive molts.

Millipedes on migration

Plagues of millipedes are rare, but sudden attacks on crops in lesser numbers are more frequent and tend to occur in times of drought following damp weather. The size of millipede populations does not seem to be governed by predators and parasites, although there are plenty of these, including spiders, toads and birds, particularly starlings. The main controlling factors seem to be physical conditions. The best conditions for the build-up of a population occur when there is plenty of moisture and organic matter in the soil, as, for example, when farmers have spread manure on the ground. If the soil then becomes dry, the millipedes move to a more congenial environment, such as a damp cavity within a sugar beet.

Sometimes the migrating masses of millipedes have been accompanied by centipedes and wood lice. Conversely, it is not unknown for millipedes to accompany the marching columns of army ants. Millipedes are sometimes found inside the nests of ants and termites, although scientists have not yet been able to establish the reason for this behavior.

The giant African millipede of the genus Archispirostreptus *is one of the largest millipedes in the world, growing up to 11 inches (28 cm) long.*

MONARCH

THE MONARCH BUTTERFLY is native to North America and South America. It has spread westward across the Pacific and is now also established in Hawaii, Tonga, Samoa and Tahiti and in Australia and New Zealand. The extension of its range began in the mid-19th century and it is possible that the spread of the species was helped by the expansion of shipping. Certainly, the monarch has sometimes been seen on ship's rigging. However, it is also possible that its migratory habit may facilitate becoming caught in winds that extend its usual migratory routes. It now seems certain that the monarch may sometimes fly across the Atlantic to Europe, helped by persistent westerly winds.

Far-flying migrant

The monarch is notable in that it makes a definite journey in one direction each year and returns along the same route the following year. In North America it is found in summer all over southern Canada and the northern United States. In the fall the monarch butterflies in the north gather in groups and begin to move south. As they go, they are joined by other monarchs, until there are thousands of butterflies on the move.

Adult monarch butterflies feed on flower nectar, showing a preference for fleabanes, asters, blazing stars and sunflowers.

Each night they settle on trees, moving on in the morning. When they get as far as Florida in the east and southern California in the west, they settle in great numbers on trees and pass the winter in a state of semihibernation, occasionally flying around on warm, sunny days. The butterfly streams farther inland fly into northern Mexico. The same trees are used as resting places year after year, and in some places, where the butterfly trees are regarded as a tourist attraction, the hibernating insects are protected by law from disturbance.

In spring the butterflies of both sexes fly northward, the females laying eggs as they go, but on this return migration they fly singly and in quite a dilatory manner, so their movement is far less easy to observe. During the summer two or three generations are born and die, and the butterflies of each generation continue to press northward. They do not reach Canada until June, and these butterflies are likely to be the second or third generation descended from those that left their southern wintering grounds in the previous fall. The journey of a monarch from the extreme north of its range to the southern hibernation trees may be as much as 2,000 miles (3,200 km).

MONARCH

ALTERNATIVE NAMES
Milkweed butterfly; common tiger butterfly

LENGTH
Wingspan: 3–4 in. (7.5–10 cm)

DISTINCTIVE FEATURES
Adult: bright orange background to upperside, with dark borders on veins and wings; paler underside; white spots on outer borders of all wings. Caterpillar (larva): black, yellow and cream stripes; 1 pair of black tentacle-like structures behind head.

DIET
Adult: flower nectar, particularly from asters, fleabanes, sunflowers and blazing stars. Caterpillar (larva): flowers, leaves and seed pods of milkweed plants.

BREEDING
Breeding season: winter; number of eggs: hundreds during lifetime of each female; hatching period: about 7–10 days; larval period: about 30 days

LIFE SPAN
Up to 9 months

HABITAT
Lowlands

DISTRIBUTION
Native to North and South America; has spread to Hawaii, Tonga, Samoa, Tahiti and Australasia; vagrants recorded in Canary Islands and Mediterranean

STATUS
Common; locally abundant in winter

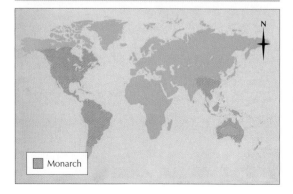

Monarch

Unfit for consumption

Like other members of its family, the monarch is distasteful and poisonous to birds and other insectivorous animals. Monarch larvae (caterpillars) are conspicuously colored with cream, yellow and black stripes and have two pairs of black fleshy filaments on the front and rear of the body, which make them even more unmistakable. The larvae feed on various plants of the milkweed family Asclepiadaceae, which contain poisonous compounds. They derive a twofold benefit from this. First, the plants are avoided by grazing animals so the larvae do not run the risk of being accidentally eaten or destroyed, a fate that may overtake insects feeding on ordinary plants. Second, the larvae are immune to the plants' toxins, and are able to absorb them into their own tissues, making them, and the adult butterflies that they grow into, toxic also. The rounded pupae, often brightly colored and with a variety of metallic gold markings, hang from a twig or similar support by a cord of silk from the tips of their tails.

The adult butterfly is strikingly marked and colored on both the upper- and underside of the wings, making it conspicuous both when it is flying and when it is at rest. By contrast, most colorful butterflies are brightly patterned only on the upperside, which is concealed when they are resting. The monarch offers a good example of warning coloration. Instead of concealing the butterfly, its colors make it conspicuous, so predators quickly learn to recognize and avoid it. The caterpillar's coloration protects it in the same way. The poison is a heart poison, or cardenolide. If retained in the predator's body, it may be fatal, but it also acts on the stomach, so a bird swallowing the insect generally regurgitates it after 10–15 minutes. In either case, the bird is unlikely to make a meal of another monarch.

The monarch caterpillar's striking coloration serves as a warning to would-be predators that it contains toxins.

A monarch's life cycle

Monarchs pass through four distinct life cycle stages: egg, larva, pupa (chrysalis) and adult butterfly. Mating takes place in the butterflies' wintering grounds or along the migratory route back to the north. Special patches on the males' wings, known as "stigmata," may help to attract partners, or aid in distinguishing species. Male and female monarchs mate by joining the tips of their abdomens together so that the male is able to pass sperm to the female. The two remain co-joined for some hours and, if disturbed, may even fly off still attached to each other.

Female monarchs lay their eggs on the underside of milkweeds, perhaps depositing them on several different plants in a milkweed patch. These eggs hatch in about 7–10 days, longer in colder temperatures. Although only about 4 millimeters long after hatching, the caterpillars are voracious eaters and grow to a length of 2 inches (5 cm) after 3 weeks, by which time they have shed their skins four times. Then the caterpillars leave the plants on which they have been feeding to search for a safe place to pupate, usually the underside of a leaf of branch.

When it has found a suitable location, the caterpillar spins a small silken pad, to which it attaches itself by its hind feet, and hangs beneath it. About a day later, it sheds its skin and enters its chrysalis. The metamorphosis into a butterfly within the chrysalis takes about 7–21 days, longer in colder temperatures. After it emerges from its chrysalis, the adult monarch hangs upside down below it and pumps fluid into its wings, which are shrivelled at this early stage, to inflate them. After about 2 hours the butterfly is able to use its wings to fly.

Deceptive viceroy

Another American butterfly, the viceroy, *Limenitis archippus*, belongs to the same family as the monarch, Nymphalidae, and is related to the European white admiral, *L. camilla*. Although it is not distasteful to birds, the viceroy is colored and patterned very like the monarch and is much the same size, so the two are difficult to tell apart except by close inspection.

There is no doubt that this butterfly gains protection from its resemblance to the poisonous monarch. In America captive jays that have never before seen a butterfly will readily kill and devour viceroys. If, however, they are experimentally offered monarch butterflies, they may eat the first, and possibly a second, but soon learn to leave them alone. Moreover, they will subsequently avoid any viceroys offered them.

On their journey northward during the spring, monarch butterflies rest in large communal groups on trees or hang from the roofs of caves.

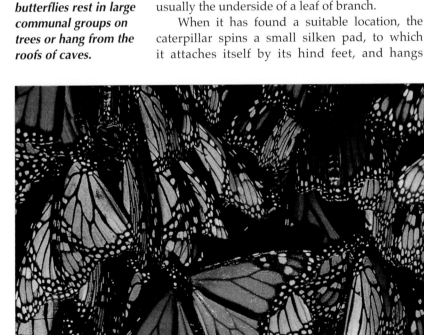

MONKFISH

The monkfish's flat body enables it to lie concealed on sandy and muddy seabeds.

MONKFISH	
CLASS	**Chondrichthyes**
ORDER	**Squatiniformes**
FAMILY	**Squatinidae**
GENUS	***Squatina***
SPECIES	**13 species, including *S. californica*, *S. squatina* and *S. argentina***

ALTERNATIVE NAMES
Angelshark; fiddle fish

LENGTH
Up to 8 ft. (2.4 m); usually 5 ft. (1.5 m)

DISTINCTIVE FEATURES
Flattened body; broad, rounded head with mouth located at tip of blunt snout; large spiracle (breathing hole) on top of head; large, winglike pectoral fins; 2 dorsal fins on tail; gray or brown above, white below

DIET
Bottom-living fish such as flatfish, croakers and mullet; also squid, shellfish and worms

BREEDING
Number of eggs: 9 to 20

HABITAT
Sandy and muddy seabeds in coastal waters; most species at 16½–330 ft. (5–100 m)

DISTRIBUTION
***S. californica*: Pacific seaboard of North and South America. *S. squatina*: north-eastern Atlantic, including Mediterranean. *S. argentina*: southwestern Atlantic.**

STATUS
Generally common

THE MONKFISH ARE true sharks in the class Elasmobranchii. Bottom-feeders, they have a diet of shellfish, flatfish and worms, although they may also take other fish, including mullet. They should not be confused with one well known species of anglerfish, *Lophius piscatorius*, which is popularly called the monkfish.

There are 13 species of monkfish sharks, all much alike. They reach up to 8 feet (2.4 m) long. The head is broad and flattened, blunt and wide in front, with the mouth at the end, not on the undersurface as in rays and other sharks. On top of the head, behind each eye, is a conspicuous crescent-shaped spiracle. The tail is more slender than that of a typical shark. There are two dorsal fins, well back on the tail. The gill slits are crowded together in front of the pectoral fin, which is large and winglike, hence one of the group's alternative names, angelsharks. Each pectoral fin is prolonged to form a "shoulder," which is free of the head. The pelvic fins are also large and flattened, and another common name, that of fiddle fish, relates to the shape of the fish when seen from above. The uppersurface is usually gray or brown, blotched and with white lines and spots. The undersurface is white.

Monkfish are found in subtropical and temperate waters. They occur on both sides of the Atlantic, in the Mediterranean, off South Africa, Australia and Japan and along the Pacific seaboard of North and South America. Monkfish sometimes wander up to beaches and into sheltered bays during the summer.

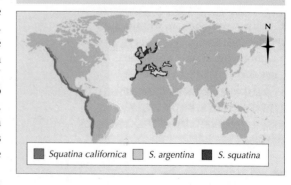

Squatina californica   S. argentina   S. squatina

Unlike the rays, which swim by flapping their large pectoral fins, monkfish swim with a sculling action of their tails. They live mainly in shallow water, but a few species live down to 4,200 feet (1,280 m) and migrate to shallower waters to give birth. The young are born alive.

MOOSE

THE LARGEST LIVING DEER, moose grow up to 10½ feet (3.2 m) long and may weigh more than 1,800 pounds (820 kg). They have long legs and reach up to 8 feet (2.4 m) at the shoulder, the rump being much lower. The antlers, grown by males only, span up to 6½ feet (2 m) and are flattened surfaces with up to 20 tines, or snags, rising from them. The summer coat is grayish or reddish brown to black above, being lighter on the underparts and legs; the winter coat is grayer. The head is long with a broad overhanging upper lip, large ears and a long, rounded muzzle. A tassel of hair-covered skin that hangs from the throat is known as the "bell." Moose's hooves are splayed, spreading the animals' great weight more evenly when they walk over swampy or muddy terrain.

The moose lives in densely wooded areas of Alaska and Canada and along the region of the Rockies in the northwestern United States.

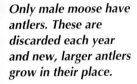

Only male moose have antlers. These are discarded each year and new, larger antlers grow in their place.

It is known as the elk in Eurasia, where it ranges across parts of Norway and Sweden and eastward through European Russia and Siberia to Mongolia and Manchuria in northern China.

Diets for winter and summer

Moose tend to be solitary, but in winter a number of them may combine to form a "yard," an area of trampled snow in a sheltered spot surrounded by tall pines and with plenty of brushwood for feeding. They stay there until the food is used up and then move on to make another yard. Moose are most at home in well-watered woods and forest with willow and scrub, and ponds, lakes or marshes. Much of their time in summer is spent wading into lakes and rivers to feed on water lilies and other water plants. By doing this, they also escape to some extent the swarms of mosquitoes and flies. They will submerge completely to get at the roots and

MOOSE

CLASS **Mammalia**

ORDER **Artiodactyla**

FAMILY **Cervidae**

GENUS AND SPECIES *Alces alces*

ALTERNATIVE NAME
Elk (Eurasia only)

WEIGHT
440–1,820 lb. (200–825 kg)

LENGTH
**Head and body: 8–10½ ft. (2.4–3.2 m);
shoulder height: 4½–8 ft. (1.4–2.4 m);
tail: 2–4¾ in. (5–12 cm)**

DISTINCTIVE FEATURES
**Largest species of deer. Broad muzzle with
overhanging upper lip; large, broad antlers
(male only); large ears; rather long legs;
splayed hooves; coat dark to reddish brown
(summer) or grayish (winter)**

DIET
**Leaves and shoots of trees and shrubs;
water vegetation; bark and twigs in winter**

BREEDING
**Age at first breeding: 18 months (female);
breeding season: September–October;
number of young: usually 1; gestation period:
215–265 days; breeding interval: 1 year**

LIFE SPAN
Up to 25 years

HABITAT
Forests with ponds, lakes and marshy areas

DISTRIBUTION
**Northern parts of North America, south
through Rockies; northern Eurasia**

STATUS
**Generally common, but rare in Mongolia;
estimated population: 2 million**

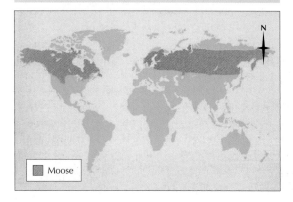

Moose

stems of water plants. Moose are good swimmers and can cross narrow sea straits in search of grazing grounds if necessary. In winter they use their great height to browse the shoots, leaves and branches of saplings. They also straddle saplings, bending them over to reach the tender shoots. Bark, particularly that of poplar trees, is also eaten. The Algonquin Native American name *musee*, from which the word moose is derived, means "wood-eater."

Although low in vitamins, proteins and sugars, the water plants that moose feed on are high in salt. By contrast, the land vegetation that they feed on lacks salt, but is high in vitamins, proteins and sugars. By taking from both food sources, moose give themselves a well-balanced diet and maximize the available food types.

Growth of antlers

The bulls (males) shed their antlers in December. In April to May new antlers begin to sprout. Initially the antlers are made of living tissue supplied with blood via a network of blood vessels. These are covered with a soft skin called velvet. By August the antlers are full grown and the moose sheds the velvet, leaving the antlers as dead matter. At first the exposed antlers are white, but after a bull has rubbed them on bushes and branches they are polished and brown. A yearling bull has spikes 6–8 inches (15–20 cm) long; in a two-year-old they are forked, and by the time he reaches 3 years he has narrow, hand-shaped antlers with four spikes.

Breeding

The breeding season takes place in the fall, during September and October. It is characterized by fighting between the bulls, which mark

Moose (female, above) feed on both land vegetation and water plants. The former provide them with vitamins, proteins and sugars, the latter with essential salt.

Moose are solitary animals. The limited resources of their native habitats are not sufficient for communal living.

out small territories for themselves and then fight each other for the right to mate with the females. They spar with their antlers, normally doing little damage. Bulls are polygamous and a mature individual will mate with several cows.

The bulls bellow for females and, on hearing their responding calls, smash their way through the thick brushwood to find them. The females may breed first when they are as young as 18 months. Males have to wait until they are older, because the rutting season is physically very demanding on them and they must ensure that they are strong enough before competing for mates. In the past, Native American hunters called up bull moose by using a birch bark trumpet to imitate the cows' calls.

The bull may stay with his chosen cow until her calf is 10 days old. The gestation is about 240 days, after which one to three calves, normally two, are born, each weighing 20–35 pounds (10–16 kg). The first time a cow gives birth she has a single calf, but after this twins are common, with triplets rare. The calf is a uniform reddish brown and can run with its mother at about 10 days old. For the first three days the calf is unable to walk much and the cow keeps close beside it, often squatting low or lying down so that the calf can reach her udder. The calf calls to bring the mother to it when it is hungry.

Moose are long-lived animals, sometimes reaching 25 years of age. However, humans have had a dramatic effect on the species and today it is estimated that 10 percent of the global moose population is killed for food every year. Moose meat provides an important source of protein for many local people, and the animals are also hunted globally for sport. In addition, several are killed each year on roads.

Preserving food supplies

The main predators of moose are bears and wolves and to a lesser extent pumas, coyotes and wolverines, which prey on the young, the elderly and the weak. An adult moose is a match for any of these predators, defending itself not with its antlers but by striking downward with its large hoofs and then trampling on its opponent.

The mother protects her young from predators for the first year of their life, by which time she may well have given birth again. She then leaves the yearlings to fend for themselves and directs her attention toward her newborn young.

Living alone

Solitary living is a characteristic of both male and female moose. One possible reason for this is that because of their size, moose have to maximize the limited food resources available to them. Collective living and feeding would make more of a demand on these resources than that made by individual animals.

During her calves' first year a mother is likely to behave aggressively toward other moose of either sex, as well as predators. It is probable that the mother's behavior is prompted by the need to preserve winter food supplies.

MUD TURTLE

MUD TURTLES AND MUSK TURTLES belong to the family Kinosternidae. There are 22 species in North, Central and South America; nine of these are found in the United States. They are mostly rather small. The largest species in North America is the Big Bend mud turtle, *Kinosternon hirtipes murrayi*. This turtle is found mostly in Mexico but extends into the United States in Presidio County, Texas. It never has a shell longer than 7 inches (18 cm).

The plastron (underpart of the shell) of mud turtles has two hinges. The central part of the plastron is fixed to the carapace (the upperpart of the shell), but the front and back parts are moveable. When a turtle withdraws its head, limbs and tail into the shell, the moveable parts close over them, so that the soft parts of the animal are entirely covered. The common mud turtle, *K. subrubrum*, which ranges from Connecticut to southern Florida, and westward into central Texas, has a dark brown carapace. The plastron is light brown in color, or sometimes yellow brown. The head is speckled with yellow spots.

Musk turtles are very similar to mud turtles in both appearance and habits, but they have only one hinge across the plastron, at the front of the shell, and their lower shells are smaller than those of mud turtles. One of the best-known species of musk turtle is the common musk turtle or stinkpot, *Sternotherus odoratus*, which ranges from New England and southern Ontario south to southern Florida and westward into Wisconsin and parts of Texas.

Mud turtles and musk turtles have scent glands that open on either side of the body. These produce a musky, foul-smelling liquid, particularly when the animals are disturbed.

An aquatic lifestyle

Mud and musk turtles live in pools, swamps and sluggish streams where there are plenty of water plants. They crawl over the bottom and occasionally wander out over the land or bask on banks and tree stumps. The common musk turtle is rarely seen out of water, but the keel-backed musk turtle, *S. carinatus*, of the southeastern United States often comes out to bask in the sun. The mud turtles are more likely to be found on land, and they often live in very small pools and roadside ditches.

Mud turtles and musk turtles feed on tadpoles, snails, worms, aquatic insects and small fish. They also eat a large amount of carrion and are unpopular with anglers because they often take their bait.

Leisurely courtship

The courtship of mud turtles usually takes place in the water, but the female comes on land to lay her eggs. A courting male approaches the female from behind and noses her tail to confirm her sex. He then swims beside her, nudging her just behind her eye. She swims with him for some distance and then stops suddenly. This is a signal for the male to climb onto her back, grasp the edges of her carapace with his toes and hold her tail to one side with the scaly patches on one of his hind legs. Several fertile clutches may result from one mating, and females isolated for 3–4 years have laid fertile eggs.

The female lays her eggs under rotten logs and stumps or in nests dug in the earth. Musk turtles sometimes lay their eggs in muskrat nests. In the coldest areas of the turtles' range, such as Canada, the eggs are dormant for a period.

The common musk turtle favors slow-running rivers, ponds and swamps. The female leaves the water only to lay her eggs.

Although most species of mud and musk turtles are primarily aquatic, some, such as the keel-backed musk turtle (above), often come on land to bask.

They hatch during the spring, when food is plentiful. Up to seven eggs with hard, brittle shells are laid in each clutch. They hatch in 60–90 days, depending on a warm temperature and the decaying vegetation around them. The newly hatched turtles have shells about 1 inch (2.5 cm) long. Males mature in 4–7 years and the females in 5–8 years. In captivity mud turtles have lived for 40 years, but in the wild they fall prey to several predators: crows attack the adults, while king snakes, raccoons and skunks eat the eggs.

Shells give support and protection

It would be easy to assume that the plastron is no more than a breastplate to protect the underside of a turtle or tortoise, but in some species it is so small that it can offer very little protection. Even so, it still has an important function. In all turtles and tortoises the ribs are incorporated into the carapace and the plastron takes over, to some extent, the work of the ribs in bracing the body and in providing an anchoring surface for the muscles of the shoulders and hips. In the snapping turtle, *Chelydra serpentina*, for instance, in which the plastron is very much reduced, scientists have calculated that this small plastron is just sufficient to give the necessary strength and support to the body. It is much the same in the mud and musk turtles when they are young: they have a soft carapace and a rigid plastron that braces the carapace. As the turtles grow older and the carapace hardens, the plastron is no longer used for this purpose. It then develops the hinges that, acting like lids, close over the turtle when it withdraws into its shell and in this way provide it with maximum protection.

MUD AND MUSK TURTLES

CLASS **Reptilia**

ORDER **Testudines**

FAMILY **Kinosternidae**

GENUS **Mud turtles, *Kinosternon*; musk turtles, *Sternotherus***

SPECIES **22, including common mud turtle, *Kinosternon subrubrum*; and common musk turtle, *Sternotherus odoratus***

ALTERNATIVE NAMES
Stinkpot, stinking-jim (*S. odoratus*); eastern mud turtle, Florida mud turtle (*K. subrubrum*)

LENGTH
Carapace (shell): up to 4½ in. (11 cm) in most species; up to 7 in. (18 cm) in Big Bend mud turtle, *K. hirtipes murrayi*

DISTINCTIVE FEATURES
Plastron (underpart of shell) has 1 (musk turtles) or 2 (mud turtles) transverse hinges; musk glands in all species

DIET
Mainly invertebrates; also fish and carrion

BREEDING
Varies according to location. Age at first breeding: 4–7 years (male), 5–8 years (female); breeding season: early summer (*K. subrubrum*); number of eggs: 9 to 11; hatching period: 60–90 days.

LIFE SPAN
***S. odoratus*: up to 40 years in captivity**

HABITAT
Ponds, swamps and slow-moving rivers; also tiny pools and ditches (mud turtles only)

DISTRIBUTION
Ontario south to Argentina

STATUS
***S. odoratus*: abundant; other species less common. Flattened musk turtle, *S. depressus*, only in Black Warrior River system, Alabama.**

Common musk turtle

MUSKRAT

Muskrats are semi-aquatic rodents found throughout North America except in some regions of treeless tundra. They have also been introduced into Europe.

THE MUSKRAT IS A LARGE vole with a head and body length of ¾–1⅕ feet (23–36 cm) and a tail of ⅗–1 foot (18–30 cm). Its name is derived from the secretions of two glands at the base of the tail. The muskrat ranges in color from silvery brown to almost black. Under the long, coarse guard hairs there is a short, dense layer of soft hair. This short undercoat is very hardwearing and muskrats are hunted or farmed on ranches for their fur. The pelt is sold under the name of musquash, the name given to the animal by Canadian Indians.

Muskrats are adapted to an aquatic life. Their scaly, almost hairless tails are flattened from side to side, so acting as a rudder. The hind feet are partly webbed and fringed with short, stiff hairs.

The muskrat, *Ondatra zibethicus*, is native to North America as is a second species, the round-tailed muskrat, *Neofiber alleni*. The round-tailed muskrat is found only across Florida and the Okefenokee Swamp area in Georgia. Somewhat smaller and less aquatic than the muskrat, with a rounded rather than a flattened tail, it is sometimes called the Florida water rat.

Two kinds of nests

The presence of muskrats in an area is shown by well-defined channels through the vegetation, slides down banks and networks of tunnels. Muskrats are seldom found away from water, except when they are searching for new feeding grounds. They live in marshes, lakes and rivers, preferably where there is dense vegetation to provide them with both food and cover.

Muskrats make two types of nest. In open swamps a pile of water vegetation is made, perhaps 4 feet (1.2 m) high and 5 feet (1.5 m) across. The walls are cemented with mud and a nest of finely shredded leaves is made in the middle. Several tunnels connect the nest with underwater exits. The other type of nest is built along the edges of ponds and rivers, where muskrats dig elaborate tunnels to a nest above the high watermark. The entrances are either underwater, below the level of the thickest ice, or above water, when they are camouflaged by vegetation.

Muskrats can stay underwater for up to 15 minutes. Normally they dive for shorter periods, only staying submerged when danger threatens.

MUSKRAT

CLASS	**Mammalia**
ORDER	**Rodentia**
FAMILY	**Muridae**
GENUS AND SPECIES	***Ondatra zibethicus***

ALTERNATIVE NAME
Musquash

WEIGHT
1.5–4 lb. (0.7–1.8 kg)

LENGTH
**Head and body: ¾–1⅕ ft. (23–36 cm);
tail: ⅗–1 ft. (18–30 cm)**

DISTINCTIVE FEATURES
**Small, round body; large face with tiny ears;
long, sharp claws; silvery brown to brown-
black coat made up of thick, short fur and
long, coarse hairs; hairless, flattened tail;
partly webbed hind feet**

DIET
**Mainly aquatic vegetation such as water
lilies, wild rice and bullrushes; also insects,
small fish, crayfish and mussels**

BREEDING
**Age at first breeding: 6–12 months; breeding
season: March–September (Canada), all year
(southern U.S.); number of young: usually 5
to 7; gestation period: 25–30 days; breeding
interval: up to 6 litters per year**

LIFE SPAN
Up to 4 years

HABITAT
**Most aquatic habitats, including streams,
rivers, marshes, lakes and ponds**

DISTRIBUTION
Most of Canada and U.S.

STATUS
Common

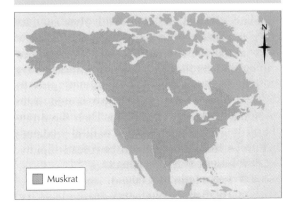

Muskrat

In the winter they keep breathing holes open in the ice by continually breaking the ice as it forms. As the ice around the hole thickens, it is plugged with plants, giving the muskrat shelter from the sight of enemies when it surfaces to breathe.

Water plants feeder

The food of muskrats consists mainly of roots and leaves of water plants such as water lilies, wild rice, cattails and arrowheads. In winter they do not feed on stored food but on the roots of water plants that they grub out from the mud. Crops such as maize, alfalfa, clover and peanuts are plundered, and some animal food is eaten, such as insects, crayfish, mussels and occasionally fish.

Rapid breeding

In the northern parts of their range, muskrats breed from spring to autumn and several litters, perhaps up to six, are raised in that time. In the south breeding continues year-round, with a peak of births from November to April. Gestation lasts just 25–30 days and the young muskrats are 2–3 inches (5–7.5 cm) long when born. There are usually five to seven in a litter,

*Muskrats often eat
on special feeding
platforms, such as on
a flat rock or a bed of
reeds. Water plants
make up the main part
of their diet, but
insects, mollusks and
fish are also taken.*

Muskrats are well adapted for life in and around water. Their tails are flattened to form a rudder, while the hind feet are partly webbed, making them good swimmers.

but there may be up 11 young. They are blind, naked and helpless at birth and are weaned when 1 month old. They will have started nibbling plants some time before weaning. At this point the mother drives the young muskrats out of the nest. She mates shortly after the young are born and so gives birth to another litter shortly after weaning the first.

Vulnerable to flooding

Muskrats are particularly vulnerable during floods and are more common in lakes and rivers that are not susceptible to flooding. As the muskrats are driven from their nests by floodwaters, they seek refuge on rafts of floating vegetation and on trees where bark and twigs form an emergency food. Fighting is common under these conditions and many muskrats die of drowning, infections and cold.

The lack of cover and the weakened condition of the muskrats during floods also makes them an easy target for their many predators. These include red-tailed hawks, great horned owls, bald eagles, foxes, coyotes and raccoons. In the water they are also attacked by alligators, snapping turtles, pike and water snakes such as the water moccasin, *Agkistrodon piscivorus*. Perhaps the muskrat's most serious predator is the mink, although it mainly kills the very young, sick or old animals.

Hunted for fur and flesh

Muskrat fur is very valuable. Each year pelts worth many millions of dollars are traded in North America. For this reason alone the muskrat is a useful animal, but muskrats are also welcomed in many places as they keep waterways open by eating water plants. They are sometimes deliberately imported for this purpose. In addition, muskrats are hunted for food in some regions and the flesh is marketed in parts of the United States as "marsh rabbit" or "Chesapeake terrapin."

A pest in some places

Elsewhere, however, muskrats are a pest because their tunneling breaches banks and dykes. After being introduced into Europe in the 1900s muskrats were raised on ranches for their fur, but many escaped and went wild. They are now prone to cause serious damage as there are few large marshes where they can live without coming into conflict with humans. Muskrats are thought to be a particularly severe pest in Holland and were only just prevented from becoming established in Britain. Their rapid rate of breeding and the absence of natural predators in Europe has allowed them to spread rapidly. For example, in 1927 five females and four males escaped from a farm in Scotland. Three years later nearly 900 of their descendants were trapped.

OCEAN SUNFISH

Several ocean sunfish off the coast of California. Sunfish, so called because of their highly distinctive shape, are the heaviest of all bony fish.

THE GENERIC AND SPECIES NAME of the ocean sunfish, *mola*, is Latin for "millstone," a reference to the fish's circular body shape. Sunfish are regarded as the heaviest of all bony fish and are distributed throughout warm and temperate waters worldwide.

The ocean sunfish, *Mola mola*, has a spinal cord that is only about ½ inch (1.3 cm) long, which is shorter than its brain. However, it is the largest of all sunfish, growing to 10¾ feet (3.3 m) and to a maximum weight of about 2¼ tons (2 tonnes). The fish's body is oval and covered with a thick, leathery skin that is bluish, gray, olive brown or nearly black with silvery reflections. The snout projects beyond the small mouth, and the teeth in both upper and lower jaws are joined to form a single sharp-edged beak. The dorsal and anal fins are large and high, and the body ends abruptly in a low tail fin. There are no pelvic fins. The tail of the ocean sunfish is rounded and wavy, but in related species it has a slightly different shape. In the sharptail sunfish, *Masturus lanceolatus*, the tail is drawn out into a point in the middle, and in the slender sunfish, *Ranzania laevis*, it has a rounded margin. The first of these species grows up to 10 feet (3 m) long and weighs about 1 ton (0.9 tonne), while the second seldom exceeds 2 feet (60 cm) in length. A fourth sunfish species, *Mola ramsayi*, is found in the Southern Hemisphere, in the waters around South Africa, Australia, New Zealand and Chile.

Floating at the surface

Ocean sunfish sometimes lie somewhat obliquely at the surface, with the dorsal fin above the surface, as if basking in the sun. They have also been seen well upstream in rivers on a number of occasions, as if they have been carried in on the tide. In October 1960, in Monterey Bay, California, a very heavy death rate was recorded among ocean sunfish close inshore. Skin divers discovered about 100 of the fish in 50 feet (15 m) of water. All of the fish had their fins bitten off and most of them had lost their eyes. On the same day, a little distance from that spot, 20 or more ocean sunfish were seen floating on the surface. These fish had also lost their fins and their eyes had been damaged. The cause of death was never confirmed, but the naturalist Daniel W. Gotshall, who investigated this event, concluded that when sunfish are seen floating at or near the surface, it is likely that they are sick or dying, rather than that they have come to the surface to bask in the sun.

Underwater observations made by the Italian naturalist L. Roghi seem to bear this theory out. He reported that when the sunfish is at rest, it lies stationary in the water with its tail down and its mouth pointing upward. While in this position, it turns a darker color, except for the fins and a large area around the throat. Roghi also reported that as soon as the fish starts to swim, it immediately, and dramatically, changes to a much lighter color. From this evidence, if sunfish came to the surface to bask, it would be logical to assume that they would be light in color and would rest nose up.

Although they have often been sighted at or near the water's surface, especially in calm weather, ocean sunfish may possibly go down to depths of about 1,310 feet (400 m). They are usually seen singly or in pairs, although they may come together in schools of a dozen or more at certain times of the year.

Steering by water jets

The ocean sunfish directs itself by waving its dorsal and anal fins in unison from side to side, in a sculling action, the fins twisting slightly as they wave. The small pectoral fins flap continually but they probably act only as stabilizers. The sunfish uses its tail as a rudder, while it steers with its gills by squirting a strong jet of water out of one gill opening or the other, or out of its mouth. Sunfish do not need to move quickly through the water because their prey is slow-moving. They feed primarily on plankton, jellyfish and other soft-bodied invertebrates, planktonic mollusks, small crustaceans and fish larvae, although they also take a variety other prey small enough to be taken in the beaklike mouth. As well as having a short spinal cord, the sunfish also has a very small brain. It is smaller than either of the fish's two kidneys, which lie just behind it instead of farther back in the body, as is more common among fish.

Prolific egg-laying

From dissection of captured sunfish scientists estimate that the female's ovary may contain 300 million eggs, making the sunfish the most fecund fish species. The larvae are about 3 millimeters long and initially have a much more conventional fish shape than the adult sunfish, with large pectoral fins. However, the dorsal and anal fins soon begin to grow and the body becomes covered with spines. At this point in their development the juveniles resemble pufferfish or boxfish, to which sunfish are related. The spiny coat is then gradually shed, until only five long spines are left. These shorten until they are lost completely, and the bulky, disc-shaped body begins to take shape when the young fish is about ½ inch (1.3 cm) long. At this stage the parrotlike beak develops also, and the fish gradually begins to assume the typical characteristics of an adult sunfish.

Ocean sunfish often drift at the water's surface, sometimes with their dorsal fins showing (below). Some naturalists regard this as abnormal behavior, and suggest that it is a sign of sickness.

OCEAN SUNFISH

CLASS	**Osteichthyes**
ORDER	**Tetraodontiformes**
FAMILY	**Molidae**
GENUS AND SPECIES	***Mola mola***

WEIGHT
Up to 2¼ tons (2 tonnes)

LENGTH
Up to 10¾ ft. (3.3 m)

DISTINCTIVE FEATURES
Large, oval body; small eyes; small, beaked mouth; dorsal and anal fins at rear; curved pectoral fins; bluish or gray-brown in color

DIET
Fish larvae, mollusks, zooplankton, jellyfish, crustaceans and brittle stars

BREEDING
Number of eggs: up to 300 million

LIFE SPAN
Not known

HABITAT
Warm and temperate zones of oceans

DISTRIBUTION
Eastern Pacific: British Columbia, Canada, south to Peru and Chile. Eastern Atlantic: Scandinavia south to South Africa; occasionally also western Baltic and Mediterranean. Western Atlantic: Newfoundland, Canada, south to northern South America.

STATUS
Not threatened

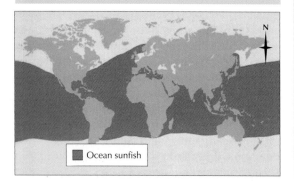

Ocean sunfish

OPOSSUM

A pair of Virginia opossums. Opossums have strong toes and a flexible tail, enabling them to scale trees with ease to hunt for prey or escape from predators.

THE OPOSSUMS ARE THE only marsupials that live outside Australasia, except for the little-known caenolestids or rat opossums of the order Paucituberculata, which live in South America. The best-known opossum is the Virginia opossum, *Didelphis virginiana*, which is common in many parts of the United States and ranges into South America. The Virginia opossum is often known simply as the "possum," but this name is also, confusingly, given to Australian marsupials of the family Phalangeridae, such as the brush-tailed possums, genus *Trichosurus*, covered elsewhere in this encyclopedia. This is why it is now usual to refer to the American species as "opossum" and the Australian animals as "possum."

Virginia opossums are the size of a small dog, with a head and body length of 12–20 inches (30–50 cm), but their appearance is ratlike, with short legs and a pointed muzzle. The tail is almost as long as the body and is naked for most of its length. The ears are also hairless and the rough fur varies from black to brown or white. The hind feet bear some resemblance to human hands. The first toe is clawless and opposable in exactly the same way as the human thumb.

The other opossums that live in Central America and South America are similar to the Virginia opossum in appearance. Some have a bushy tail, and the water opossum, or yapok, *Chironectes minimus*, has webbed hind feet and a waterproof pouch. Most species are not known at all well, except for the common mouse or murine opossum, *Marmosa murina*, which sometimes damages banana and mango crops and is occasionally found in consignments of bananas.

Resilient marsupial

The spread of the Virginia opossum from the southeastern United States north to Ontario in Canada is remarkable for an animal that originated in tropical and subtropical climates. It is even more remarkable as it belongs to the marsupials, a group that in most parts of the world has become extinct in the face of competition from the placental mammals. The opossum's spread may be due to a decrease in the number of its predators, many of which have been killed off by humans. It is surprising that opossums have survived in the northern parts of their expanded range, as they are vulnerable to the cold and are sometimes found with parts of their ears or tail lost through frostbite. Although they do not hibernate, opossums become inactive in very cold spells, subsisting on fat stored during the fall.

Opossums generally live in wooded country, where they forage on the ground, climbing trees only to escape predators and to find food. They can, however, climb well, gripping with their opposable toes, while their tail is nearly prehensile. A young opossum can hang from a branch with its tail, but adults can use their tail only as brakes or as a fifth hand for extra support.

Each opossum has a home range of about 6–7 acres (2.4–2.8 ha), although it is sometimes twice as large as this. They feed mainly at night and

OPOSSUMS

CLASS **Mammalia**

ORDER **Didelphimorpha**

FAMILY **Didelphidae**

GENUS **15 genera**

SPECIES **About 70, including Virginia opossum, *Didelphis virginiana*; water opossum, *Chironectes minimus*; and common mouse opossum, *Marmosa murina***

ALTERNATIVE NAMES
D. virginiana: common opossum; C. minimus: yapok; M. murina: murine opossum

LENGTH
Head and body: 12¾–19¾ in. (32.5–50 cm); tail: 4–21 in. (10–53 cm);

DISTINCTIVE FEATURES
Ratlike body; large, forward-facing eyes; pointed muzzle; long, almost naked tail; most species gray brown in color

DIET
Mainly leaves, shoots, buds, seeds and invertebrates; some species also small vertebrates, carrion and garbage

BREEDING
Genus *Didelphis*. Age at first breeding: 1 year; breeding season: spring and summer; number of young: up to 20; gestation period: about 12 days; breeding interval: usually 1 or 2 litters per year.

LIFE SPAN
Up to about 3 years

HABITAT
Generally forest, wooded country and scrub; *C. minimus*: lakes and streams

DISTRIBUTION
Southern Canada south to Argentina

STATUS
Some species threatened; others common

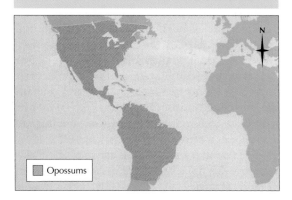
☐ Opossums

spend the day in a nest in hollow tree trunks, in abandoned burrows or under piles of dead brushwood. The nest is made of dead leaves that are carried in a most unusual way: they are picked up in the mouth and passed between the front legs to be held against the belly by the tail, which is folded under the body.

The Virginia opossum's fur consists of a thick undercoat concealed beneath longer, white-tipped protective hairs.

Varied diet

Opossums have sometimes been described as scavengers, mainly because they are often found feeding on garbage around human habitations. This simply provides an example of their adaptability, for they will eat a very wide variety of foods. Small ground animals such as earthworms, grasshoppers, beetles, ants, snails and toads are taken in large numbers in the summer and fall, together with voles, mice, snakes and small birds. Opossums also raid poultry runs from time to time and take plants such as pokeberries and persimmon, usually at night. They are particularly likely to take plant food during the late fall and winter, when their usual animal prey is becoming scarce, although they sometimes feed on carrion.

Opossums are preyed upon by many animals, including dogs, bobcats, coyotes, foxes, hawks and owls. They are also commercially trapped for their coats, which are of poor quality but are used to make simulated beaver or nutria (coypu) fur.

Carrying the babies

After a very short gestation of 12–13 days, the tiny young, numbering 8 to 18 in the case of the Virginia opossum, emerge from the mother's body in quick succession and crawl into her pouch to grasp her nipples. As she usually has 13 nipples, some of the litter may not be able to gain access to the mother's milk and soon die. The young remain in the pouch for 10 weeks, and after this they sleep huddled together in the nest. When the mother goes out foraging, she carries the young clinging to her back. They are now the size of brown rats, *Rattus norvegicus*. If the mother has a large litter, she may find it difficult to walk. The young are weaned shortly afterward and become independent at about 14 weeks. Females breed before they are 1 year old, producing one litter in the northern part of their range but sometimes two in the south.

Playing possum

The phrase "playing possum" comes from the opossum's habit of feigning death when frightened. The habit is not confined to opossums and has also been noted in foxes, African ground squirrels and various snakes. When an opossum is confronted by a predator and cannot escape quickly, it turns at bay, hissing and growling and trying to attack. If the predator succeeds in grabbing and shaking it, the opossum suddenly collapses, rolling over with its eyes shut and its tongue lolling out as if it is dead. The attacker frequently loses interest in the opossum at this, presumably because many of the opossum's natural predators do not eat carrion. After its attacker has left, the opossum gradually recovers and is able to make its escape.

This ruse must be effective at persuading predators to leave opossums alone, otherwise the latter would only be playing into the predators' hands. However, there is still some scientific debate as to how the opossum manages to simulate death so effectively. It has been suggested that harmless paralyzing chemicals are automatically released into the opossum's brain in reaction to high stress levels. Scientists believe that these cause the opossum's muscles to contract, producing an effect similar to rigor mortis. According to this theory, when the danger has passed the chemicals diffuse and the opossum recovers.

More recently, experiments have been made on opossums using an electroencephalogram. This machine records the patterns of minute electric currents in the brain, showing differences between waking and sleeping states. Recordings made of opossums feigning death showed that far from being in a state of catalepsy, the marsupials are wide awake and alert.

The common mouse, or murine, opossum, found only in South America, is one of the smallest opossums.

OSPREY

THIS REMARKABLE BIRD OF prey, which lives almost exclusively on fish, is a highly efficient hunter, with up to 90 percent of its dives being successful. The osprey, also known as the fish hawk in North America, is the size of a small eagle, and in flight its long, narrow wings can span more than 5 feet (1.5 m). Its large toes have long, curved claws, and the undersides of the toes are covered with spiny scales that help to hold the fish. The head and short crest are white with a black band running through the eye to join the chocolate brown plumage of the back. The underparts are white except for a dark band across the breast. The plumage of the sexes is similar, but the females are larger.

The osprey is almost cosmopolitan. It breeds in North America, northern Asia and much of China and northern and eastern Europe, as well as in scattered places such as southern Spain and the coasts of the Red Sea. In the Southern Hemisphere it breeds regularly only in Australia and adjacent islands to the north, but it often migrates to South America and South Africa.

In the higher latitudes of the Northern Hemisphere the osprey is migratory. Birds nesting in northern Europe overwinter in sub-Saharan Africa, returning the next spring. Migratory ospreys usually follow rivers or coasts but occasionally fly cross-country. Many die en route, especially young birds. Ospreys can cover great distances quickly. One migrating bird was satellite-tracked from Ireland to Spain in September 2000. In a 36-hour period it flew 626 miles (1,008 km) across the Atlantic and Bay of Biscay. In their winter range ospreys may have territories that they defend against other ospreys.

Spectacular diving

Ospreys spend most of their time circling over water or perched on rocks or trees where there is a good view over the water. They are usually found on the coast, but they also haunt lakes and rivers. In Australia they live on the coral islets of the Great Barrier Reef.

When it hunts, this spectacular fisher circles over the water on its long wings at a height of 50–100 feet (15–30 m) until it spots a fish. It hovers for a moment, then plunges, hitting the water with a great splash. It then surfaces triumphantly to bear its catch back to a perch. The osprey appears to strike the water headfirst, but just before the final impact, it throws its feet forward and enters the water talons first, grabbing the fish with both feet, one in front of the other. Sometimes its dive is so violent that it disappears beneath the water, but at other times

An osprey soars over Florida, where there is a year-round resident population. Ospreys tend to nest high in trees or on rocks, but in Florida they also nest on the ground beside highways.

The osprey's feet are well adapted for catching fish. Not only do they have horny spines, or spicules, on the underside of the toes, but the outer toe on each foot can be turned until it faces backward, improving the grip still further.

OSPREY

CLASS	**Aves**
ORDER	**Accipitriformes**
FAMILY	**Pandionidae**
GENUS AND SPECIES	***Pandion haliaetus***

ALTERNATIVE NAME
Fish hawk (North America only)

WEIGHT
2½–4½ lb. (1.1–2 kg)

LENGTH
Head to tail: 21⅜–22¾ in. (55–58 cm); wingspan: 57–67 in. (1.45–1.7 m)

DISTINCTIVE FEATURES
Large size; long, relatively narrow wings; powerful, strongly hooked bill; long flight feathers form "fingers" at tips of wings; long, strong, feathered legs; bluish feet; white below; chocolate brown above; white head with black line through eye

DIET
Almost exclusively fish

BREEDING
Age at first breeding: 2–3 years; breeding season: April–May (North America and northern Europe), virtually all year (rest of range); number of eggs: 2 or 3; incubation period: 34–40 days; fledging period: 49–56 days; breeding interval: 1 year

LIFE SPAN
Up to 30 years

HABITAT
Sea coasts, estuaries, rivers, inland lakes and marshes with open water

DISTRIBUTION
Breeds in much of North America, northern Eurasia, eastern China, North Africa, the Middle East, Southeast Asia and Australasia

STATUS
Locally common

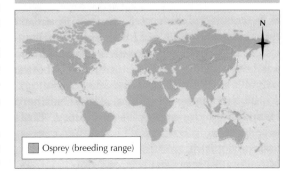

Osprey (breeding range)

it descends gently from the air to pick up its prey from the surface. The angle of the bird's dive is usually about 45°, but it can be almost horizontal.

The fish the osprey catches are usually those, such as pike, that bask near the surface, but bream, carp, perch, roach and trout are also frequently caught, depending on the locality. They are taken at a depth of no more than 40 inches (1 m). One osprey fishing at sea was found to eat mainly needlefish. On rare occasions ospreys have been found to eat mice, beetles, wounded birds and even chickens, but these items are probably taken only when the ospreys are very hungry.

There is a remarkable record of an osprey that met its death from being too good a fisher: a carp netted in a lake in Germany had the skeleton of an osprey firmly attached to its back. Presumably the carp, which weighed almost 10 pounds (4.5 kg), pulled the osprey underwater and drowned it. The talons were so deeply embedded that the corpse could not be freed, so it decomposed while trailing behind the carp.

Where they are common, ospreys nest in colonies, with the nests sometimes as little as 180 feet (55 m) apart. The nest is constructed mainly of seaweed, heather, moss, sticks and dead branches, sometimes stripped off trees while the bird is in flight. Ospreys usually nest in trees or among rocks but may build on the ground. Some have been persuaded to build their nests on artificial platforms such as cartwheels set on stakes. Occasionally ospreys become a nuisance by building on telephone poles and pylons.

In Europe and North America, the usual clutch of two or three white eggs with brown markings is laid in late April or May. The female does most of the incubation, which lasts 34–40 days, and during the first 30 days of the chicks' lives she stays in the nest, brooding or shading them. During this period all her food is brought to her by the male. At first the chicks are fed with small lumps of semidigested fish, but later they are given raw strips and when 6 weeks old they are left to tear up fish for themselves. They make their first flights at 7–8 weeks, and they either learn to catch their own fish or perish. Many ospreys die in their first year.

The eggs and chicks fall prey to nest-robbers, especially when the parents leave the nest through being disturbed. Crows and raccoons are known to steal eggs, and eagles and gulls may do so. The parents often try to lure potential predators away from their nest with a distraction display. They utter loud calls and stagger about in the air with their feet dangling, making themselves conspicuous and taking attention away from the nest.

Ospreys in Britain

Ospreys were once fairly abundant in the British Isles but were almost exterminated by the increase in the numbers of shooting and fishing estates patrolled by gamekeepers. The birds were finally wiped out by human egg collectors. In 1954 the ospreys made a comeback in Scotland. Conservationists thwarted the efforts of nest-robbers, and numbers of ospreys breeding in Scotland continued to increase. In 2000, 120 pairs of ospreys nested in Scotland.

An adult osprey watches from its nest built at the top of a tree in Scotland. An osprey nest is about 6½ feet (2 m) across and is reused year after year.

PACIFIC SALMON

In common with the Atlantic salmon, most Pacific salmon return to their natal rivers to spawn. Species such as this chinook may travel upstream for hundreds of miles, leaping waterfalls and other obstacles as they go.

There are 11 species of salmon in the North Pacific, by contrast with the North Atlantic, where there is just one, the Atlantic salmon, *Salmo salar*. Except for the Japanese species, the cherry salmon or masu, *Oncorhynchus masou*, Pacific salmon range from around Kamchatka in Siberia to the West Coast of the United States, occurring as far south as California. Of these, the chinook, *O. tshawytscha*, also known as the tyee, quinnat, king, spring, Sacramento or Columbia River salmon, is the largest, reaching some 5 feet (1.5 m) and weighing up to 135 pounds (61 kg). Other salmon species are much smaller, the sockeye, *O. nerka*, also called the red or blueback salmon, weighing up to just 15 pounds (7 kg) and the pink or humpback salmon, *O. gorbuscha*, being a similar size. The coho or silver salmon, *O. kisutch*, grows to about 3¼ feet (1 m) and weighs up to 33 pounds (15 kg) as does the chum, *O. keta*, also known as the keta or dog salmon.

Color changes for spawning

Pacific salmon mainly return to spawn in their natal river, the same river in which they hatched. When they do so, breeding males change color. In the case of the pink and the chum salmon, the silvery sides become pale red with green-brown blotches, while the head and back often become darker. In the coho salmon, males become a darker blue green with a red stripe on the sides. Breeding males also grow long, hooked snouts. In most species the returning salmon are 4 or 5 years old. The pink salmon matures the earliest, at 2 years, the coho salmon at 2–4 years. However, some of the sockeye and chinook salmon may be as much as 8 years old before they return to fresh water to spawn.

Do not feed in fresh water

The salmon return in early summer, even in late spring or in the fall, depending on species and location. They head for the coast, away from their feeding grounds out in the Pacific, and stop feeding as they near fresh water and their digestive organs deteriorate. On reaching the mouth of a river, Pacific salmon head upstream, except the chum, which usually spawns near tidal waters. The coho salmon moves only a short distance upstream. The chinook, on the other hand, has been known to travel as much as 2,250 miles (3,620 km) up rivers. One exception to this is a subspecies of the sockeye that is nonmigratory. In contrast with the Atlantic salmon, Pacific

CHUM SALMON

CLASS	**Osteichthyes**
ORDER	**Salmoniformes**
FAMILY	**Salmonidae**
GENUS AND SPECIES	***Oncorhynchus keta***

ALTERNATIVE NAME
Keta salmon; dog salmon

WEIGHT
Up to 33 lb. (15 kg)

LENGTH
Up to 3¼ ft. (1 m)

DISTINCTIVE FEATURES
In sea: steel blue or blue green above; silvery sides; white below. Breeding male (in fresh water): dark head and back; pale red sides with green-brown blotches.

DIET
Marine crustaceans such as copepods, tunicates and euphausiids; also mollusks, squid and small fish. Adult ceases feeding in fresh water.

BREEDING
Age at first breeding: usually 3–5 years; breeding season: depends on location; number of eggs: 700 to 7,000; hatching period: about 8 weeks; breeding interval: all adults die after spawning

LIFE SPAN
Up to 6 years

HABITAT
Adult: oceans for most of life; coastal streams to spawn. Migrating fry (juvenile): estuaries, close to shore, before entering sea.

DISTRIBUTION
North Pacific: Korea, Japan, Okhotsk Sea, eastern Russia and Bering Sea; Arctic Alaska south to San Diego, California

STATUS
Threatened in the U.S.

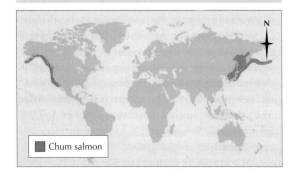

Chum salmon

salmon almost never survive the spawning run, although they may live for a few weeks after spawning. In only the pink salmon species do some of the adults survive and return to the sea.

Adults die after spawning

Because they are no longer feeding, the salmon are usually very thin as they near the spawning grounds. The males often look worse because they become aggressive, driving off other males and fighting with each other during this time.

The females, meanwhile, look for a place in the sandy or gravelly shallows where the water is clear and has plenty of oxygen. Then they start digging redds (troughs) in the riverbeds with their tails, each one lying on her side and flapping her tail. When the redd is deep enough, she drops into it to spawn, her mate swimming over to her to shed his milt (sperm-containing fluid), fertilizing the eggs. Each female lays several batches of eggs, 1,200 to 1,800 in the pink or humpback salmon, 700 to 7,000 in the chum salmon. Batches are laid in different redds, and by the end of spawning the female is completely exhausted. With her tail fins worn to stubs, her skin blackening with blotches of gray fungus, she dies. Males will often seek out other females, but eventually share the same fate. The carcasses of both sexes drift downstream or are stranded at the edge of the river or stream.

Sockeye salmon on migration along the Pacific coast of North America. The males of some Pacific salmon species become a brilliant red color as they migrate to fresh water for spawning.

Sockeye salmon return to the Adams River, a branch of the Fraser River, British Columbia, to spawn in October. It is not known exactly how Pacific salmon navigate their way back to the rivers where they were hatched.

Down to the sea as infants

The female Pacific salmon cover each batch of eggs with sand and gravel. Thus protected, the orange-pink eggs hatch 8 weeks later. The alevins, or young salmon, remain under the gravel feeding on their yolk sacs for some weeks before wriggling to the surface as fry (juvenile fish). They feed on water fleas and other small animals and in the following spring are carried downstream by the current. The pink salmon and chum go to the sea as fry, but the sockeye may go as fry or as 1–3 year old fish, and the chinook and coho go when 1–2 years old.

Finding their way home

There has always been a great interest in how salmon find their way back to the streams where they were hatched. There is now evidence to show that the thyroid gland plays a part in the salmon's changing preference for water of varying salinity. When a coho was injected with a certain hormone, it sought seawater. When the injections were stopped, it sought fresh water. The opposite effect was found in the pink salmon. Other glands are probably involved, as well as the length of day and possibly the diet. The sense of smell may also play a part, as it does in finding food. In addition, temperatures influence the fish, certainly once they have entered fresh water. When temperatures are too low or too high, the fish make no effort to surmount obstacles. There is some evidence also that celestial navigation, using the sun by day and the stars by night, as in migrating birds, keeps the salmon on their runs along the coast to the mouths of the rivers in which they were spawned.

Controlled fishing

Many people living a long way from the Pacific are familiar with the Pacific salmon, but in canned form. The salmon fishery is commercially highly valuable. Sockeye salmon, for example, are taken in gill nets, reef nets and purse seines on their way to the Fraser River in British Columbia. Unrestricted fishing could kill the industry, so by an agreement between Canada and the United States, 20 percent of each subspecies of fish are allowed through to continue their journey to the spawning grounds. This is taken care of by a joint International Pacific Salmon Fisheries Commission, which also arranges for the catch to be divided equally between the two countries. There also is cooperation in providing concrete and steel fishways to assist the salmon up the rivers. The Pacific salmon fishery is close to an actual husbandry of a wild resource. Moreover, research is being carried out to produce strains of salmon that can tolerate less favorable rivers than they use at present and to transplant fry, which, when mature, will return to spawn in waters earmarked for cultivation.

PELICAN

be distended considerably. The pouch of the brown pelican, *P. occidentalis*, can hold about 3 gallons (13.5 l) of water and is used as a dip net for catching fish rather than to store food.

Apart from the brown pelican, in the majority of pelican species the adult plumage is mainly white, tinged with pink in the breeding season in some species such as the pink-backed pelican, *P. rufescens*, of Africa. The primary feathers are black or dark. Some species have crests and in some there is yellow, orange or red on the bill, pouch and bare parts of the face.

Only one marine species

The brown pelican is the smallest member of the pelican family, with a wingspan of up to 9¼ feet (2.8 m) and weighing 4½–8¾ pounds (2–4 kg). It has a white head with a yellow tinge to it. In the breeding season the neck turns a rich brown with a white stripe running down each side. The wings and underparts are dark brown. The brown pelican is a seabird, but does not venture far from the shore. It is found along the southern Atlantic and Gulf coasts of North America through the Caribbean to the Guianas. Along the Pacific it ranges from central California to Chile, with one population on the Galapagos Islands. The brown pelican is the only truly marine pelican. The remaining pelican species are found on lakes, estuaries, river deltas and lagoons. The other New World species is the American white pelican, *P. erythrorhynchos*, which breeds on inland lakes from western Canada to southern Texas.

Brown pelicans nest in colonies in trees, bushes or on the ground. Tree nests are made of reeds, grasses, straw and sticks.

THERE ARE SEVEN SPECIES of pelicans, all of which belong to the same genus. Two of these species occur in the New World and five in the Old World, distributed over the tropical and warm temperate parts of the globe. Both sexes are alike and all have massive bodies, supported on short legs with strong webbed feet. They have long necks, large heads and a thick, tough plumage. Pelicans are among the largest living birds. The largest of all pelican species is the silvery white Dalmatian pelican, *Pelecanus crispus*, which reaches 5¼–6 feet (1.6–1.8 m) in length, with a wingspan of 10¼–11½ feet (3.1–3.5 m). It weighs 22–26½ pounds (10–12 kg). The most conspicuous feature is the enormous bill: the upper part is flattened, and the lower part carries a pouch, known as a gular pouch, that can

In the Old World there are pelicans in Africa, southern Asia, the Philippines and Australia, and in southeastern Europe there are isolated colonies of the Dalmatian pelican, which ranges eastward into Central Asia, visiting Egypt and northern India in winter. The breeding range of this species has contracted and today only about 100 pairs nest in Europe, with about 1,400 to 2,000 pairs in Turkey, Central Asia and Mongolia. It winters from the Balkans east through Iran and the Persian Gulf to Pakistan and India. Classed as vulnerable by the World Conservation Union (I.U.C.N.), the Dalmatian pelican has become extremely localized.

BROWN PELICAN

CLASS	**Aves**
ORDER	**Pelecaniformes**
FAMILY	**Pelecanidae**
GENUS AND SPECIES	*Pelecanus occidentalis*

ALTERNATIVE NAMES
Chilean pelican; Peruvian pelican

LENGTH
**Head to tail: 4–4½ ft. (1.2–1.4 m);
wingspan: up to 9¼ ft. (2.8 m)**

DISTINCTIVE FEATURES
**Huge, long bill with extendible pouch
suspended below; large head; broad, heavy
body; long, broad wings; webbed feet.
Adult: grayish brown to brown-black overall;
blackish throat patch; golden yellow head
and neck sides (whiter when not breeding).**

DIET
Mainly fish; some crustaceans

BREEDING
**Age at first breeding: 3–5 years; breeding
season: mainly March–April (U.S. Pacific
coast), December–June (U.S. Gulf coast), all
year (Chile and Peru); number of eggs: 2 or
3; incubation period: 30–32 days; fledging
period: 75–84 days; breeding interval: 1 year**

LIFE SPAN
Probably up to 40 years

HABITAT
**Coastal waters; also on inland fresh waters.
Nests on slopes, islands and sandy beaches.**

DISTRIBUTION
**Coasts from California south to Chile, and
Maryland south to northern South America**

STATUS
**Locally common (Florida, California, Peru);
uncommon (rest of U.S.); varies elsewhere**

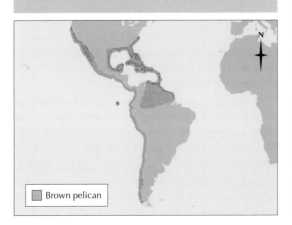

Brown pelican

A pair of Australian pelicans, Pelecanus conspicillatus. *The huge pouch beneath the pelican's bill has a capacity two or three times greater than that of the bird's stomach.*

Pelicans feed almost entirely on fish but a few crustaceans are also taken. White pelicans fish while floating on the surface or wading about in the shallows. They thrust their heads under the water, using their pouches as dip nets to catch the fish.

Community breeding

Pelicans are very sociable and all the species nest in large colonies sometimes consisting of tens of thousands of birds. Most of the white species breed on isolated islands in large inland lakes, usually making their nests on the ground but occasionally they nest in low trees. On the ground the nest is sometimes just a depression scooped out of the earth. The brown pelican, which breeds on small islands on the coast, makes a loose nest of sticks in mangrove trees and low shrubs or sometimes on the ground.

In all species the breeding season varies from place to place and from year to year. In some tropical areas, such as parts of the Caribbean and Chile and Peru in the case of the brown pelican, the birds may even breed throughout the year. The eggs are chalky white in appearance, and the number laid varies according to species. Both parents help to incubate the eggs for 29–35 days, again according to species. Such a period is fairly

Great white pelicans fish cooperatively. They form a line across the water and beat the surface, driving small fish into shallow water to scoop them up.

short for such a large bird. The chicks are born naked and blind but quickly grow a soft white down. Both parents feed the young, at first dribbling regurgitated food out of the ends of their bills into the chicks' open mouths, but after a few days the chicks are strong enough to stick their heads into their parents' pouches to get the food. Before the chicks are 2 weeks old they leave the nest and form noisy juvenile groups, but the parents continue to feed them for some time. The young mature slowly, only acquiring adult plumage after several years. They seldom breed until they are 4 years old. Pelicans are long-lived birds and have a low adult mortality rate: the accepted record for pelican longevity is 40 years.

Many hazards for the young

Mature pelicans have few natural enemies. Sometimes they may be killed by sea lions in the Pacific or occasionally eaten by sharks, but among the young mortality is very high. About 70 percent of young pelicans die within their first year, a figure that goes some way toward counterbalancing the pelican's long reproductive lifespan. When the young birds congregate after leaving the nest, many fall from trees or get caught in the branches or even trampled by clumsy adults. The adult birds do little to protect their young, and sometimes entire nesting colonies are wiped out by predatory animals. Fishers have been known to destroy colonies of pelicans to prevent them from taking too

many fish. Today pelican colonies are commonly endangered by marsh drainage, water pollution, habitat loss or from lakes drying up as the result of large water schemes. Variable fish stocks also contribute toward a high chick mortality.

Strong in flight

When a pelican has managed, after much effort and flapping to become airborne, it is a strong and graceful flier, and it is no less graceful in the water. With legs up, head well back on the shoulders and its large bill resting on the front of the neck, it can sail through the air with little effort.

Many pelican species are part-migratory, or nomadic, and regularly move feeding grounds and breeding grounds. The ability to fly steadily over some distance is essential to them. Pelicans fly at about 26 miles per hour (42 km/h) and there is an authentic record of their having maintained this speed for 8 miles (13 km), so it seems they also have the quality of endurance in flight. There is one record of the great white pelican, *P. onocrotalus*, having achieved 51 miles per hour (82 km/h).

Pelicans regularly fly in formation, either in single file or in V-formation, all members of the flight beating their wings in perfect unison. They also use thermal currents, in the manner of vultures, soaring in spirals to a great height, perhaps as high as 8,000 feet (2,400 m), where by alternately flapping and gliding they may circle for hours.

PIKA

PIKAS ARE SMALL MAMMALS related to the rabbits and hares. They are known by a variety of names, including mouse-hares, rock rabbits, rock conies, calling hares, piping hares and whistling hares. There are two species in North America and 24 species in Asia; the largest is 1 foot (30 cm) long, and the smallest is less than half this. Pikas look like rabbits or hares with short rounded ears and no tail. Each foot has five toes, and the soles of the feet are hairy, enabling them to run easily over smooth rock surfaces. The fur of pikas is usually grayish brown above and lighter on the underparts; it is reddish in one species. In general, the coat is lighter colored in dry areas and darker in more humid regions. Some species have two molts a year, giving a summer coat that is reddish or yellowish and a gray winter coat.

The North American pikas live in and around the Rockies, in the Sierra Nevada, Utah and New Mexico, and in southeastern Alaska and the Yukon in the north. In northern Asia pikas range from the Volga River and Ural Mountains to Korea and the Japanese island of Hokkaido, and in southern Asia from Iran to Nepal.

From lowlands to Mount Everest

One species of pika lives on Mount Everest up to 17,500 feet (5,250 m), the highest altitude at which any mammal has been found. Pikas live in a variety of habitats: on plains, in deserts, in forests and on rocky mountainsides.

One of the most noticeable features of pikas is their voice, which is usually a whistle or a sharp bark, *ca-ak*, repeated many times. Both calls are remarkably ventriloquial, the body being jerked forward and upward at each cry. Pikas rely for safety on remaining hidden, dropping into a crevice and there lying still. Among rocky screes they use the crevices and cavities as shelters, while on the plains they burrow.

Making hay while the sun shines

Pikas usually live in places where the winters are cold, but they do not hibernate. Instead they have the remarkable habit of cutting vegetation with their chisel-like teeth, drying it in the sun and storing it for winter fodder. A pika may travel several hundred feet from home to cut herbs and grasses, carrying these in its mouth to a chosen spot to dry and adding a fresh layer each day. Some pikas climb into the lower branches of young trees to take young green shoots. In winter bark is sometimes eaten as the pikas tunnel under snow, but the main food even then is the dry

fodder. This fodder is stored under an overhanging shelf of rock or under a fallen tree, a single store holding a bushel of hay. Pikas feed in the early morning and late afternoon. Midday is spent basking. During the day the droppings are small, green and dry. At night they are black and wrapped in a jellylike layer that keeps them soft and wet. These droppings are swallowed again and kept in the stomach to be mixed with fresh food and redigested, a habit first noticed in rabbits. It has been found that if rabbits are prevented from eating their soft night droppings they will die in about 3 weeks. The droppings are their only source of certain essential vitamins, formed by the activity of bacteria breaking down partly digested plant material in the droppings.

The miners of the Yukon and elsewhere in the western half of North America called the pika the starved rat. Although strictly vegetarian, pikas must nevertheless be well fed and are far from deserving this nickname. Animals in the

In summer, the pika collects grass stems and other vegetation, leaves them to dry in the sun and then piles them into small haystacks. These dried food stores are eaten during the winter months.

A distinctive whistle or bark is a characteristic feature of the pika. The animal is something of a ventriloquist, since neither call seems to emanate from the creature itself.

PIKAS

CLASS	**Mammalia**
ORDER	**Lagomorpha**
FAMILY	**Ochotonidae**
GENUS	***Ochotona***
SPECIES	**26, including Pallas' pika, *O. pallasi*, and Rocky Mountain pika, *O. princeps***

ALTERNATIVE NAMES
Rock rabbit; mouse-hare; rock coney; calling hare; piping hare; whistling hare

WEIGHT
4⅖–14 oz. (125–400 g)

LENGTH
Head and body: 5–12 in. (12.5–30 cm)

DISTINCTIVE FEATURES
Resemble a small rabbit or hare, but with shorter, rounder ears and shorter legs; no visible tail; feet have hairy soles; grayish brown fur, lighter on underparts

DIET
Grasses, herbs, shoots and bark

BREEDING
Age at first breeding: 6 weeks; breeding season: varies with species and location; gestation period: 30 days; number of young: usually 2 to 5; breeding interval: up to 3 litters per year

LIFE SPAN
Usually 3 years, occasionally up to 7 years

HABITAT
Varied, includes open plains, deserts, mountains and steppes; usually on rocky terrain

DISTRIBUTION
Western North America and Asia

STATUS
Some species common (including both U.S. species); at least 4 Asian species threatened

North Temperate Zone can stand up to cold so long as they are well fed. It is not the hard winters that kill, but food shortages caused by freezing conditions. Pikas can keep going even when the ground is covered with snow because they have their food stores. They even sun themselves on rocks in temperatures of 0° F (-17° C).

Small, naked babies

The breeding season is often between May and September, when each female has two or three litters. The gestation period is 30 days and there are usually two to five babies in a litter. Each young is born naked and helpless and is put in a nest of dried grass. They weigh 1 ounce (28 g) at birth; adults weigh up to about 14 ounces (400 g). The young reach full size in 6–7 weeks, having been weaned when about a quarter grown. The life span of the pika is 1–3 years. During that time their predators are weasels and other small carnivores as well as hawks.

A modern guinea pig?

Pikas enjoyed a measure of obscurity for a long time, but they now seem to be emerging to fame as laboratory animals. They were first discovered in North America in about 1828. Naturalist Thomas Nuttal recorded how he heard, in the Rockies, "a slender but very distinct bleat, like that of a young kid or goat. But in vain I tried to discover any large animal around me." Finally he located the little animal "nothing much larger than a mouse." The first pika was discovered in Asia in 1769. However, little more was known of them, except their habit of storing hay and their ventriloquial voice, until the middle of the 20th century. Since then scientists in the former Soviet Union have been using them as laboratory animals because they are so easy to maintain.

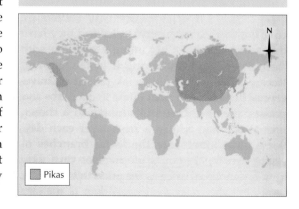

Pikas

POLAR BEAR

Their broad, hairy feet provide polar bears with a good grip on ice. When they are pursued the bears can run at speeds of 18–24 miles per hour (30–40 km/h).

THE POLAR BEAR IS THE largest land carnivore. The males average 6½–8¼ feet (2–2.5 m) long and may reach 9 feet (2.7 m) standing erect on their hind legs, with a shoulder height of about 5¼ feet (1.6 m). Male polar bears may weigh up to 1,720 pounds (780 kg), although the females are smaller, with an average weight of about 660 pounds (300 kg). Polar bears have a long head with small ears and a straight nose, a long neck, powerful limbs, broad feet with hairy soles and a stumpy tail 3–5 inches (7.5–12.5 cm) in length. Although it appears to be white, polar bear fur consists of hollow, colorless hairs. These conduct heat to the polar bear's skin, which is black and therefore a highly efficient heat absorber. The coat becomes more yellow in the summer, and with age.

Polar bears live along the southern edge of the Arctic pack ice. They are carried southward by the ice in spring and summer and return northward when the ice breaks up.

A home of ice and water

Polar bears are expert divers and swim strongly, reaching a maximum speed of about 7 miles per hour (12 km/h), using only the front legs and trailing the hind legs. A thick layer of fat under the skin, 3 inches (7.5 cm) thick on the haunches, helps to insulate the bears and to keep them buoyant in the water. Polar bears have been seen swimming strongly 200 miles (320 km) from land and can cover more than 62 miles (100 km) in one go. The bears usually swim with the head stretched forward, but when the sea is rough they put their heads underwater, lifting them periodically to breathe. When polar bears come onto land, they shake themselves dry as dogs do. They swing their heads from side to side as they walk, as if searching or smelling out prey. The bears are essentially nomadic, and wander for miles in search of food.

Hunting seals

Polar bears' favorite food is seals, especially the ringed seal, *Pusa hispida*, which the bears stalk by taking advantage of snow hummocks. A seal asleep on the edge of the ice is easy prey. The polar bear swims underwater to the spot, comes up beneath the seal and crushes its skull with one blow of the powerful forepaw. When a ringed seal is about to give birth, she digs an igloo in a hummock of snow over her breathing hole. Polar bears sniff out seal igloos and take the pups and also catch seals when they come up for air at breathing holes. Polar bears kill young walrus, *Odobenus rosmarus*, but in a fight with a grown walrus the bear is likely to lose. The bears also eat fish, seabirds and their eggs and carrion.

POLAR BEAR

CLASS	**Mammalia**
ORDER	**Carnivora**
FAMILY	**Ursidae**
GENUS AND SPECIES	***Ursus maritimus***

ALTERNATIVE NAME
Ice bear

WEIGHT
Up to 1,720 lb. (780 kg), male much larger than female

LENGTH
Head and body: 6½–8¼ ft. (2–2.5 m); shoulder height: about 5¼ ft. (1.6 m); tail: 3–5 in. (7.5–12.5 cm)

DISTINCTIVE FEATURES
Large, powerful bear; long head and neck; small ears; broad feet with hairy soles; stumpy tail; thick white coat, becoming cream colored with age; dark nose

DIET
Mainly seals and carrion; occasionally young walrus and musk-ox; also fish, lemmings, vegetation and berries

BREEDING
Age at first breeding: 10–11 years (male), 5 years (female); breeding season: March–April; number of young: usually 2; gestation period: 195–265 days, including delayed implantation; breeding interval: usually 2–4 years

LIFE SPAN
Up to 30 years

HABITAT
Summer: Arctic tundra grassland; winter: frozen pack ice

DISTRIBUTION
Arctic coasts

STATUS
Threatened

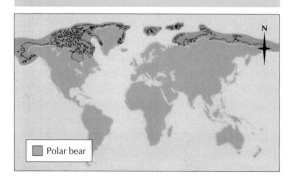

Polar bear

A stranded whale draws bears from a large area. At certain times of the year, usually in late spring or early summer, polar bears eat large quantities of grass, lichens, seaweed and moss. They also take crowberries, bilberries and cranberries.

The cubs of polar bears are able to walk around 47 days after their birth, but are not fully weaned until they are 3 months old.

A long gestation

Mating is in April or May. The implantation of the fertilized egg in the uterus, and its development, are delayed. Consequently, polar bears have a fairly long gestation period of 195–265 days. Two cubs are usually born in December or January. At birth each cub is 1 foot (30 cm) long and weighs 1½ pounds (0.7 kg). It has a coat of short, sparse hair. The eyes open at 33 days, and the ears open at 26 days, although hearing is imperfect until the cub is 69 days old. Male polar bears are sexually mature at about 10 years, although females mature in about half this time.

It is often said that cubs are born while the mother is hibernating. Polar bears, like other bears, do not hibernate in the strict sense, and it is now usual to speak of their sleep as winter dormancy. The pregnant she-bear seeks out a bank of snow in the lee of a hill and digs into it. There is some scientific debate as to whether the males hibernate. It seems likely that some do, although for shorter periods than the females.

Humans are the main threat

Apart from humans, the polar bear has no predators, although a walrus may gore a polar bear in self-defense. Young bears die of accidents, by drowning or by being crushed by ice during storms; old males also kill and eat cubs. Polar bears have long been hunted by Inuits for their meat and pelts. Their long canine teeth are also used for ornaments. Indigenous peoples also make bed covers, sleigh robes and trousers from polar bear pelts.

Although Inuits eat the flesh of polar bears, they do not make use of the liver, even to feed their dogs. It is poisonous, due to the fact that it contains high concentrations of vitamin A, which causes headaches and nausea and sometimes a form of dermatitis (skin inflammation).

Conserving the polar bear

The earliest known record of polar bears being taken into captivity may date from 880 C.E., when two cubs were taken from Iceland to Norway. At the time polar bears were often offered as gifts to European rulers, who rewarded the donation with valuable goods or titles.

Intensive hunting of the bears began in the 17th century, when whalers reached the Arctic pack ice. Two centuries later the population of polar bears was decreasing in many parts of the Arctic. Subsequently, sealers also made an impact on polar bear numbers, and in 1942 alone Norwegian sealers killed 714 bears. More recently the Inuits have hunted polar bears in order to trade their pelts. In parts of arctic North

America it was relatively easy for hunters to land by airplane and shoot the bears for sport in the past, but legislation controlling this is now in place and under fairly constant review.

In 1965, the world population of polar bears was estimated at over 10,000, with a total annual kill of about 1,300. In 1968 research scientists from five Arctic nations—the Soviet Union, the United States, Canada, Norway and Denmark—established the Polar Bear Group to study the life history, ecology, seasonal movements and population of the species. As a result of the work of this group, the International Agreement on the Conservation of Polar Bears and their Habitat was signed between the five participating nations in 1973. The agreement prevented the hunting and capture of polar bears unless for strictly defined purposes and banned the use of motorized vehicles or aircraft to hunt them, although indigenous peoples were permitted hunting rights for subsistence purposes. It also outlawed the sale of the skins of any polar bears caught within the agreed conditions and stated that any ecosystems polar bears belong to should also be protected.

In 2008, the U.S. government declared the species threatened because of the loss of sea-ice habitat resulting from climate change. Contemporary estimates put the worldwide polar bear population at 20,000 to 25,000.

Polar bear cubs stay with their mother until they are at least 10 months old. When she is ready to mate again, the mother drives away any cubs that still remain with her.

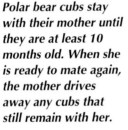

PRAIRIE DOG

P RAIRIE DOGS ARE hamsterlike, short-tailed ground squirrels, so named because of their barking calls. Apart from being slightly flattened, the prairie dog's tail bears little resemblance to that of a squirrel, although its head is more squirrel-like, apart from its small ears. The length of the head and body averages about 1 foot (30 cm) with a 3½-inch (9-cm) tail. The prairie dog's fur is yellowish brown, gray or slate gray with paler cream or white underparts. In some species the tip of the tail is black. All five species are very similar in appearance.

Prairie dogs inhabit grassland and pasture on the plains and plateaus of North America, from the Dakotas to Texas, and from Utah and Arizona in the west to Kansas and Oklahoma in the east. They are also found in southern Canada and northern Mexico. The black-tailed prairie dog,

Cynomys ludovicianus, is the most wide-ranging throughout this area. The other four species occur more locally in the southern part of this range.

Prairie citizens

Prairie dogs used to live in vast populations, called towns. In 1901 one prairie dog town was estimated to cover an area 100 by 240 miles (160 by 390 km) and to contain 400 million animals. Nowadays towns are much smaller, because large concentrations of prairie dogs inevitably came into conflict with humans by competing for land with grazing cattle.

As with other colonial or social animals, prairie dogs have a social organization, which, as must be expected with such vast colonies, is very complex. A single town is divided into a number of wards, the boundaries of which depend largely on the geography of the area and linear features such as streams. The wards are then divided into a number of coteries (groups of individuals), each covering less than 1 acre (0.4 ha). The coterie is the base unit on which each prairie dog's life is founded. Each family unit defends its territory, and individuals rarely venture outside the boundaries. If they do, they are likely to be chased back by members of neighboring coteries.

A typical coterie consists of an adult male, three adult females and a variable number of young prairie dogs. The members of a coterie recognize each other and are on friendly terms and, except for the very young ones, they jealously guard the coterie's boundaries. Apart from squabbles along the borders, members of the coterie, including the youngsters, advertise their territories with a display. Each animal rears up on its hind legs, with its nose pointing to the sky, then delivers a series of two-syllable calls.

Each coterie has a network of burrows with a large number of entrances. From the entrance the burrow descends steeply for 3–4 yards (2.7–3.6 m) before meeting radial tunnels with nests at the end. From a distance a prairie dog town appears pockmarked with craters because each burrow entrance is surrounded by a volcano-like cone. This is more than the casual accumulation of excavated soil:

A Gunnison's prairie dog, Cynomys gunnisoni, *Bruce Canyon National Park, Utah. Prairie dogs used to be found in vast towns across the plains of North America but are now mostly confined to National Parks.*

PRAIRIE DOGS

CLASS	**Mammalia**
ORDER	**Rodentia**
FAMILY	**Sciuridae**

GENUS AND SPECIES   **Black-tailed prairie dog,** *Cynomys ludovicianus;* **white-tailed prairie dog,** *C. leucurus;* **Gunnison's prairie dog,** *C. gunnisoni;* **Utah prairie dog,** *C. parvidens;* **Mexican prairie dog,** *C. mexicanus*

WEIGHT
1½–3 lb. (0.7–1.4 kg)

LENGTH
Head and body: 11–13 in. (28–33 cm); tail: 1–4½ in. (3–11.5 cm)

DISTINCTIVE FEATURES
Hamsterlike appearance; squirrel-like head with small ears; yellow-brown, gray or slate gray upperparts; paler cream or white underparts; flattened, often black-tipped, tail

DIET
Grass seeds and shoots

BREEDING
Age at first breeding: 18–24 months; breeding season: January–May (southern U.S.), February–April (northern U.S.); number of young: usually 3 or 4; gestation period: 27–35 days; breeding interval: 1 year

LIFE SPAN
Up to 8 years in captivity

HABITAT
Open grassland and pasture

DISTRIBUTION
Southern Canada; western U.S. south to northern Mexico

STATUS
Some species locally common; conservation dependent: Utah prairie dog; endangered: Mexican prairie dog

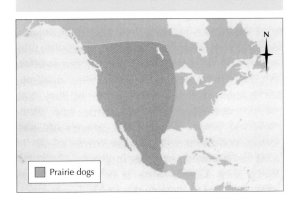

Prairie dogs

it is actually a carefully built rampart of soil 1–2 feet (30–60 cm) high and up to 6 feet (1.8 m) across. The soil is gathered from the surface, brought to the entrance and patted into place, where it serves as a lookout post and a protection against floods after heavy rain.

Prairie dogs, such as this black-tailed prairie dog, are named for their barking alarm call. This is specialized to defend against different predators.

Unintentional agriculture

Prairie dogs are vegetarian, feeding on grass shoots and seeds, and other plants that grow on the prairies. Not surprisingly, the crowds of prairie dogs have a profound effect on the vegetation inside the town limits. Taller plants are completely eliminated, being cut down and left to wither if they are not eaten. Meanwhile, the continual cropping of the grasses and herbs encourages fast-growing plants with abundant seeds and also encourages high herbaceous plant diversity. As a result, the optimal vegetation, from the prairie dog's point of view, is produced. There is a second advantage to this unintentional agriculture. The removal of tall plants deprives predators of cover and allows the prairie dogs a clear view from their mounds.

Prairie dogs live in close-knit family groups known as coteries. When food is plentiful, a female will suckle any pup within the coterie.

Perhaps the main advantage of the coterie system is that each group of prairie dogs has sufficient area for feeding, and overgrazing is prevented by not allowing other prairie dogs onto the pasture. When the population gets too large, some members of the coterie emigrate.

Keeping the balance

The rate of reproduction in prairie dogs is slow compared with that of many other rodents. Each female produces only one litter each year, usually of three or four pups, although there may be up to eight young. Breeding takes place from January to May in the southern United States and between February and April in the north. The young are born after a gestation period of 27–35 days. The pups' eyes open at 33 days and they are weaned in 7 weeks.

Although comparatively few pups are born each year, the population can still increase rapidly, for example, growing from 4 to 15 prairie dogs per acre in 3 months. Such an increase would threaten the food supply if it were not for emigrations to "overspill" towns or suburbs. When the population rises, the behavior of the prairie dogs changes. Usually any member of a coterie can enter any burrow, and any female will suckle any pup. However, when the population becomes too high, the females defend their nests. The other adults and last year's young, meanwhile, dig burrows and feed at the edge of the town, commuting home at night. As the

young prairie dogs appear, the traveling animals move permanently into their new homes. The population is thus redistributed without disturbing the boundaries.

Early warning system

Prairie dogs fall prey to many predators, particularly coyotes and raptors (birds of prey). As with marmots (discussed elsewhere in this book), prairie dogs have an alarm call that sends them all bolting for cover. This is the bark that is responsible for their name. It is a short nasal yip and is specialized for different predators, such as the black footed ferret. The alarm call also has several shades of meaning. When high-pitched, it is the signal for immediate flight. The territorial call, however, is used as an all-clear signal.

The depredations of so many predators does not seriously affect prairie dog numbers, but the prairie dog's use of the grassy plains has led to its being nearly wiped out by humans. Ranchers want the grasses for their livestock, which are also in danger of breaking their legs in prairie dog burrows. In the past, poisoning has been so effective that prairie dog towns have been wiped out across much of their former range and they now survive mainly in national parks and other protected areas. While some species are still locally common, with prairie towns of up to several thousand animals in places, the Utah prairie dog, *C. parvidens,* is now conservation dependent and *C. mexicanus* is endangered.

PRONGHORN ANTELOPE

THE PRONGHORN IS THE sole living representative of an ancient family, Antilocapridae, that arose and developed in North America. Usually called the pronghorn antelope, the pronghorn is not a true antelope, as these are found only in Eurasia and Africa. It stands 32–41 inches (81–104 cm) at the shoulder and is 3⅓–5¼ feet (1–1.6 m) in length, with a tail that grows 3–7 inches (7.5–18 cm) long. The pronghorn's weight is in the range of 79–154 pounds (36–70 kg), with the bucks (males) about 30 pounds (13.5 kg) heavier than the does (females). The upper parts of the coat are reddish brown to tan with a black mane and the underparts and rump are white, with two white bands across the neck.

Pronghorns have long, pointed ears and large eyes that are set out on the sides of the head, allowing a very wide range of vision. The buck has a black face and a patch of black hair on the side of the neck, characteristics that are less pronounced, or missing, in the female. Both sexes carry horns, which in the male are longer than the ears, consisting of a permanent, laterally flattened bony core, as in true antelopes, covered by a sheath of fused hairs. Like the antlers of deer, these horns are shed annually at the end of the breeding season, the bucks losing theirs first and the does shedding theirs a little later. The horns are erect, backward-curving and reach up to 20 inches (50 cm) in length, although most are about 15 inches (38 cm) long on average. The pronghorn's common name is derived from the short, forward-pointing branch, which is really part of the sheath, arising from the upper part of its horns.

Pronghorns live in rocky desert and grassland in western Canada, the western United States and northern Mexico.

Renowned for its speed

The pronghorn can leap up to 25 feet (7.6 m) at one bound. It is the swiftest mammal in North and South America, capable of cruising at a speed of 30 miles per hour (48 km/h), and is able to attain a speed of 50 miles per hour (80 km/h) over distances of up to ¾ mile (1.2 km). It is also

In winter the pronghorn antelope uses its forefeet to dig through snow cover to reach shrubs and also to scrape holes in which to deposit its droppings.

The black face mask and patches beneath the ears of male pronghorns are used in courtship and dominance displays.

PRONGHORN ANTELOPE

CLASS	**Mammalia**
ORDER	**Artiodactyla**
FAMILY	**Antilocapridae**
GENUS AND SPECIES	***Antilocapra americana***

ALTERNATIVE NAMES
Pronghorned antelope; American antelope

WEIGHT
79–154 lb. (36–70 kg)

LENGTH
Head and body: 3⅓–5¼ ft. (1–1.6 m); shoulder height: 32–41 in. (0.81–1.04 m); tail: 3–7 in. (7.5–18 cm)

DISTINCTIVE FEATURES
Coarse outer coat, areas of which can be isolated to protect skin from oncoming breeze in cold weather; reddish or tawny upperparts; 1 or 2 broad white rings around neck; white underparts; black cheek patches (male); laterally flattened horns (both sexes)

DIET
Cacti, lichens, sedges, grasses and shrubs

BREEDING
Age at first breeding: 15 months (female), 2–3 years (male); breeding season: July–October; number of young: 1 or 2; gestation period: about 250 days; breeding interval: 1 year

LIFE SPAN
Up to 11 years in captivity

HABITAT
Grassland, prairie and rocky desert

DISTRIBUTION
Western Canada south to northern Mexico

STATUS
Conservation dependent; estimated population: 1 million

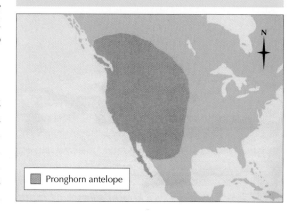

Pronghorn antelope

a powerful swimmer. The woolly undercoat is covered by long, coarse guard hairs, which can be maintained at different angles by the flexing of certain skin muscles. Cold air is excluded when the hairs lie smooth and flat, but these can be raised to allow air movements to cool the skin in the heat of the desert sun. Cartilaginous pads on the hooves, particularly those of the forefeet, act like foam rubber soles, helping the pronghorn to travel quietly and quickly.

Winter nomads

The pronghorn eats a variety of low-growing grasses, shrubs, cacti and weeds and can get all the moisture it needs from this diet if necessary, although it will drink freely when water is available. The daily feeding range may be as much as 2 square miles (5.2 sq km). Apart from the old bucks, which are sometimes solitary, pronghorns are gregarious animals and roam in small, scattered bands throughout the summer. In winter they mass in herds of up to 100 or more and several times a year they shift from one area to another in search of food.

Solitary birth

The rut begins in late summer when fights break out between the bucks. When the harems, which may consist of up to 15 does, have been collected, mating takes place, the season lasting 2–3 weeks. For a first birth there is normally a single fawn, but in later births twins or, more rarely, triplets may be born. The doe seeks solitude for the birth,

in rocky areas or open country with low vegetation. Young pronghorns are born with a wavy grayish coat. They can walk within a few hours of birth and start grazing after 3 weeks. The coloring and texture of the coat breaks up the light, making the fawn difficult to distinguish and affording it some protection against predators. By the age of 3 months the first adultlike coat has grown and at 15–16 months the does mate, although the bucks probably do not breed until they are 2 or 3 years old. Pronghorns have lived up to 11 years in captivity.

White for danger
The pronghorns' main predator is the coyote, especially in winter, when the snow makes rapid movement impossible, and bobcats sometimes take the young. When a pronghorn becomes aware of danger, the hairs of its white rump patch are raised, alerting other pronghorns. This white flash can be seen by humans over 2 miles (3.2 km) away. Pronghorns have excellent distance vision. They are also naturally curious animals and will often approach an unfamiliar object if not startled by a sudden movement or alarmed by its scent. As is the case in many herbivores, the eyes of pronghorns are sensitive

to movement. They will approach stationary predators unless alerted by some movement by the latter.

Curious pronghorn
The family Antilocapridae dates back 20 million years to the Middle Miocene period in North America, when the pronghorn population is estimated to have been 40 million. Hunting for sport, trophies and meat greatly reduced their numbers, which fell to 20,000 in 1925. Today, however, as the result of a policy of careful conservation, pronghorns are on the increase, the present population standing at about 1 million.

The pronghorn's acute inquisitiveness was quickly noticed by the early pioneers in North America. A pronghorn will inspect any moving object, such as a bush waving in the wind or small dust devils raised by the wind, or anything unfamiliar such as dogs, goats, cattle and even machinery. Early settlers attracted the pronghorn's attention by pushing a stick into the ground and tying a white handkerchief on it, which flapped in the wind. Its interest piqued, the pronghorn would come closer to inspect the moving object, bringing it within range of the settlers' guns.

Their tan and white coloration enables pronghorns to blend in well with their native prairie and grassland. The coat is unique among large North American mammals.

RACCOON

RACCOONS ARE ONE OF the best known North American animals, if only because of their appearance in folklore and stories. Their adaptability has allowed them to withstand drastic changes in their native environment. Raccoons have a head and body length of 16–24 inches (41–60 cm), with a tail of 8–16 inches (20–41 cm), and they weigh up to 26½ pounds (12 kg). Their fur is gray to black with black rings on the tail and a distinctive black "burglar mask" over their eyes. Their feet have long toes, while the front paws are almost handlike and exceptionally dexterous.

Raccoons are relatives of pandas, kinkajous and coatis. There are six species, the best-known of which is the common or North American raccoon, *Procyon lotor,* which ranges from Canada to Central America. The crab-eating raccoon, *P. cancrivorus,* lives in much of South America, from Venezuela south to Argentina. The other raccoon species are the Tres Marías raccoon (*P. insularis),* the Cozumel Island raccoon (*P. pygmaeus*) and the Guadeloupe raccoon (*P. minor*), all of which are are found on islands in the Caribbean. The Bahama raccoon (*P. maynardi*) is critically endangered, while a seventh species, the Barbados raccoon (*P. gloveranni*) is now believed to be extinct.

An adaptable species

Raccoons originally lived in woods and brush country, usually near water, but as the woods were cut down, they successfully adapted to life in open country. Raccoons are generally solitary animals, each one living in a home range of about 40 acres (16 ha), with a den in a hollow tree or a rock crevice. Occasionally they live in extended families and share dens, although it is rare for more than one adult male to belong to a den. Raccoons are mostly nocturnal creatures, although in some areas they may be diurnal (day-active), and are good climbers and swimmers. In the northern part of their range raccoons grow a thick coat and sleep through cold spells. The raccoons of the southern United States and southward are active throughout the year; they are also smaller than those in the north.

Where trees have been cut down raccoons move into fox burrows or barns, and they have been known to spread into towns, even to the middle of cities, where they live in attics and sheds and raid garbage bins for food. This last characteristic is one of the raccoons' less popular traits. Apart from the mess they cause, raccoons sometimes carry entire bins away so that they can search them at their leisure. There are stories of ropes securing the bins being untied by

Raccoons often respond to danger by raising the fur and arching the back, making themselves appear larger and more threatening to predators.

RACCOONS

CLASS	**Mammalia**
ORDER	**Carnivora**
FAMILY	**Procyonidae**

GENUS AND SPECIES **North American raccoon,** *Procyon lotor;* **crab-eating raccoon,** *P. cancrivorus;* **Tres Marías raccoon,** *P. insularis;* **Bahama raccoon,** *P. maynardi;* **Cozumel Island raccoon,** *P. pygmaeus;* **Guadeloupe raccoon,** *P. minor*

LENGTH
Head and body: 16–24 in. (41–60 cm); shoulder height: 9–12 in. (23–30 cm); tail: 8–16 in. (20–41 cm)

DISTINCTIVE FEATURES
P. lotor. Gray fur, often with red tinge; 4 or 5 black rings on tail; black eye stripes; sparsely furred paws; long toes.

DIET
Fruits, birds, eggs, fish, frogs, small mammals and invertebrates; also carrion and scraps

BREEDING
Age at first breeding: 1–2 years; breeding season: December–August (*P. lotor*), July–September (*P. cancrivorus*); number of young: usually 4; gestation period: 60–75 days; breeding interval: 1 year

LIFE SPAN
Up to about 5 years

HABITAT
Scrub and forest; also suburban areas (*P. lotor*)

DISTRIBUTION
P. lotor: Canada south to Panama; introduced to northeastern Europe. *P. cancrivorus:* much of South America. Other species: Caribbean.

STATUS
P. lotor, P. cancrivorus: common. *P. minor, P. insularis, P. pygmaeus:* endangered. *P. maynardi:* critically endangered.

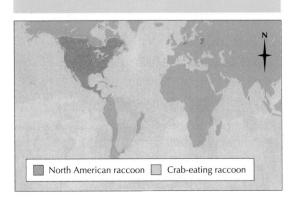

■ North American raccoon □ Crab-eating raccoon

raccoons rather than being bitten through, an example of their dexterity. Experiments have shown that raccoons' sense of touch is very well developed and that they are almost as skillful with their hands as monkeys.

Raccoons are agile climbers and spend nearly as much of their time in trees as they do on the ground.

A wide-ranging diet
Raccoons eat a very wide variety of both plant and animal food and it is the ability to take so many kinds of food that is probably the secret of their success and explains their ability to survive changes in the countryside. Raccoons are primarily carnivores; earthworms, insects, frogs and other small creatures are included in their diet, and they also search in swamps and streams for crayfish and along the shore for shellfish. The eggs and chicks of birds, both ground- and tree-nesters, are eaten, and raccoons are sometimes pests on poultry farms and in waterfowl breeding grounds. They are also pests on agricultural land, due to the fact that they invade fields of corn, ripping off the ears and scattering them, half eaten. Fruits, berries and nuts are also taken.

Mother rears the young
Raccoons mate from December to August, each male mating with several females and then leaving them to raise the family. The young, usually about four in a litter, are born from April to June, after 60–75 days' gestation. Newborn raccoons weigh 2½ ounces (71 g) and are clad in a coat of fuzzy fur, already bearing the characteristic black raccoon mask. Their eyes open in 18 days, and at about 10 weeks they emerge from the nest for short trips with their mother. These trips become longer as the young learn to forage

for themselves, but they stay with their mother until they are about 1 year old. Raccoons have lived up to 20 years in captivity, although in the wild they generally live for about 5 years.

Coonskin currency

Raccoons are a match for most predators and when hunted with dogs they may come off best, especially if they can lure their pursuer into water, where it may drown. Raccoons have been trapped and hunted in large numbers for some time in North and South America, first by Native Americans and subsequently by European settlers. The animals were hunted primarily for their hard-wearing fur, but also because of their attacks on crops. Even in the 17th century taxes and bans were imposed to prevent too many raccoon pelts from being exported. At one time the skins were used as currency, and when the frontiersmen of Tennessee set up the State of Franklin, the secretary to the governor received 500 coonskins a year, while each member of the assembly acquired three a day. Nowadays coonskin is not widely considered valuable.

Why so fastidious?

In the *Systema Naturae*, the Swedish naturalist Carl Linnaeus called the raccoon *Ursus* (later *Procyon*) *lotor*, or the "washing bear." The animal's common name originates from the Native-American word *aroughcan*, or *arakun*, meaning "one that scratches with its hands." It is similarly named in other languages: *ratons laveur* in French, Spanish *ositos lavadores* in Spanish and *Waschbaren* in German. These names testify to the habit raccoons have of apparently washing their food before eating it.

Some books state that raccoons always wash their food, whereas others say that the habit may be more common in captive animals. The first scientific study of food washing was made by a scientist at London Zoo, who showed that raccoons do not really wash their food but immerse it, manipulate it and then retrieve it. He suggested that the habit should therefore be called dousing.

The scientist gave a large variety of foods to a number of raccoons. Animal food was doused more often than plant food, yet earthworms, the only food that needed cleaning, were doused least of all. In another series of experiments it was shown that the shape, smell and size of food objects governed dousing to some extent, but that the most important criterion was the distance of the food from water. The nearer the water, the more likely the raccoon is to douse its food. Scientists now believe that raccoons wash food that they consider to be dirty before they consume it, and also that they remove the fleas from mammalian prey by immersing it in water.

Raccoons are born with their eyes closed and covered in fuzzy fur. They are weaned and start to hunt for themselves after 2 months, but stay with their mother for up to 1 year.

RATTLESNAKE

R ATTLESNAKES ARE HEAVY-BODIED and usually highly venomous snakes, best known for the rattle at the tip of the tail, which is also known as the buzzer, whirrer, bell or cloche. When it is disturbed, a rattlesnake vibrates its tail, which causes the sound from the rattle. Rattlesnakes are found only in the New World. There are about 30 species, most of which occur between southern Canada and the south of Mexico, but three species have ranges that extend into South America as far as Argentina.

There are two groups of rattlesnakes, each represented by one genus. Pygmy rattlesnakes (*Sistrurus*) rarely exceed 2 feet (60 cm) in length and have tiny rattles. True rattlesnakes (*Crotalus*) are usually 3½–5 feet (1–1.5 m) in length, although one eastern diamondback, *C. adamanteus*, was measured at 8 feet (2.4 m), the greatest recorded length for a rattlesnake. In common with other pit vipers (described elsewhere in this encyclopedia) rattlesnakes are able to tolerate low temperatures, and the ranges of several species extend to altitudes of more than 11,000 feet (3,350 m).

A rattlesnake's rattle

The rattle is made up of a number of loosely interlocked shells, each of which was originally the scale that covered the tip of the tail. Usually in snakes this scale is a simple hollow cone that is shed with the rest of the skin at each molt. In rattlesnakes it is larger than usual, much thicker, and has one or two constrictions. Except at the first molt, the scale is not shed but remains loosely attached to the new scale, and at each molt a new one is added.

The rattle does not grow in length indefinitely. The end scales tend to wear out, so there can be a different number of segments to the rattle in different individuals of the same age, depending on the extent to which the end of the rattle is abraded. It seldom exceeds 14 segments in wild rattlesnakes, no matter how old they may be, but snakes in zoos, which lead a less hazardous life and do not rub the rattle against hard objects, may have as many as 29 pieces in a rattle. The longer the rattle, the more the sound is deadened, eight segments being the most effective number to produce the loudest noise.

The species C. viridis *is the most widespread rattlesnake in the United States. It is also the most variable, with 9 subspecies, including the prairie rattlesnake,* C. v. viridis *(above).*

A Mohave rattlesnake, C. scutulatus. The rattle probably evolved so the snakes could warn large grazing mammals such as bison of their presence, and avoid being trampled.

The volume of sound varies not only with the size of the snake and the length of the rattle, but also from species to species.

Variation among species

It is as difficult to generalize about the size and effectiveness of the rattle as it is to do so about any other feature of rattlesnakes. For example, these snakes have a reputation for attacking people and being bad-tempered, but this applies only to some species. Unless provoked or roughly treated, the red diamond rattlesnake, *C. ruber*, may make no attempt to strike when handled. It may not even sound its rattle. By contrast, the eastern diamondback, *C. adamanteus*, and the western diamondback, *C. atrox*, not only rattle a warning but also pursue intruders, lunging at them again and again. How poisonous a snake is also depends on several things, such as its age (the younger it is, the less the amount of poison it can inject) and whether it has recently struck at another victim (if it has done so, the amount of venom it can use will be reduced). Snakes have been known to take nearly two months to replenish their venom to full capacity. Rattlesnakes of the same species from one part of the range may be more venomous than those from another part. For example, prairie rattlesnakes, *C. viridis*, that live in the plains are about three times as venomous as those of California and half again as venomous as those of the Grand Canyon.

Waterproof skin

Rattlesnakes feed on much the same prey as other pit vipers, mainly small, warm-blooded animals, in particular rodents, cottontail rabbits

RATTLESNAKES

CLASS **Reptilia**

ORDER **Squamata**

SUBORDER **Serpentes**

FAMILY **Crotalidae**

GENUS AND SPECIES **Eastern diamondback rattlesnake, *Crotalus adamanteus*; western diamondback rattlesnake, *C. atrox*; timber or banded rattlesnake, *C. horridus*; red diamondback rattlesnake, *C. ruber*; tiger rattlesnake, *C. tigris*; Aruba Island rattlesnake, *C. unicolor*; prairie rattlesnake, *C. viridis viridis*; Massasauga, *Sistrurus catenatus*; pygmy rattlesnake, *S. miliarius***

ALTERNATIVE NAMES
Rattlers (all species); coontail rattler (*C. atrox*); ground rattler (*S. miliarius*); swamp rattler, black snapper (*S. catenatus*)

LENGTH
Usually 3½–5 ft. (1–1.5 m)

DISTINCTIVE FEATURES
Stout body; large fangs; tail rattle

DIET
Mainly small mammals

BREEDING
Viviparous. Number of eggs: usually 10 to 20; breeding interval: often 2 years.

LIFE SPAN
Not known

HABITAT
Very varied, from forest to arid desert

DISTRIBUTION
Southern Canada south to Venezuela; northeast coastal regions of South America; southern Brazil; northern Argentina

STATUS
Some species locally common; endangered: *C. horridus*; threatened: *C. unicolor*

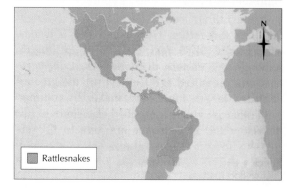

Rattlesnakes

and young jack rabbits. Young rattlesnakes, including the pygmy rattlesnakes, take a larger proportion of cold-blooded animals, such as frogs, salamanders and lizards. Rattlesnakes' water needs are not as great as those of active and warm-blooded animals because the water loss from the body is not high. They need only about one-tenth as much water as a mammal of similar size.

In one test scientists found that twice as much water is lost from a rattlesnake's head, mainly in its breath, as from the whole of the rest of its body, which suggests that its skin is almost waterproof. When it does drink, the snake sucks up water from a pond or stream. There is no evidence that it laps it up with the tongue, as is sometimes stated, or that it drinks dew.

Two years to be born

All rattlesnakes give birth to live young. Whether they have one litter a year or less depends on the climate. The prairie rattlesnake has one litter a year in the southern part of its range, but in the northern part it may be two years before the young are ready to be born. Mating takes place in spring, and the number in a litter may vary from 1 to 60 according to the size of the mother, the usual number being between 10 and 20.

Their venom does not prevent rattlesnakes from being killed and eaten. Hawks of all kinds kill them, as do skunks and snake-eating snakes. Pigs, deer and other hooved animals trample them, especially the young ones, and many die of cold, excessive heat or starvation. Indeed, few rattlesnakes from a litter survive their first year.

A snake's senses

Snakes are known to be deaf, yet they often seem to react to sounds. However, in his experiments on rattlesnakes the American herpetologist Laurence Klauber found that this was not the case. Having placed a red diamond rattlesnake under a table, Klauber first clapped two sticks together, making sure his hands and the sticks could not be seen by the snake. It reacted, apparently to the sound. Klauber was puzzled by the reaction at first. However, he finally worked out the cause. He was sitting on a stool, his feet dangling, and every time he clapped the sticks together his feet moved and the snake reacted to the sight of them. Following this discovery, Klauber placed a screen between the snake and his feet before repeating the test. To his surprise, the snake reacted once again when he clapped the sticks, this time because it could see a reflection of Klauber's feet in a nearby window.

Klauber found that the rattlesnake was highly sensitive to footsteps up to 15 feet (4.6 m) away on a concrete floor. The snake still reacted to footsteps this distance away after Klauber had placed it on a blanket, in an effort to absorb any vibrations that the snake might pick up from the floor. Deciding to test this further, he put the snake in a fiberboard box, suspended this by a rubber band from a stick and held each end on a pillow to insulate it from vibrations through the ground. It still reacted to clapped sticks and to a nearby radio that was switched on. Klauber finally determined that the snake was picking up the heat from the valves of the radio as they warmed up, and it was reacting to vibrations in the floor and sides of the fiberboard box, against which its body rested. The box was changed for a Chinese woven bamboo basket and hung from the same stick. The snake still appeared to react to sound, but further tests showed it was reacting to Klauber's hand movements seen through the very tiny cracks between the bamboo.

Klauber's experiments indicate how hard it sometimes can be to test a particular animal sense. They also show, among other things, how sensitive a snake's eyes are to small movements.

The western diamond-back injects venom into its prey through a pair of hollow fangs. Like all snakes, it is able to dislocate its jaws and swallow its prey, usually small mammals, whole.

ROADRUNNER

The greater roadrunner is a nonmigratory bird of the southwestern United States and northern Mexico. It is the state bird of New Mexico.

nasal gland instead of via the urinary tract. Furthermore, their predatory habits enable these birds to obtain much vital moisture from their prey.

Roadrunners rely on running for catching their food and escaping from danger. They were given their name before the days of automobiles, when they used to run alongside horses and carriages. Although a roadrunner was reportedly clocked at a speed of 26 miles per hour (42 km/h) when being chased by a car, reliable measurements put the bird's top speed at 18 miles per hour (29 km/h). It has been calculated that a roadrunner moving at 15 miles per hour (24 km/h) takes 12 steps per second. At speed the roadrunner's feet barely seem to touch the ground, and it uses its wings and long tail to maintain its balance and help it turn. A roadrunner flies only in extreme danger and is unable to remain airborne for long.

LARGE, GROUND-DWELLING members of the cuckoo family (Cuculidae), roadrunners are famous for being able to run fast. They have strong legs and zygodactile feet, which means that two toes face forward and the other two backward. The wings are short and rounded, and roadrunners seldom fly.

Roadrunners are found in dry, open habitats, including deserts, of the United States and Central America. There are two species: the lesser roadrunner, *Geococcyx velox*, ranges from Mexico into northern Central America, while the greater roadrunner, *G. californianus*, the subject of this article, is confined to the southwestern United States and northern Mexico. Also known as the chaparral cock, the greater roadrunner is 23 inches (58 cm) long from the bill to the tip of the long tail. It is is brown, streaked with buff and white, with black iridescent feathers in the tail and a short, uneven crest. It has a blue-and-orange streak of bare skin behind the eye.

Rapid runners

Greater roadrunners live in hot, dry country. They survive hot weather by reducing their activity by half during the hottest parts of the day, seeking shade and becoming fully active again only when the air has cooled. Other physiological adaptations to their environment include the abilities to reabsorb water from their feces before they void it and to expel surplus salt via a

Pounded prey

Roadrunners eat a wide variety of small animals, including beetles, spiders, scorpions, grasshoppers, small birds, rodents and lizards. The birds simply snap up small items such as insects from plants, or flush them out first by beating their wings. Roadrunners are also known to follow deer, picking up the insects they disturb. The birds catch larger prey by a quick sprint, seizing the prey and dashing it against the ground to kill it before swallowing it whole. If the prey's body is tough, it is pounded repeatedly until it is reduced to an easily swallowed morsel.

Roadrunners are known for their habit of catching snakes, and they enjoy the same reputation as snake killers as the mongooses (family Viverridae) of Africa and Eurasia. While both roadrunners and mongooses undoubtedly kill venomous snakes, the numbers they kill are often exaggerated. For example, examinations of the stomachs of more than 80 roadrunners showed that 70 percent of the birds' food was insects and only 4 percent lizards and snakes. Nevertheless, the idea of their being ruthless enemies of snakes is deeply rooted and forms the basis of extravagant legends. One is that a roadrunner advances with a prickly cactus leaf held in its bill as a shield and builds up a wall of cactus spines around a sleeping snake. A roadrunner deals with a snake in the same way as does a mongoose. It circles about it, keeping clear

GREATER ROADRUNNER

CLASS	**Aves**
ORDER	**Cuculiformes**
FAMILY	**Cuculidae**
GENUS AND SPECIES	***Geococcyx californianus***

ALTERNATIVE NAME
Chaparral cock

WEIGHT
Up to 13½ oz. (380 g)

LENGTH
Head to tail: 23 in. (58 cm)

DISTINCTIVE FEATURES
Large size; fairly long legs; brown overall with shaggy, streaked appearance; tail long, white-edged and usually held at upward angle; crest short, ragged and often raised; white stripe and patch of blue-and-orange skin behind each eye

DIET
Invertebrates, lizards, snakes, small birds and rodents

BREEDING
Age at first breeding: 2 years; breeding season: eggs laid April–May; number of eggs: 2 to 6; incubation period: 18–20 days; fledging period: about 18 days; breeding interval: usually 1 year, but 2 broods per year in Sonoran Desert, Arizona

LIFE SPAN
Up to 8 years

HABITAT
Dry, open habitats, including rocky deserts, chaparral and grasslands

DISTRIBUTION
Southwestern U.S. and northern Mexico

STATUS
Common

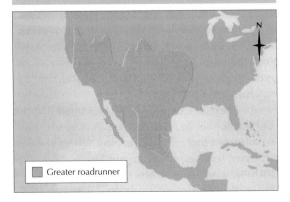

Greater roadrunner

of the snake's fangs using its superior speed and agility. Then, when the opportunity arises, the bird rushes in and strikes at the snake with its pointed bill, stunning the reptile with repeated blows before seizing it, dashing it to the ground and swallowing it gradually, head first.

Wooing with a patter

Little was known about roadrunner breeding until quite recently, and even now scientists' knowledge is based on the behavior of captive birds. Although naturally furtive, roadrunners settle down in captivity and become very tame. At the beginning of the breeding season, the male stakes out a territory, advertising his presence with a song that consists of a series of *coos* descending the scale. Courtship begins with the male offering the female food, which he does not hand over immediately. After presenting this offering he raises his crest, flicks his tail and patters his feet, cackling rapidly at the same time. Then he bows and coos, repeating the whole performance until the female accepts him. Only after mating has taken place does the male part with the food.

The female builds a nest from twigs, which she weaves into a shallow basket in low vegetation. There are usually two to six eggs in a clutch, sometimes more, and they are incubated by both parents for 18–20 days. Incubation begins as soon as the first egg is laid, so the chicks hatch at intervals. At first they are black and almost naked. They are fed by both parents and sometimes swallow lizards as large as their own bodies. They leave the nest when 1 month old.

This greater roadrunner has caught a lizard. Roadrunners belong to the cuckoo family, but unlike some cuckoo species, they build their own nests instead of laying their eggs in the nests of other species.

ROBIN, AMERICAN

The American robin is a common sight in suburban gardens, where it forages for food such as insects and their larvae and earthworms.

THE EARLY COLONISTS IN America gave the name robin to a red-breasted bird that reminded them of the European robin, *Erithacus rubecula*, of their homeland. American and European robins are both members of the thrush family, as is suggested by the speckled breast of the young birds, but the American robin is more closely related to the song thrush (*Turdus philomelos*), blackbird (*T. merula*), fieldfare (*T. pilaris*) and eyebrowed thrush (*T. obscurus*) than to the European robin. Indeed, the American robin was originally called the fieldfare by some of the early colonists.

The American robin is the largest North American thrush, reaching 10 inches (25 cm). The head, back, wings and tail are brownish gray, the tail being darker and the head dark brown to black, with a black-and-white speckled throat and a white eye-ring. The breast and belly are brick red; the lower body and vent are white.

Distribution and habits

The range of the American robin covers most of the United States, as well as much of Canada. The bird is found far to the north, breeding just beyond the northernmost limit of tree growth, and in the southeastern states its range is gradually extending southward, toward the Gulf of Mexico and the western Atlantic Ocean. While the American robin is more common in deciduous woodland, it is tolerant of climate extremes and may be found anywhere from dense forests to open plains.

The American robin is a migratory bird, the whole population shifting southward during the fall. Consequently, the northernmost robins spend the winter where their more southerly neighbors breed. In the spring, the robins are among the first migrants to return to any area. As a result, they have come to be known as the harbingers of spring.

AMERICAN ROBIN

CLASS **Aves**

ORDER **Passeriformes**

FAMILY **Muscicapidae**

GENUS AND SPECIES *Turdus migratorius*

ALTERNATIVE NAMES
**Canada robin; northern robin;
robin redbreast**

WEIGHT
2⅓–3 oz. (65–84 g)

LENGTH
**Head to tail: about 10 in. (25 cm);
wingspan: 15–16½ in. (38–42 cm)**

DISTINCTIVE FEATURES
**Largest North American thrush; grayish
brown back and wings; blackish brown head
and tail; white eye-ring; whitish streaks on
throat; brick-red breast and belly; white on
lower belly and vent**

DIET
Invertebrates; also berries and other fruits

BREEDING
**Age at first breeding: 1–2 years; breeding
season: April–July; number of eggs: usually
3 or 4; incubation period: 12–14 days;
fledging period: 14–16 days; breeding
interval: 2 or more broods per year**

LIFE SPAN
Up to 11 years

HABITAT
**Gardens and woodlands; mountains up to
12,000 ft. (3,600 m) in west of range**

DISTRIBUTION
**North and Central America, from Canada
south to Guatemala**

STATUS
Common

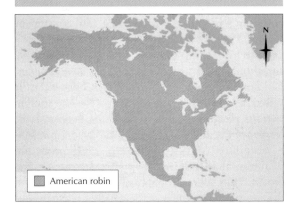
American robin

The largest member of the North American thrush family, the American robin is about twice the size of its European namesake.

Although it is primarily a woodland bird, the American robin has adapted its habits to share human environments, and in doing so has become popular with many householders. It often searches for food on garden lawns and sometimes builds its nests in houses and sheds.

American robins feed on a mixture of berries and insects, probably opting for whichever is most readily accessible. An examination of the stomach contents of a sample of American robins revealed that 42 percent of their diet was made up of insects; half of these were accounted for by beetles and half by grasshoppers.

Female builds the nest

Across its range the American robin is one of the first birds to begin laying. Nests are usually built 2–20 feet (0.6–6 m) from the ground, but may be found as far as 80 feet (24 m) up in a tree.

Newly hatched chicks are defenseless. The parents feed them constantly during their first two weeks, after which time they are able to fly.

Usually there are two broods each year, although rarely there are three. In more northerly areas the nest for the first brood is usually made in coniferous trees, because the deciduous trees that the robin would prefer for the second brood are bare at this time.

The nest is built by the female, with the male assisting only in the collection of material. Even so, he makes fewer trips and carries less material in any trip than his industrious mate. Moreover, if she is busy shaping the nest when he arrives, he is likely to drop his load rather than wait to give it to her.

Building the bowl-shaped nest may take as little as 1 day's activity on the part of the female. There are three stages in its construction. First, the rough outer foundations are laid down, long coarse grass, twigs, paper and feathers being woven into a cup-shaped mass. Then the bowl itself is made out of mud and laid inside the main mass. If there is no readily available source of mud the robin makes her own, either by soaking a billful of dry soil in water, or by wetting her feathers then rubbing them in earth. If there is no hurry and no egg is imminent, the nest construction will stop for a day or two to let the mud dry. Finally, the nest is lined with a layer of soft grasses.

The female may lay from one to six eggs, although three or four is a more usual figure. The eggs are blue green and are incubated for a fortnight, by the female only. She continues brooding the chicks while they are very young. Later she does so only during bad weather and at night. Sometimes her mate helps feed the chicks.

Predators

At one time the American robin was regarded as a game bird in some southern states. Although it is unlikely to have provided much sport, it was often slaughtered in enormous numbers. Today, the robin is protected over its entire range.

Cowbirds frequently parasitize American robins. Domestic cats catch adult birds and young, and the introduced house sparrows often plunder the robins' nests.

Robin in name only

The United States is not the only country where European settlers gave a bird the name robin because of its appearance. In Australia and New Zealand several birds, mainly flycatchers belonging to the genus *Petroica*, are known as robins. There is an Indian robin, *Saxicoloides fulicata*, while the Pekin robin, *Leiothrix lutea*, commonly kept as an aviary bird, is a babbler. The small, dumpy Jamaican tody, *Todus todus*, is called a robin because of its red breast and in various places there are robin-chats, bush-robins, scrub-robins and magpie robins. These represent a diversity of birds, having little more in common than red feathers somewhere on the breast. They were probably all so named because they reminded settlers of their native country.

SEA HORSE

THE SEA HORSE IS AN unusual fish that looks almost like the knight of a chess set. It hangs suspended in the water, with its tail wrapped around seaweed or eelgrass. Another peculiar feature is that each of its eyes is on a turret that can move independently. Although many other fish can also move their eyes independently, this ability is more pronounced in sea horses. A final oddity is that the male carries the fertilized eggs, and later the baby sea horses, in a pouch.

A sea horse has a large head positioned, unusually for a fish, at a right angle to the body. It has a tubular snout, a mobile neck, a rotund body and a long, slender tail. Size ranges from the pygmy sea horse, *Hippocampus bargibanti*, and the tiny western Atlantic dwarf sea horse, *H. zosterae*, both of which are just ¾ inch (2 cm) long, up to the large White's sea horse, *H. whitei*, which measures 13¾ inches (35 cm) in total length. The neck, body and tail are marked with circular and longitudinal ridges, on which there are bony bumps, so the fish looks almost like a wood carving. There is a pair of small pectoral fins and a single small dorsal fin. There are often fleshy strands, which may serve as camouflage.

There are 32 species of sea horses, distributed worldwide. The majority of species live in Southeast Asia and Australasia. The others live off the Atlantic coasts of Europe, Africa and North America, with two species on the Pacific Coast of America.

Swimming upright

Sea horses live in shallow inshore waters among seaweeds or in beds of eelgrass in estuaries. They swim in a vertical position, propelling themselves by rapid waves of the dorsal fin. When they swim at full speed, this fin may oscillate at a rate of 35 times a second, making it look a bit like a revolving propeller. The pectoral fins oscillate at the same rate, and the head is used for steering, the fish turning its head in the direction it wants to go. They are able to rise or sink in the water by altering the volume of air in the swim bladder. If the fins are damaged, they can be regenerated relatively quickly.

Pipette mouth

Sea horses eat their prey in an unusual manner. The long snout acts like a pipette, and the food is drawn in rapidly by a slight inflation of the sea horse's body. The fish approach their tiny prey in a very leisurely way, peer at it for a couple of seconds, and then, having placed their snout in a convenient position, suddenly engulf the meal. Prey is mainly tiny crustaceans such as copepods, but baby fish are also eaten.

Sea horses such as this Pacific or yellow sea horse, Hippocampus ingens, are among the weakest of swimmers. Even in slight currents they anchor themselves to gorgonian corals with their prehensile tails.

The curious body form of sea horses can serve both as armor and as camouflage, as in the case of the pygmy sea horse (above), one of the smallest species.

LONGSNOUT SEA HORSE

CLASS	**Osteichthyes**
ORDER	**Syngnathiformes**
FAMILY	**Syngnathidae**
GENUS AND SPECIES	***Hippocampus reidi***

ALTERNATIVE NAME
Longnose sea horse

LENGTH
Up to 6 in. (15 cm)

DISTINCTIVE FEATURES
Yellow to reddish-brown body; solid color, spotted or speckled

DIET
Zooplankton (animal plankton)

BREEDING
Breeding season: 8 months in the laboratory; number of eggs: 100 to 200; hatching period: 10–60 days, incubated in the pouch of the male

LIFE SPAN
A few years

HABITAT
Surface of gorgonian corals, *Zostera* eelgrass or floating *Sargassum* seaweed, attached by the tail, or free swimming in shallow water to 50 ft. (15 m)

DISTRIBUTION
Coastal waters of western Atlantic, from Nova Scotia south to São Paulo, Brazil

STATUS
Vulnerable

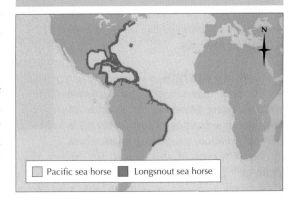

Pacific sea horse Longsnout sea horse

Father carries the young

Breeding starts when a male finds a female and begins courtship. Depending on the species, either he swims in front of her without actually touching her, or the two entwine tails. He seems to be bowing to her, but this is actually a pumping action to drive the water out of the pouch on his belly. The female then inserts her long ovipositor into the opening of the pouch to lay her eggs. When laying is finished, the mouth of the pouch closes to a minute pore and stays like this until the baby sea horses are ready to be born. The young sea horses are ⅓–½ inch (0.8–1.3 cm) long at birth and are perfect miniatures of their parents. The first thing baby sea horses do is to swim to the surface and gulp air to fill their swim bladders. They then feed ravenously on extremely small crustaceans, such as newly hatched brine shrimps, and grow rapidly.

Placental fishes

The inside of the pouch changes just before and during courtship. The walls thicken and become spongy, and they are enriched with an abundant supply of blood vessels. As the female lays her eggs, the male fertilizes them and they become embedded in these spongy walls. The network of blood vessels in the wall of the pouch probably acts like a placenta, passing oxygen to the eggs and taking up carbon dioxide from them. Also, food probably passes from the paternal blood into the eggs, just as it does from the mother's blood in the mammalian placenta.

Male labor

We are accustomed to the idea that the actual bearing of offspring is always done by the female. In sea horses it is the reverse. As each batch of eggs is laid in his pouch, the male sea horse goes through violent muscular spasms. These work the eggs to the bottom of the pouch to make room for more. It seems also that there is a physiological reaction as the eggs sink into the spongy tissue, and he shows signs of exhaustion. When the young have hatched and are ready to leave the pouch, the mouth of the pouch opens wide. The male alternately bends and straightens his body in convulsive jerks, and finally a baby sea horse is shot out through the mouth of the pouch. After each birth the male rests. In aquaria the males often die after delivering their brood, but this does not seem to happen in the wild.

Hippocampus hippocampus, *which lives in the Mediterranean Sea, can be recognized by its short snout. This one has chosen a peacock worm as an anchorage point.*

SEA LION

T HE SEA LION THAT traditionally featured in circus performances is the California sea lion, *Zalophus californianus*, the smallest of the five species, all of which resemble the fur seals (discussed elsewhere). Both sea lions and fur seals have small external ears and both turn the hind flippers forward to move by bounding on their flippers. Sea lions, however, have broader muzzles than fur seals. Male California sea lions measure 7 feet (2.1 m) and females about 6 feet (1.8 m); the males lack the lionlike mane characteristic of other sea lions. When the fur is wet it appears black, but it dries to a chocolate brown. California sea lions are found on the coasts of California and northern Mexico, on offshore islands, on the Galapagos Islands and on islands off the Japanese coast.

The other northern sea lion is Steller's sea lion, *Eumetopias jubatus*, which lives in the northern Pacific from Japan around to California. Adult males measure about 11 feet (3.3 m) and weigh around 1 ton (1,015 kg). Females are very much smaller, measuring about 7½ feet (2.3 m) and weighing only 600 pounds (270 kg). Adult males develop very thick necks and have

Depending on their geographical location, California sea lions breed between June and September each year, usually producing a single pup.

shaggy manes. The southern sea lion, *Otaria flavescens*, is similar to Steller's sea lion but is smaller, except for the Australian sea lion, *Neophoca cinerea*. The Australian sea lion is found on the coasts of southwestern Australia. Hooker's sea lion, *Phocarctos hookeri*, is restricted to Auckland, Campbell and Snares Islands, all to the south of New Zealand. The southern sea lion is found on the coasts of South America from northern Peru, around Cape Horn to southern Brazil and the Falkland Islands.

Outside the breeding season sea lions live in large mixed herds on rocky shores, but some migrate. California sea lions and Steller's sea lions often move northward in winter, some of the latter reaching the Bering Strait, but they return south when the sea freezes.

Cartilaginous ribs

Except when they are defending their pups or territories, sea lions are usually quite tame and it is possible to walk close to them. They are generally wary rather than aggressive, and sometimes a whole herd will panic and rush into the sea. On reasonably smooth ground they can outpace a

SEA LIONS

CLASS **Mammalia**

ORDER **Pinnipedia**

FAMILY **Otariidae**

GENUS AND SPECIES **California sea lion,** *Zalophus californianus*; **Steller's sea lion,** *Eumetopias jubatus*; **southern sea lion,** *Otaria flavescens*; **Australian sea lion,** *Neophoca cinerea*; **Hooker's sea lion,** *Phocarctos hookeri*

WEIGHT
Up to 2,500 lb. (1,120 kg)

LENGTH
Head and body: 5–11 ft. (1.5–3.3 m)

DISTINCTIVE FEATURES
Streamlined body; blunt snout; small ears; powerful flippers; short, dark brown coat

DIET
Fish, squid and crustaceans

BREEDING
California sea lion. Age at first breeding: 6–9 years; breeding season: June–September; number of young: usually 1; gestation period: 11 months, including 3-month delayed implantation; breeding interval: 1 year.

LIFE SPAN
Up to about 35 years

HABITAT
Coastal waters; rest and breed on islands and sandy or rocky shores

DISTRIBUTION
West Coast of U.S.; Alaska; northwestern Mexico; Galapagos Islands; South America; Japanese islands; southwestern Australia

STATUS
Hooker's sea lion: vulnerable. Steller's sea lion: endangered or threatened in the U.S. Other species: locally common to uncommon.

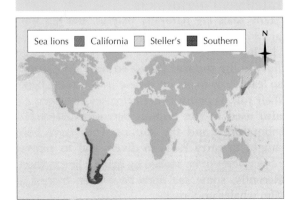

Sea lions ▮ California ▯ Steller's ▮ Southern

human, although they are less maneuverable. In the Falkland Islands sea lions trample paths through the tall, dense tussock grass and, when disturbed, they rush down these paths to safety in the sea. Sea lions display remarkable agility in leaping over rocks and down steep slopes, and may even jump over a low cliff. The shock of the fall is absorbed by the front flippers, the blubber and the soft, cartilaginous ribs, a real advantage when swimming around rocks in heavy seas.

Eyesight and echolocation

Although their eyesight is bad, sea lions are expert fishers. In murky water they probably use their long whiskers to detect their prey and other objects. Recently it has been found that sea lions, and probably other seals, use echolocation, or sonar, as well. Steller's sea lion, which scientists have studied in detail, eats a wide variety of food, including squid, herring, pollack, halibut, sculpin and salmon. Wherever sea lions live near a commercial fishery they are blamed for damage both to fish and to equipment. In the Alaska

Sleek and streamlined, and with large front and hind flippers, Australian sea lions are perfectly adapted for their underwater activities.

The number of Steller's sea lions in the Alaska region fell by 85 percent in 35 years, from 230,000 in 1965 to 34,000 in 2000. The decline was caused by overfishing of the sea lions' main prey by the local fishery.

region, for example, there is a battle between environmentalists, who are trying to save Steller's sea lions, and the U.S. fishing industry. A rise in the catch numbers of pollack has matched a regional decline in the number of sea lions. An injunction has been granted to prevent fishers trawling in areas off the Alaskan coast.

California sea lions, also unpopular with fishers, appear to prefer squid to salmon. Around the Falkland Islands, southern sea lions eat fish although crustaceans and squid are the main food.

Breeding habits

At the start of the breeding season, the mixed herds split up as each mature bull attempts to stake out a territory. As with elephant seals and fur seals, only the old bulls can form a territory; the younger bulls are driven off the beach and spend their time just offshore or on common ground where the sea lions mix.

Each bull gathers a harem of 10 to 20 cows in his territory. The cows come ashore 2–3 weeks after the bulls, when the territory boundaries have been decided and most of the serious fighting has finished. Within a day or two the

single pups are born. A few days later the cows mate again with the bull in whose territory they have pupped and then return to the sea to feed, returning every so often to suckle their pups. The pups swim at an early age and are suckled for up to a year. Many pups die in storms, although their mothers carry them by their scruffs away from the waves. Depending on the species, females are sexually mature at about 6 years and males at 9 years, when they are large enough to hold a territory.

Intelligent performers

Many seals are naturally playful, and sea lions are especially so. They have even been observed chasing their own streams of air bubbles as they float to the surface. They also have the capacity to learn how to act on simple instructions, hence their role as performers in circuses. Sea lions are also used to run errands between underwater laboratories and the surface. They have been taught to carry tools to divers and to recover objects lost on the seabed by fixing a line to them. Recently, some sea lions have been trained to film whales underwater.

SEA OTTER

Using its chest as a dining table, the sea otter skillfully uses rocks as tools to break open its shellfish prey. In this case, the victim is an abalone.

THE SEA OTTER WAS ONCE hunted in American waters to the brink of extinction for its valuable fur. It is an exclusively marine animal whose head and body measure up to 47 inches (1.2 m) long. It has a 10–14½-inch (25–37-cm) tail and weighs up to 99 pounds (45 kg). It has one of the densest furs of any mammal. The fur is thick and glossy, varying in color from rufous to dark brown and sprinkled with white-tipped hairs. The head, throat and chest are creamy gray. The sea otter has a large, blunt head, a short, thick neck with short, pointed ears almost hidden in the fur, and small eyes. Its hind feet are long, broad, webbed and flipperlike, whereas its forefeet are comparatively small and have retractile claws.

The sea otter is the only carnivore with four incisor teeth in the lower jaw. Its molars are broad, flat and well adapted for crushing the shells of crabs, sea urchins and other shellfish on which it feeds. Unlike most marine animals, a sea otter has no layer of fat or blubber under the skin to keep it warm. When resting or sleeping, the sea otter would lose too much body heat but for the air trapped in its fur. This insulating layer is so essential that if the fur is damaged, the sea otter may die from cold and exposure.

Hunted ruthlessly

The sea otter once ranged along the Pacific coasts in vast numbers, from the Kurile Islands, along the coast of the Kamchatka Peninsula and Alaska, among the Commander and Aleutian Islands and down the western coast of North America to lower California. In the 18th century they were ruthlessly exploited by fur hunters, and thousands were killed for their valuable fur until very few were left. By the beginning of the 20th century the sea otter had become so rare that its pelts were regarded as the most valuable of all furs, fetching as much as $1,000.

In 1910 the United States government introduced a law prohibiting the capture of sea otters within U.S. waters, and by 1911 other interested governments had followed suit. The Northern sea otter has been increasing and has returned to many of its colonies from the Kuriles to southern Alaska. The Southern sea otter population off the coast of California is not recovering as well.

Feeds in kelp forests

The sea otter spends its time, usually in small groups, in shallow waters off the rocky mainland or island shores, particularly favoring the waters

SEA OTTER

CLASS	**Mammalia**
ORDER	**Carnivora**
FAMILY	**Mustelidae**
GENUS AND SPECIES	***Enhydra lutris***

WEIGHT
33–99 lb. (15–45 kg)

LENGTH
Head and body: 39–47 in. (1–1.2 m);
tail: 10–14½ in. (25–37 cm)

DISTINCTIVE FEATURES
Stocky body; large, blunt head; short, thick neck; short, pointed ears; small eyes; webbed hind feet; very dense, glossy fur; mainly rufous to dark brown in color, with creamy-gray head, throat and chest

DIET
Mainly shelled invertebrates such as abalones, sea urchins, clams, mussels and crabs; occasionally small fish and octopuses

BREEDING
Age at first breeding: 5–6 years (male), 3–4 years (female); breeding season: all year, peaking January–May and early autumn; number of young: 1 to 3, but only 1 survives; gestation period: 120–160 days; breeding interval: usually 2 years

LIFE SPAN
Up to 23 years

HABITAT
Rocky coasts, usually within ½ mile (800 m) of shoreline; strongly associated with kelp forests of California

DISTRIBUTION
Eastern coasts of Japan, Canada and U.S.

STATUS
Threatened in the U.S.; estimated worldwide population up to 1 million

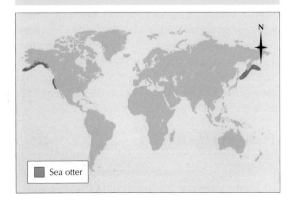

■ Sea otter

around kelp beds. Although it only occasionally ventures more than 1 mile (1.6 km) from land, it rarely comes ashore, except in violent storms. The sea otter is active in the day, feeding, playing, swimming or floating on its back. It swims belly-down only when in a hurry or to avoid a predator. When resting, the sea otter wraps strands of kelp around its body to serve as anchors and stop it drifting off in its asleep. Sometimes it sleeps with its hands over its eyes as if to shade them from the moonlight.

Using tools

The sea otter feeds mainly in the early morning and evening on sea urchins, clams, crabs, mussels, abalones and other shellfish. Fish and octopuses are occasionally taken. It dives for its food, sometimes to depths of as much as 160 feet (48 m), and floats on its back while eating, using its chest as a table. It is one of the few mammals to make deliberate use of a tool; when diving for food, it will sometimes bring up a flat stone and, placing this on its chest, use it as an anvil to smash the shells of mussels and other shellfish. It holds up the mollusk between its paws and crashes it down repeatedly onto the stone until the shell breaks. Large crabs are eaten piecemeal, their legs torn off one by one, and are devoured while the crab runs about on the otter's chest. Sea otters require a lot of food. They eat around a quarter of their body weight each day: in some individuals as much as 20 pounds (9 kg).

The sea otter remains an endangered species although its numbers are recovering in some areas.

Slow breeders

Mating, which takes place throughout the year and in the water, is preceded by an elaborate courtship. There is delayed implantation, so the true gestation period is 120–160 days, after which one to three pups are born, of which only one survives. The pup is born on shore in an advanced stage of development, well furred, with its eyes open and with a complete set of milk teeth. The mother immediately carries her pup into the water and gives it constant and careful attention, nursing and grooming it on her chest as she swims or floats on her back. The pup does not leave her until it is about 8 months old, probably relying on her to teach it to hunt. The reproductive rate of sea otters is slow because males do not breed until they are 5–6 years old, whereas females are 3–4 years old before they breed, and they bear pups only every other year.

Humans were its worst enemy

The sea otter has formidable natural predators in the killer whale and various sharks, but in the past its worst predator was humans, who hunted it for its fur. The Native Americans made little difference to the sea otter's numbers. It was a different story once the animal was exploited for the fur trade by European settlers.

Holding without hands

Very few animals, only two dozen or so, use tools, yet many could do so. Two things are needed for this: the ability to hold the tool and the "idea" of using it. One of Darwin's finches, the woodpecker-finch, *Camarhynchus pallidus*, probes insects from holes using a cactus spine held in its bill. All birds have bills, many feed on insects and a number of them live where cacti grow. Yet the woodpecker-finch is the only one with the necessary behavior pattern that leads it to break off a spine and use it as a probe.

There are many mammals, apart from monkeys and apes, with handlike forefeet, and yet they use no tools. The toes on a raccoon's forefeet, for example, are very supple and finger-like, and a raccoon can even untie knots in string. Yet it does not use a tool. Some mammals will pick things up with their forefeet, the beaver being an example, but they do not use their feet to wield tools.

The paws of a sea otter are small and the toes are very short. In fact, the paws are little better than stumps at the ends of the forelegs. Nobody could guess from looking at them that the sea otter could manipulate a tool. Yet the sea otter uses a stone to crack open mollusk shells on its chest as efficiently as it possibly could with these stumps, because it has the inborn impulse (or innate behavior pattern) to do so.

It makes one wonder what the sea otter might have been able to do if it had long, slender fingers and opposable thumbs. Perhaps it would have been capable of nothing more than it does now, because its behavior pattern is limited to cracking open clams, mussels, sea urchins, crabs and other shellfish.

Sea otters are strong swimmers in the open sea, where they are sometimes threatened by oil pollution. Oil clogs their layer of insulating fur, rendering it useless.

SHIELDBUG

Mating shieldbugs,
Graphosoma lineatum.
The bold colors of their
wing covers tell other
animals it is unwise to
make a meal of them.

Shieldbugs are insects mainly of warm climates and are most numerous and diverse nearer the Tropics. For example, fewer than 40 species occur in Britain. Many more are found on the continent of Europe, especially toward the south, and the diversity increases greatly toward tropical Africa.

Useful and harmful selection

Almost all shieldbugs are found crawling about on the foliage of trees or bushes, or in low herbage, and many of them are found attached to particular species of plants on whose sap or fruit they feed. The birch, hawthorn and juniper shieldbugs take their names from their food plants, and the last two types feed mainly on the berries. Some are agricultural pests. One of the tortoise bugs, *Eurygaster integriceps*, is a serious pest of wheat in Russia, the Ukraine and western Asia. The green vegetable bug, *Nezara viridula*, has a worldwide distribution in the warmer countries, including southern Europe, and does great damage to beans, tomatoes and other vegetables. It is sometimes encountered in imported vegetables in northern European countries, but it does not establish populations in these countries.

In contrast to these harmful species, some of the shieldbugs are predatory and may be of service in destroying harmful insects. The North American genus *Podisus* is a useful predator of the Colorado beetle. The common northern European species *Picromerus bidens* feeds throughout its life on caterpillars but has no preference for any particular kind.

Broody shieldbugs

Shieldbugs lay their eggs either on their food plant or on the ground. The eggs look rather like those of butterflies and moths. They are usually developed in the insect's body, a few at a time, with the eventual total reaching 100 or more. A few shieldbugs develop their eggs in dozens and lay them in two neat rows of six. In many species the eggs hatch by the opening of a lid on the top, so that under a microscope the egg cases look like little empty barrels.

The young grow by stages, changing their skins usually five times before reaching full size. Although the development is gradual, there is often a startling change in color and pattern when the adult stage is reached. *Sehirus dubius,*

SHIELDBUGS ARE ALSO called stinkbugs, and with good reason. Their often bright colors warn predators of their potent and smelly chemical defenses. Shieldbugs represent a group of plant bugs comprising four families of the suborder Heteroptera. All are flattened in shape and some have an outline like that of an heraldic shield. Most are ¼–½ inch (6–13 mm) long, but the colorful red, black, orange and blue *Oncomeris flavicornis* of Australia, is 2 inches (50 mm) long. Shieldbugs are included in the great order of insects called the Hemiptera, which is the scientific name for bugs. All bugs are characterized by mouthparts formed for piercing and sucking, and are hemimetabolous, that is, they grow into adults by incomplete metamorphosis from nymphs, without a pupal stage.

Most shieldbugs have a superficial resemblance to beetles, but beetles have biting mouthparts, and they develop by complete metamorphosis, involving distinct larval and pupal stages. Shieldbugs also resemble beetles in using the hind wings for flying and the forewings as a protective covering for the hind wings. Not all shieldbugs can fly, and most of those that can fly, do so only in hot weather. In the shieldbugs each forewing is divided into two parts, a thick leathery basal part and a thin membranous area toward the tip. This results in the backs of these insects being broken up into patterns of triangles, which clearly distinguish them from beetles.

SHIELDBUGS

PHYLUM	**Arthropoda**
CLASS	**Insecta**
ORDER	**Hemiptera**
SUBORDER	**Heteroptera**
FAMILY	**Acanthosomidae, Cydnidae, Scutelleridae and Pentatomidae**
SPECIES	**Approximately 5,500**

ALTERNATIVE NAME
Stinkbug (applied to all species)

LENGTH
⅖–2 in. (1–5 cm)

DISTINCTIVE FEATURES
Shieldlike shape; flattened body; some species with striking colors; nymphs similar in appearance to adults

DIET
Plant sap and fruit; some species carnivorous

BREEDING
Hemimetabolous insects; nymphs molt several times (usually 5) before adulthood; number of eggs: up to 100 or more

LIFE SPAN
Weeks to years

HABITAT
The surfaces of plants

DISTRIBUTION
Worldwide except polar regions; most species in Tropics

STATUS
Some species abundant, many unknown

around the empty egg shells for a few days while the mother actively protects her young, a behavior very unusual in insects. The family group then moves away in search of the birch catkins that form the main part of the diet.

A clutch of young shieldbugs, such as these pentatomids in Sweden, may be actively protected by their mother before hatching, and even after hatching in some species.

Why stinkbug?

Many of the shieldbugs have glands from which they can eject an evil-smelling and ill-tasting fluid if molested. Anyone picking a berry and not noticing the shieldbug on it may get an unpleasant taste in the mouth. A bug held in one's fingers will usually resort to this same mode of defense. The smell is so strong and offensive that they are called stinkbugs, especially in North America. Some kinds feed on fruits and berries and render any they touch inedible to humans. The forest bug *Pentatoma rufipes* sometimes infests cherry orchards and spoils a great deal of the fruit in this way. It can be prevented from climbing up the trunks of the trees in spring by grease-banding the trunks.

Some species having this defense capacity are conspicuously colored, usually black with white, yellow or red patterns. They are undoubtedly examples of warning coloration. By making themselves conspicuous to predators, especially birds, they derive protection from the fact that a bird, once it has tasted one of the bugs, will remember its distinctive appearance and avoid trying to eat others of the same species.

Shieldbugs not protected in this way are preyed on by birds, especially tits (Paridae), which seek out the hibernating bugs in winter. Far more serious predators are the tachinid flies, whose larvae live as parasites inside the bodies of the developing bugs, killing them just before they reach maturity. These predators are in no way deterred by the bugs' repugnant fluids or lurid colors.

quite a common shieldbug of continental Europe, is variable in color. In one form the young have bold black and red markings. After the last skin change, the adult is at first brilliant red, but after only a couple of hours its color darkens until it assumes its final livery of steely black.

A number of the shieldbugs are known to brood their eggs, attending and protecting them up to the time they hatch. The parent bug *Elasmucha grisea*, which lives in birch woods, goes further than this. The female lays a batch of about 40 eggs on a birch leaf, the egg mass being diamond-shaped and compact, the right shape for her to cover with her body. She broods the eggs rather as a hen does, for 2–3 weeks until the young hatch. The mother and small larvae stay

SKUNK

THE SKUNKS ARE MEMBERS of the family Mustelidae, along with the badgers, minks, otters and weasels. All mustelids have musk or stink glands at the base of the tail, but the skunk is perhaps the best-known mustelid and is able to squirt a nauseating fluid at its enemies.

The bold black-and-white color pattern of the skunk's fur makes it highly conspicuous and acts as a warning to any would-be predators. All 10 species of skunks have long fur and long, bushy or plumed black-and-white tails. The legs are short and the hind feet are plantigrade (both sole and heel are in contact with the ground when the animal walks). The soles of the feet are nearly naked; the five toes are webbed and each foot has strong, curved claws that are used for digging. The skunk has a small skull that is similar in shape to that of the Eurasian badger, *Meles meles*; there is only one molar in the top jaw and two in the bottom jaw.

Limited to the New World

The commonest skunk species is the striped skunk, *Mephitis mephitis*, ranging from southern Canada through most of the United States to northern Mexico. It grows up to about 30 inches (75 cm) long, including a tail that reaches about 12 inches (30 cm) in length. The females are usually smaller than the males. The fur, which is long and harsh with soft underfur, is black with white on the face and neck, dividing into two white stripes diagonally along the sides of the body. The hooded skunk, *M. macroura*, which is native to the southwestern United States and Central America, is similar to the striped skunk but the tail is longer than the head and body and the white stripes are more widely separated. The three species of spotted skunks, *Spilogale pygmaea*, *S. gracilis* and *S. putorius*, range from British Columbia through most of the United States and Mexico into Central America. They are distinguished by their small size, being only 22 inches (55 cm) maximum length, of which 9 inches (22.5 cm) is accounted for by the tail. They also have a white spot on the forehead and a pattern of white stripes and spots.

The five species of hog-nosed skunks, *Conepatus mesoleucus*, *C. leuconotus*, *C. semistriatus*, *C. chinga* and *C. humboldti*, are not as well known as the other species of skunks. They are

Skunks are able to adapt to a wide range of habitats, provided there is a food source nearby. However, they are most commonly found near woods.

The striped skunk has two distinctive white stripes running down its sides. Its bold black-and-white marking is intended to dissuade would-be predators.

SKUNKS

CLASS	**Mammalia**
ORDER	**Carnivora**
FAMILY	**Mustelidae**

GENUS AND SPECIES   **Striped skunk, *Mephitis mephitis*; hooded skunk, *M. macroura*; spotted skunks, *Spilogale pygmaea, S. gracilis* and *S. putorius*; hog-nosed skunks, *Conepatus mesoleucus, C. leuconotus, C. semistriatus, C. chinga* and *C. humboldti***

WEIGHT
7–14 oz. (200–400 g)

LENGTH
Head and body: 4⅓–19⅓ in. (11–49 cm); tail: 2¾–17⅓ in. (7–44 cm)

DISTINCTIVE FEATURES
White markings on black coat, spotted with lines in spotted species, small white patches or distinct white lines from head to tail in others; small head; short legs; long tail

DIET
Small rodents and birds; insects; vegetation

BREEDING
Striped skunk. Age at first breeding: 1 year; breeding season: February–April; number of young: usually 5; gestation period: about 65 days; breeding interval: usually 1 year.

LIFE SPAN
Up to 5 years; more than 12 years in captivity

HABITAT
Varied, including scrub, woodland, desert and rocky habitats

DISTRIBUTION
Mainly North and Central America; some hog-nosed skunks also in South America

STATUS
Striped skunk and several other species: common. *S. pygmaea*: rare; subspecies *C. mesoleucus telmalestes*: probably extinct.

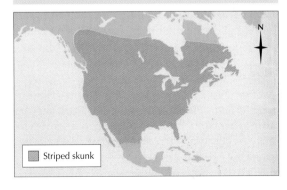

Striped skunk

found in the southwestern United States and are the only genus of skunks with representatives in South America. They are much the same size as the striped skunk but with shorter, coarse hair; the top of the head, back and tail is usually white. They have a long, naked, piglike snout that they use for rooting up insects.

Noxious spray

Skunks are found in a variety of habitats, including woods, plains and desert areas, although they avoid wetlands and dense forest. They live in burrows that they dig for themselves or in the abandoned burrows of badgers, foxes or woodchucks, or under buildings, denning up by day and only coming out at night to forage. Although they are not true hibernators, most skunks, especially those in the northern parts of their range, settle down in their dens and sleep for long periods during the cold weather. The dens are lined with dry leaves and grass. Occasionally several skunks den together. Spotted skunks, however, are active throughout the year.

When it is disturbed or attacked, a skunk lowers its head, erects its tail and stamps a warning with its front paws. It may also chirp, growl, bark or purr by way of warning. If the intruder remains undeterred, the skunk turns its back and squirts an amber-colored, foul-smelling fluid, composed of a chemical called mercaptan, from glands situated on either side of the anus. It is able to project the fluid for as far as 12 feet (3.6 m) with unerring accuracy and can repeat the spray seven or eight times if necessary. This pungent spray can cause temporary blindness if it touches the eyes and its odor can be detected half a mile (0.8 km) away. It is highly potent and extremely difficult to remove. A striped skunk turns its back to a predator and eject its fluid at it, while a spotted skunk may discharge from a handstand position.

Skunks have very poor eyesight. They can only see well up to about 3 feet (90 cm). This may explain why the animal is ready to act so defensively at the first hint of a predator.

Carnivorous feeder

Skunks feed mainly on vegetation and insects such as beetles, crickets, grasshoppers and caterpillars. They also take mice, frogs, eggs, small birds and crayfish, and occasionally they cause damage by entering poultry runs, killing the birds and taking the eggs. As the winter approaches, the striped skunk becomes fat, adding leaves, grain, nuts and carrion to its diet. Some skunks feed on snakes. The hog-nosed skunks in the Andes are immune to the venom of pit vipers, and spotted skunks may be resistant to rattlesnake venom.

Blind and hairless kits

The striped skunk breeds between February and April, and the mating season is preceded by boisterous but relatively harmless fighting among the males. After a gestation of 60–77 days, 4 or 5 young, occasionally up to 10, are born in the den. The young skunk, or kit, weighs about an ounce (28.3 g) at birth and is blind, hairless and toothless, but the black-and-white pattern shows plainly on its skin. Its eyes open in 21 days and it is weaned in 6–7 weeks. Toward the end of this period it is taken on hunting trips by its mother. By the fall the family breaks up and each youngster goes its own way to fend for itself. Skunks become mature in about a year and have lived for 10–12 years in captivity.

The young of spotted skunks are usually born in late May or June although they may be born at any time in the southern parts of their range, where two litters may be raised in a year. As in the striped skunk, the usual litter size is four or five, but the young weigh only ⅓ ounce

(9.4 g) at birth and are only 4 inches (10 cm) long. They are not weaned until they are 8 weeks old, when they begin to take insects.

Left alone by most predators

Most predators give skunks a wide berth, but pumas and bobcats occasionally kill and eat them when their usual prey is scarce. Only the great horned owl preys regularly on the skunk, and it generally bears the noticeable odor of skunk about it. Many skunks are killed every year on the road by cars, particularly at dusk. They appear not to have learned to run away from a car and instead sometimes stand their ground and eject their fluid in futile defiance, as they would at a living predator.

Some skunks are still trapped for their fur, and in South America the hog-nosed skunk is hunted by the local people, as its meat is said to have curative properties. The skin is used for capes and blankets.

This striped skunk has assumed a defensive posture from which it can emit its potent musk at an intruder.

SNAPPING TURTLE

THE SNAPPING TURTLES OF North and South America are named for their powerful bite and need to be handled with caution. A full-grown snapping turtle can easily break a pencil in two or severely maul a person's hand. Snapping turtles are heavily built, with large heads and strong, hooked jaws; they are unable to retract their limbs into the shell. The common snapping turtle, *Chelydra serpentina*, usually known simply as the snapping turtle, has a shell length of up to 15 inches (38 cm) but it is proportionately very heavy and may weigh up to 50 pounds (23 kg). It is drab in color, with a gray, black or brown top. The tail is half the length of the shell and bears a row of scales like a crest on the upper surface. The feet are partly webbed and bear strong claws. The skin is greenish and the shell is often covered with green algae. The plastron, the underside of the shell, is reduced in size and forms a crosslike shape, with the turtle's limbs fitting between the arms of the cross.

The common snapping turtle is the most widespread turtle in North America, ranging from southern Canada to Florida and southern Texas, and in parts of Mexico and south to Ecuador. The other species of snapping turtle, the alligator snapper, *Macroclemys temmincki*, is restricted to the United States, where it is found in the Mississippi basin, from Kansas, Iowa and Illinois eastward as far as Georgia and northern Florida. It is also found in parts of Texas. It is one of the largest freshwater turtles and can grow to 200 pounds (20 kg). The shell may be nearly 2½ feet (75 cm) in length; it is extremely rough and features three ridges. The eyes of the alligator snapper are on the side of its head, unlike those of the common snapping turtle.

Snapping turtles have a more aquatic lifestyle than most other freshwater turtles and spend most of their lives in muddy ponds, lakes and rivers. Snapping turtles are usually only aggressive when they are encountered on land. They hibernate but can sometimes be seen swimming in lakes under ice during the winter months.

Active and passive hunters

The common snapping turtle actively hunts for its food, which consists of plants, carrion, insects, fish, frogs, ducklings and young muskrats. Live prey is caught with a quick thrust of the head and snap of the jaws and is then pulled apart by the mouth and claws. The fish-eating habits of snapping turtles often bring them into conflict with anglers or the owners of fish farms. Too many snapping turtles in a fish pond can lead to too few fish, but some studies have suggested that the harmful effect of snapping turtles on fish populations is often exaggerated. In many places, however, snapping turtles are trapped either because of their supposed depredations or so that they may be used for snapper soup.

Unlike the common snapping turtle, the alligator snapper is a passive hunter. It lies in wait for its prey, half-buried in the mud and camouflaged by the algae growing on its shell which, combined with its rough texture and ability to remain motionless for some time, gives the shell a rocklike appearance. From this concealed position the alligator snapper lures small fish into its mouth using a remarkable piece of deception.

This adult male snapping turtle is making a threat display with its powerful hooked jaws.

Common snapping turtles are poor swimmers and usually prefer to walk across the bottoms of rivers and lakes rather than swimming.

The tongue is forked and the two branches are fat and wormlike; moreover, when filled with blood, the tongue becomes bright pink. The turtle moves its tongue, making the wormlike tips wriggle, and this action attracts small fish, which are then promptly snapped up. Larger prey, including ducklings, are also caught, but by more active hunting, not by means of the lure.

Alligator snappers are virtually omnivorous. As well as taking fish, amphibians and reptiles, including other turtles, they raid henhouses in search of eggs, chicks and even adult birds. They also eat carrion, but do not usually eat plants.

Overwintering eggs

Common snapping turtles may crawl some distance from water to find a suitable place to make a nest. They seem to prefer open areas and even cultivated land. The nest is dug with the hind feet. The usual size of a clutch is 20 to 30 eggs, but there is one report of a very large female producing 83. Hatching takes place during the late summer, and eggs that are laid late may not hatch until the following spring.

As with many species of turtles, the sex of the hatchlings, is determined by the temperature at which the eggs have developed. If the average temperature is above about 86° F (30° C) or below 68° F (20° C), they will be females. If it is between these temperatures, they will be males. Breeding habits of the alligator snapper are similar but it lays its eggs, which may number from 17 to 44, nearer to the water.

SNAPPING TURTLES

CLASS   **Reptilia**

ORDER   **Testudines**

FAMILY   **Chelydridae**

GENUS AND SPECIES   **Snapping turtle, *Chelydra serpentina*; alligator snapper, *Macroclemys temmincki***

ALTERNATIVE NAMES
Common snapping turtle; snapper (*C. serpentina* only)

LENGTH
***C. serpentina* shell length: up to 15 in. (38 cm); *M. temmincki* shell length: up to 30 in. (75 cm)**

DISTINCTIVE FEATURES
Large head; long tails; powerful bite. *C. serpentina*: sawtooth projections on dorsal surface of tail. *M. temmincki*: smooth tail; three prominent ridges along back of shell.

DIET
***C. serpentina*: nearly all animal and plant material, living or dead; *M. temmincki*: variety of foods, but not usually plants**

BREEDING
Breeding season: eggs laid during summer; hatching period: about 4 months, but *C. serpentina* eggs may overwinter

LIFE SPAN
Not known

HABITAT
***C. serpentina*: almost all freshwater habitats; also in slightly salty water near estuaries and the sea. *M. temmincki*: mostly deep rivers and lakes with muddy bottoms.**

DISTRIBUTION
***C. serpentina*: southern Canada south to Ecuador; *M. temmincki*: U.S., in Mississippi basin and surrounding areas**

STATUS
Both species common

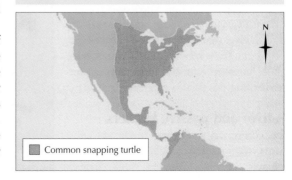

Common snapping turtle

SOFT CORAL

This soft coral, genus **Siphonogorgia,** *is a branching form that lives around Papua New Guinea. It can grow on vertical walls on the seaward side of fringing coral reefs.*

SOFT CORALS ARE MEMBERS of a group of *octocorals,* so called because they have polyps divided radially into eight sections. Other octocorallian groups, to which soft corals are closely related, include the sea pens, sea fans (gorgonians) and organ pipe corals. These are all part of a larger group called the Cnidaria, which includes hard corals, jellyfish, anemones and sea firs. Cnidarians are all composed of single or group-living polyps with stinging cells. The soft corals, of which there are around 800 known species, are at their most diverse and abundant in tropical waters, in the Indian and Pacific Oceans and the Red Sea, although there are cold water examples, such as dead man's fingers, *Alcyonium digitatum,* which is described in a separate article. In the Caribbean, gorgonians dominate instead, and there are few soft corals.

Soft corals are varied in color and form, but their basic construction is constant. They are group-living organisms whose surface is covered by numerous relatively small polyps, usually less than ½ inch (1 cm) across, embedded in a soft material. The polyps are all interconnected by a series of vessels, and can share resources such as food and oxygen. In most species the structure is stiffened by regular, mineralized bodies called sclerites, spicules or ossicles. In many cases, the shape, size and ornamentation of the sclerites are essential in identifying the species.

Feeders and pumpers

The more obvious polyps in a colony are feeding polyps called autozooids. They have eight featherlike tentacles, instead of the smooth tentacles of hard corals. The tentacles bear stinging cells with which they capture their prey, small planktonic organisms. These are passed to the mouth then to the stomach, which is divided into eight chambers. There are also polyps with very poorly developed tentacles and whose stomachs are not divided into chambers. These are called siphonozooids. They pump water into the colony, primarily for oxygenation, but in many species they also play an important role in maintaining internal pressure, to keep the colony relatively stiff and erect.

Soft corals are generally found in shallow waters between low tide and about 160 feet (50 m), very few having successfully colonized deep waters. There are numerous species that favor dimly lit caves and overhangs, but others that need well-lit areas. They are particularly abundant at 33–100 feet (10–30 m) on coral reefs. Possibly due to the lack of need to deposit the mineralized skeleton, soft corals are often much faster growing than hard or stony corals that form reefs. In many cases, when reefs have been destroyed, soft corals are among the first large organisms to reappear. On occasion they appear in such densities that they greatly hinder the establishment of hard corals.

Soft corals rarely have encrusting growths of plants or animals, unlike many other reef organisms, in part because they secrete potent chemicals that inhibit the growth of marine organisms. For this reason, medical researchers eager to find possible tumor inhibitors have intensively studied soft corals.

Microalgal partners

Many species of soft corals have embedded within them extremely numerous tiny micro-algae, or *zoothanthellae.* These photosynthesize like all plants, and can release significant quantities of food into the host coral. In some species of *Xenia,* the zoothanthellae are the only source of food, the action of the polyps being solely aimed at pumping water. This is more common in the hard corals. Hard and soft corals also share the phenomenon of coral bleaching, where zoothanthellae are expelled under conditions of stress, particularly high temperatures. However, this phenomenon is less widespread than in hard corals, and perhaps less likely to lead to the ultimate death of the colony.

Some soft coral species are hermaphroditic (male and female organs in the same colony). Sexual reproduction is common, with the eggs and sperm being shed into the water, where fertilization takes place. The *planula* larvae that hatch from the eggs are radially symmetrical,

ELEPHANT'S EAR CORAL

PHYLUM **Cnidaria**

CLASS **Anthozoa**

ORDER **Alcyonacea**

FAMILY **Alcyoniidae**

GENUS AND SPECIES *Sarcophyton trocheliophorum*

LENGTH
Polyps: ½ in. (1.3 cm); colonies: 40 in. (1 m)

DISTINCTIVE FEATURES:
Colony of polyps supported on short, massive stalklike structure, 5 to 10 large, waved lobes spread from stalk. Polyps long and tube-shaped.

DIET
Plankton; nutrient uptake from symbiotic zoothanthellae; direct nutrient uptake from sea water

BREEDING
External fertilization; breeding season varies geographically, often year-round; ciliated planula larvae spend days or weeks in plankton before settling

LIFE SPAN
Probably more than 10 years in wild

HABITAT
On rocks and other corals in open, sunny positions, from low water to 100 ft. (30 m)

DISTRIBUTION
Indian and Pacific Oceans; Red Sea

STATUS
Locally common

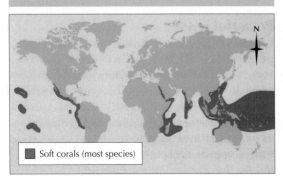

Soft corals (most species)

ciliated and free swimming. After some days or weeks in the zooplankton the planulae settle and develop into polyps. Each polyp soon begins to bud new polyps, and a new colony is begun. Unlike hard corals, some species of which can remain as solitary polyps, soft corals are always group-living. Some species can also reproduce by fragmentation: drifted pieces of colonies, perhaps broken off during storms, can reattach elsewhere and continue to grow, so forming new colonies.

Varied and beautiful

Soft corals are often vividly colored. Shades of red, pink, purple, yellow, green and brown are common, often reflecting the colors of the zoothanthellae. They also come in a dazzling variety of shapes: encrusting forms, mushroom shaped, lobed, or branched to varying degrees of complexity. *Sarcophyton* species, such as the massive, gently lobed elephant's ear coral, *S. trocheliophorum*, are probably the largest, regularly reaching over 40 inches (1 m) across. Many soft corals can be mistaken for stony corals until a gentle waft of current reveals how soft and flexible they really are.

Most soft corals feed mainly at night, perhaps to avoid the action of feeding fish, which like to bite off the polyps. A number are conspicuously active during the day, however, including the genera *Xenia* and *Heteroxenia*. Many of these have polyps extended for 24 hours per day, except when disturbed. These open and close for feeding at typically 40 times per minute in rhythmic pulses. This creates regular waves of contractions that spread over the colony surface.

The polyps of these soft corals are visible as red or pink objects on the white structure, called the coenenchyme. Swimming among the corals are black-margin sweepers, Pempheris mangula, and copper sweepers, P. oualensis.

SPADEFOOT TOAD

THE SPADEFOOT TOADS ARE named after the spadelike horny projection on the side of each hind foot with which they dig their burrows. The family of spadefoot toads is widely distributed over Europe, northwestern Asia and North America. They are usually 2–4 inches (5–10 cm) long with a soft skin that is moist like that of a common frog rather than dry and warty like that of a common toad. The color of the skin varies greatly between species. It may be gray, brown or green with red, white or black markings. There is also some variation in markings between the individuals of a single species.

The common spadefoot toad of Europe is found over much of Europe south of southern Sweden and extends into Asia as far as Iran. The best-known spadefoot toads live in North America. They are related to the European common spadefoot toad.

In Asia there live relatives of the spadefoot toads that are sometimes placed in the same family, but in a separate subfamily called the Megophryinae. Some of these Asian frogs species are called horned frogs, *Megophrys nasuta*. They have three unusual pointed projections of skin on the head, one on the snout and one above each eye.

Spicy toads

Spadefoot toads are nocturnal, spending the day in burrows that they excavate by digging themselves in backward, pushing soil with their spadelike feet, while rotating their bodies. As they disappear beneath the surface, the entrance of the burrow caves in, concealing it. The burrowing and nocturnal habits of spadefoot toads make these animals hard to spot, even though they may be quite abundant. However, during the brief and sporadic breeding seasons, when the males can be heard calling, they are much more conspicuous. Spadefoot toads are mainly found in sandy areas where burrows are easy to dig. In dry weather they may burrow 6–7 feet (around 2 m) down to find moist soil.

Some spadefoot toads give a shrill cry when handled, which may be a means of deterring predators. They may also give off secretions from glands in the skin. In certain species, such as the Mexican spadefoot toad, *Scaphiopus multiplicatus*, small glands give off an unpleasant-tasting secretion that also irritates the lining of the nose and mouth. The common spadefoot toad is called the *Knoblauchskrote*, or garlic toad, in Germany because of the strong smell of its skin secretions. The food of spadefoot toads is mainly insects and other small invertebrates. A few small lizards are also taken.

Explosive breeding

While the European spadefoot toads are relatively unspecialized in their breeding behavior, among the North American spadefoot toads there are some very remarkable adaptations. These toads live in the dry parts of the southwestern United States and breed when shallow ponds are temporarily filled with rainwater. They therefore have to start breeding as soon as the ponds fill, and their offspring have to be independent before they dry up again.

Shortly after a storm the males search for water, and when they have found a suitable stretch of standing water, they start to call. Their calls attract other males, so a chorus builds up that eventually attracts the females, and pairs form for mating. The louder the chorus from any

The eastern, or Hunter's spadefoot toad, Scaphiopus holbrooki, *is a typical explosive breeder of North American arid habitats, meaning the breeding season is sudden, brought on instantly by seasonal heavy rains.*

The common spadefoot toad of Europe does not possess the extreme arid-habitat adaptations of its North American relatives. Nevertheless, as a land-living amphibian, water conservation is always a concern.

SPADEFOOT TOADS

CLASS	**Amphibia**
ORDER	**Anura**
FAMILY	**Pelobatidae**
GENUS	***Pelobates, Scaphiopus*, others**
SPECIES	**European common spadefoot toad, *P. fuscus*; Couch's spadefoot toad, *S. couchii*; others**

LENGTH
2–4 in. (5–10 cm)

DISTINCTIVE FEATURES
Flange, or spade, of hard skin on rear feet; eyes with vertical slit pupil

DIET
Mainly insects; a few small lizards

BREEDING
***Scaphiopus*: breeding season: after heavy rain; number of eggs: 10 to 500; hatching period: a few days; larval period: 2 weeks. *Pelobates*: slower development.**

LIFE SPAN
***S. couchii*: up to 13 years**

HABITAT
***Scaphiopus*: burrows in sandy or loose soils in arid areas; visits surface only in heavy rain, to breed**

DISTRIBUTION
***Pelobates*: Europe and northwestern Asia. *Scaphiopus*: North America. Other genera (Megophryinae): China; Southeast Asia.**

STATUS
Many species common

pond, the more females are attracted to it, which is an efficient way of ensuring rapid pairing. The eggs hatch in 2 days, a much shorter time than that known for any other frog or toad. The tadpoles grow very rapidly. The tadpoles of Couch's spadefoot toad are the fastest developers, completing development within eight days if conditions are optimal. Even so, sometimes the temporary pools dry up before they can change into toadlets. In some species the tadpoles gather in compact groups if the water level is dangerously low and wriggle together to form a depression in the mud, where the remaining water can collect. This mud-stirring action can also expose food on the bottom.

The tadpoles also eat the bodies of other tadpoles that have died from starvation. This means that in bad conditions a few survive instead of all of them dying. It has also been found that when a pond is drying up, tadpoles that have fed on other tadpoles complete their development more rapidly, so increasing the chances of the strongest youngsters' survival.

Each to its own

In the western United States there are four species of spadefoot toads that are very similar but only rarely interbreed. Where two or more species live in the same place, interbreeding is usually prevented by females responding only to the calls of males of their own species and by the slightly different behavior of different spadefoot toad species. For instance, Hunter's and Couch's spadefoot toads breed in the shallows, whereas the Plains, *S. bombifrons*, and Hammond's, *S. hammondi*, spadefoot toads prefer deeper water. There is also a great difference in the kinds of soil in which the American spadefoot toads prefer to live, and this also results in the species being kept apart. In Texas, Hunter's spadefoot toad

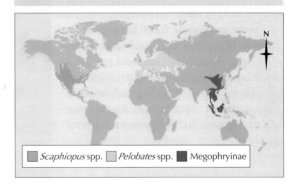

Scaphiopus spp. ▢ Pelobates spp. ◼ Megophryinae

likes sandy areas, whereas Couch's spadefoot toad prefers soil that is not sandy. This is a sufficient barrier to keep them apart, except where humans have disturbed the soil. At one place disturbed ground supports both species, and they interbreed occasionally.

SPONGE

THE SPONGE SEEN IN the bathroom is often, in fact, the fibrous skeleton of an animal. In life the gaps in the skeleton are filled with a yellowish flesh, the whole organism being covered with a dark purple skin. A sponge has no sense organs and few specialized organs apart from chambers containing collared cells. At best, there are a few scattered muscle cells and very simple nerve cells.

Although there are nearly recognized 3,000 species of sponges, the most familiar is the group of half a dozen species of horny sponges in the genus *Spongia*. On the market, bath sponges are given common names, such as fine turkey, brown turkey, honeycomb for Mediterranean sponges, and wool, velvet, reef, yellow and grass for Bahamas sponges. These names express mainly the varying textures of the fibers. There are many other names, but the fine turkey and the honeycomb are those most often seen for sale. They are found only in warm seas, to depths of 600 feet (180 m). They are most numerous in the Mediterranean, particularly the

Crowding the surface of a Red Sea sponge are many small gemmules, or asexually produced offspring. Also visible are two of the vents from which waste water is expelled after feeding.

eastern part, and off the Bahamas and Florida. Elsewhere, in tropical and subtropical waters, sponges are found of similar type but less durable or pleasing texture, although in places, as in Southeast Asia, there may be limited fisheries supplying a local market.

Sitting pretty

A sponge normally draws all it needs from the sea without departing from the spot on which the larva settled. The beating of the protoplasmic whips, or flagella, of its collared cells, which are grouped in rounded chambers in the network of canals running through the body, draws in currents of water through many minute pores in the skin. Having passed through the chambers, the water is driven back toward the surface and expelled with moderate force through craterlike vents that are usually larger and less numerous than the inlet pores. In its course through the sponge, the water yields food particles and oxygen, and it ferries away waste products of digestion and respiration.

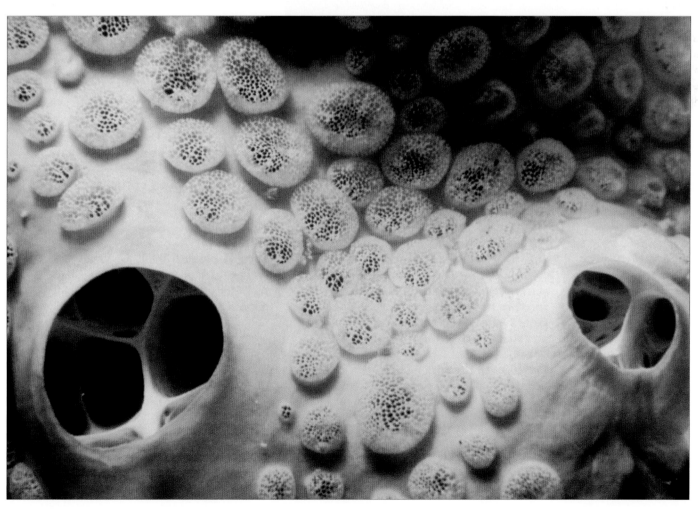

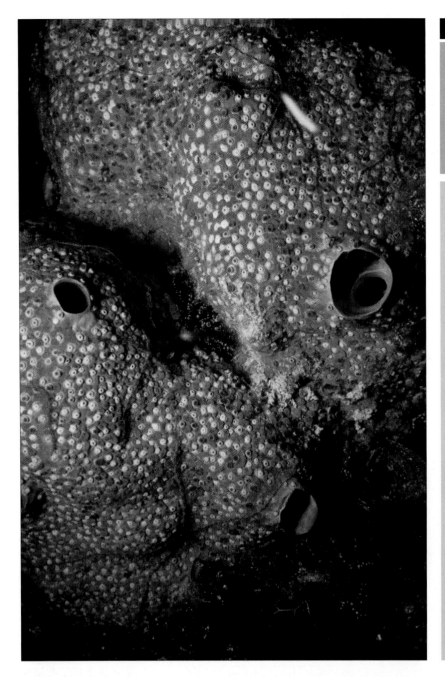

A mature sponge in the Caribbean. After several years sponges may become colonized by other marine animals, such as anemones. Some crabs also pick up small sponges to use as shell camouflage.

BATH SPONGE

PHYLUM	**Porifera**
CLASS	**Demospongiae**
ORDER	**Dictyoceratida**
FAMILY	**Spongidae**
GENUS AND SPECIES	*Spongia officinalis*

SIZE
Up to 20 in. (50 cm) across; normally about 12 in. (30 cm)

DISTINCTIVE FEATURES
Pale brown to yellow color; many holes of various sizes on surface; spongy texture

DIET
Filter feeder on tiny organic particles

BREEDING
Each sponge produces both eggs and sperm; sperms released into water and inhaled by another sponge for internal fertilization to occur; tiny larvae, released a few days later, spends hours or days swimming with plankton before settling and developing into new sponge

LIFE SPAN
Probably up to 30 years or more

HABITAT
Rock surfaces to depths of 150–180 ft. (45–55 m) in warm waters

DISTRIBUTION
Coastal waters of Pacific, Indian and Atlantic Oceans; also in Mediterranean

STATUS
Locally common; also cultivated

Sponges are almost completely sedentary once the free-swimming larva has settled on a solid substrate—usually a steady boulder. There is, however, evidence of limited movement, specially in young sponges, their speed being about 1 inch (2.5 cm) in 2 weeks. The movement may be a response to adverse conditions.

Particulate feeders

Sponges feed on bacteria and minute particles from the breakdown of plant and animal bodies. Sponges are therefore particulate feeders and scavengers. Because sponges have no separate digestive system, food particles are taken into the collared cells, which digest them and reject any inedible scraps. The food is then passed into the body by migrating, amoeba-like cells.

Ciliated larva

There is no such thing as a male or a female sponge: each sponge produces eggs and sperm. At various points in the body of the bath sponge, *Spongia officinalis*, one of the body cells is fed by neighboring cells so that it grows noticeably large. Of the many thousands that undergo this process, some are destined to become egg cells.

The other cells subdivide repeatedly until masses of tiny cells are formed. These are the sperms. When ripe, each bursts from its capsule into the water canals and escapes by the vents into the sea. The sperms swim around until, drawing near another sponge, they are sucked in by the water current entering through its pores. Inside, they travel through the canals until they meet an egg, which one of them fertilizes.

The fertilized egg divides repeatedly to form an oval mass of cells: the embryo. Some of these put out flagella, and as they beat, they cause the embryo to rotate. This breaks its capsule, and the embryo, now a free-swimming larva, swims out through one of the vents. For the next 24 hours it swims in a spiral motion with its flagella. Then the flagella weaken, and the larva sinks to the seabed. There, it develops into a small platelet of tissue the size of a pinhead. This is a new sponge.

Sponges also reproduce by asexual means, in which gemmules, budlike aggregates of cells, form on the surface of the parent sponge.

From seabed to bath

From the moment that the larva changes into the pinhead-sized sponge to the time this has grown large enough to be put on the market, seven years must elapse. By then it has developed into a sponge the size of two clenched fists. If left to its own devices, a sponge may live much longer and grow considerably larger. Bath sponges 20 inches (50 cm) in diameter have been brought up. These were probably 20 or more years old.

If a living bath sponge is cut into two, each piece heals the cut and grows into a new sponge. The same powers of regeneration will take place in a sponge cut into 4, 6, 12 or even more pieces: it produces 4, 6, 12 or more new sponges in due course. More than a century ago Oscar Schmidt, an Austrian zoologist, proposed that sponges be grown from cuttings, like plants. Early in the 20th century the idea was adopted by the British Colonial Office. Experiments in growing sponges from cuttings were carried out in the Bahamas and in the Gulf of Mexico. Each sponge was fastened to a concrete disc, and all were laid out in rows on the seabed.

Misfortune dogged the experiments. One year, when rows of cuttings had been laid down, a hurricane swept them all away. The farmers persevered, and in 1938 some 600,000 tons (545,000 tonnes) of sponges were harvested from the Gulf of Mexico alone. Though sponges have few predators except nudibranches (sea slugs), they can suffer from a fungal disease. This struck in 1938, causing 90 percent mortality among sponges in the Bahamas and Florida.

A diver investigates a large barrel sponge, genus Petrosia, *off Papua New Guinea. Sponges commonly settle on submarine cliffs such as these.*

SWAN

THE SEVEN SPECIES OF swans are closely related to geese. Together they make up the tribe Anserini, which belongs to the subfamily Anserinae, part of the order Anseriformes. Swans look much alike in terms of structure. However, the South American coscoroba swan, *Coscoroba coscoroba*, which is the smallest swan and has a comparatively short neck, is somewhat different from the other six species (genus *Cygnus*). The coscoroba swan has several characteristics in common with the whistling or tree ducks (tribe *Dendrocygnini*).

Familiar, much-loved birds

The most familiar swan is the mute swan, *Cygnus olor*, which originally was native to parts of Europe and Asia but has been domesticated and introduced into many parts of the world, such as North America and Australia, where it has gone wild. It is thought that the species was introduced into Britain by the Romans. The mute swan is about 5 feet (1.5 m) long. Its plumage is

all white and the bill is bright orange with a prominent black knob at the base. Bewick's swan, *Cygnus columbianus bewickii*, and the whooper swan, *C. cygnus*, are the other two swans that breed in Eurasia. Bewick's swan breeds in the marshy tundra of northern Russia and Siberia and migrates south to temperate wetlands in Europe and Central and eastern Asia for the winter. The whooper swan breeds farther south, including in northern Scandinavia and Iceland, with a few pairs nesting sporadically in Scotland. Both types of swans have black bills with a yellow base, the pattern differing slightly between the two. Bewick's swan is rather smaller than the whooper, with a shorter neck.

Two swans are found in North America. The tundra swan, *Cygnus columbianus columbianus*, is the American counterpart of Bewick's swan, and was formerly known as the whistling swan (tundra and Bewick's swans are subspecies, or races, of the same species). The tundra swan has much less yellow on the bill than its Eurasian

Swans (mute swan, below) defend their cygnets aggressively, attacking anything that comes too close for comfort.

TUNDRA SWAN

CLASS **Aves**

ORDER **Anseriformes**

FAMILY **Anatidae**

GENUS AND SPECIES *Cygnus columbianus*

ALTERNATIVE NAME
Bewick's swan (Eurasian subspecies, *C. c. bewickii*); whistling swan (former name for American subspecies, *C. c. columbianus*)

WEIGHT
9½–21⅔ lb. (4.3–9.6 kg)

LENGTH
Head to tail: about 4⅓ ft. (1.3 m); wingspan: 6½–7 ft. (2–2.2 m)

DISTINCTIVE FEATURES
Very long neck, held vertically with a kink at bottom; black legs and feet. Adult: pure white plumage; small yellow spot of variable size at base of bill (*C. c. columbianus*); entire upper half of bill yellow (*C. c. bewickii*); rest of bill black. Juvenile: gray overall; pink bill.

DIET
Mainly aquatic plants; also grasses and crops

BREEDING
Age at first breeding: usually 3–4 years; breeding season: eggs laid late May–June; number of eggs: 4 or 5; incubation period: 30–32 days; fledging period: 60–75 days; breeding interval: 1 year

LIFE SPAN
Up to 25 years

HABITAT
Summer: small lakes and ponds in tundra; winter: estuaries, marshes and shallow lakes

DISTRIBUTION
Breeds across tundra of far north; migrates to localized winter sites in temperate latitudes

STATUS
Locally common

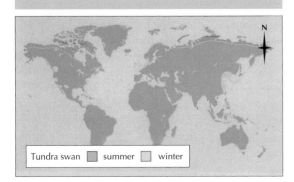

Tundra swan ▊ summer ▊ winter

relative: no more than a yellow spot at the base. It breeds mainly north of the Arctic circle and migrates to southern Canada and the United States for the winter. The second North American swan, the trumpeter swan, *C. buccinator*, used to breed over much of Canada and the United States but it is now confined to Alaska, southwestern Canada, the northwestern United States and parts of the Midwest. In 2000 the total wild population was only about 13,500. Trumpeter swans resemble the slightly smaller tundra swans but lack the yellow spot on the bill, and the eyes are almost totally enclosed by black.

The only swans in the Southern Hemisphere, apart from the coscoroba swan, are the black swan, *C. atratus*, of Australia, and the black-necked swan, *C. melanocoryphus*, which is found from Brazil south to Tierra del Fuego and the Falkland Islands. The black swan is all black but with white primary wing feathers and a bright red bill. It has been introduced into New Zealand. The black-necked swan has a black head and neck, a white eye stripe and a red bill.

A pair of trumpeter swans, Kenai Peninsula, Alaska. The trumpeter swan, which is one of the world's heaviest flying birds, suffered a dramatic population decline during the last century.

Black swans are highly nomadic, flying large distances across the arid inland plains of Australia in search of temporary wetlands. Flocks of hundreds or even thousands of black swans gather at rich feeding grounds.

Not so mute

Compared with other swans, the mute swan is quiet, but its name is a misnomer because it has a variety of calls. A flock of mute swans can be heard quietly grunting to each other as they swim along a river or across a lake. When disturbed or in defense of the nest, mute swans hiss violently. The sighing noise during flight is caused by the wings.

The whooper swan has a buglelike call when flying and a variety of quiet calls when ground-ed. Bewick's swan has a pleasant variety of honks and other sounds, and the trumpeter swan is named after the trombonelike honking calls produced in the long, coiled windpipe. It is said that the swan song, the legendary song of a dying swan, is based on a final slow expiration producing a wailing noise as it passes through the long windpipe.

Heavyweights of the air

Despite their great weight, swans are strong fliers. They have four times the wing loading (the body weight divided by the surface area of

the wings) of a herring gull, *Larus argentatus*, or American crow, *Corvus brachyrhynchos*, and they have to beat their wings rapidly to remain airborne. A high wing loading makes takeoff and landing difficult, and swans require a long stretch of open water over which they can run to gain flying speed or surge to a halt when landing. Swans are also unable to maneuver in flight, and one of the chief causes of mortality in built-up parts of the world is collision with overhead power cables.

Shallow water feeders

Swans feed mainly on plants but they also feed on animals such as tiny fish, tadpoles, insects and mollusks. They often feed on land, grazing on grasses, herbs and sedges like geese, but more often they feed on submerged aquatic plants, which they may collect from the bottom by lowering their long necks underwater, some-times upending like ducks. This limits the swans' distribution to stretches of shallow water because they very rarely dive and are only occasionally seen on deep water.

Aggressive in defense of the nest

Swans nest near water. Male mute swans set up territories, each defending a stretch of river from which they drive other males and young swans. Intruders are threatened by an aggressive display in which the neck is drawn back, the wings are arched over the back and the swan propels itself in jerks with the webbed feet thrusting powerfully in unison, instead of alternately as in normal walking. There are a variety of displays between the cob (male) and the pen (female), involving tossing and swinging the head and dipping it into the water.

Mute swans mate for life and nest in the same territory each year, some violent fights taking place if a new pair tries to usurp the territory. The nest is a mass of water plants and twigs, roughly circular and cone-shaped with a depression in the center. Wild mute swans nest among reeds on small islands in pools, but semi-domesticated ones may nest on the banks of ponds in parks or in other inhabited places. Mute swans occasionally nest in colonies rather than in spaced-out territories, such as the large colony at Abbotsbury in southern England. There usually are about five eggs, rarely up to twice as many,

and they are incubated mainly by the female, the male taking over only when she leaves to feed. In the smaller swans incubation lasts about 4 weeks, but it is 5 weeks in the larger species and 5½ weeks in the black swan. While the last eggs are being brooded by the female, the male takes the cygnets (young) to the water. The family stays together until the cygnets fledge at 4–5 months. When young, they swim together in a tight bunch with the female leading and rooting up plants for them to eat.

Swan-upping

By the 13th century the mute swan no longer existed as a wild bird in England. All swans were the property of the Crown or certain individuals and bodies who owned swans under royal license. The sovereign had a swan master, who enforced the practices of swan keeping. Individual swans were marked on the bill or feet with a series of notches or more elaborate marks to indicate ownership. This practice still survives on the Thames River, where cygnets are marked annually in a practice known as swan-upping, and the Abbotsbury swans are still marked on the webs of the feet.

In spring, Bewick's, tundra, whooper and some trumpeter swans fly north to taiga or tundra regions to breed. They nest on small ponds or lakes. Pictured are two pairs of whooper swans.

TERN

ERNS ARE LIGHTLY BUILT seabirds, characterized by their fluttering flight. Together with the noddies (discussed elsewhere), they are classed in a subfamily of the gulls. There are over 30 species, usually smaller than gulls but differing little in their general habits. The bill is narrow and pointed and the legs are short. Most have a white plumage with light gray on the wings and back and dark crowns. Some are darker, such as the black tern (*Chlidonias niger*), which is black in summer except for gray wings and white coloration under the tail, but much lighter in winter; the white-winged black tern (*C. leucopterus*), which is black on the head and on most of the body in summer; and the sooty tern (*Sterna fuscata*), which has black upperparts and white underparts. The Inca tern, *Larosterna inca*, has a gray plumage with long, trailing mustaches.

The similarity in plumage of black-capped terns makes identification very difficult. In winter, the dark color, including the dark cap, is often reduced, which adds to the difficulties of identification. The main distinguishing feature of many species is the bill color. The gull-billed tern, *Gelochelidon nilotica*, is identified by its heavier bill. Some terns have crests, such as the Caspian tern, *Hydroprogne caspia*. This is the largest tern, 21 inches (52.5 cm) long compared to 10–15 inches (25–37.5 cm) in most other species.

Terns are widely distributed throughout the world. Most species are found in the Tropics, but the common tern, *S. hirundo*, and Arctic tern,

S. paradisaea, breed beyond the Arctic Circle as well as in more temperate parts of Europe, Asia and the Americas. Four species breed in the Southern Ocean, and the Antarctic tern, *S. vittata*, breeds as far south as the South Shetlands.

Marathon migration

Despite their similarities, terns are immediately distinguishable from gulls at a distance, both by their long wings and forked tail and, even more certainly, by their slow, buoyant, rather butterflylike flight. The wing tips appear to travel through a wide arc, and there is less gliding than in the flight of a gull. The head is usually carried in flight with the bill pointing down. Although terns are more tied to water than gulls are and many lead a pelagic (open-sea) existence outside the breeding season, most of them swim very rarely. Four species, the black tern, white-winged black tern (*C. leucopterus*), whiskered tern (*C. hybridus*) and Forster's tern (*S. forsteri*), breed on inland swamps and on the banks of sluggish rivers, whereas the remainder nest mostly around coasts and on islands, usually on areas of sand, gravel or pebbles.

All terns are migratory, those that nest in higher latitudes moving to the Tropics for the winter. The Arctic tern, however, goes one stage further and crosses the equator to spend the northern winter or southern summer among the pack ice surrounding the Antarctic continent. Here it is easily confused with the Antarctic tern,

Tapering wings and a forked tail have given terns the nickname sea swallows. Pictured here is a common tern.

The Arctic tern (above) and the common tern both have a red bill, although that of the Arctic tern is shorter. The Arctic tern also has a shorter neck and slightly slimmer body.

ARCTIC TERN

CLASS	**Aves**
ORDER	**Charadriiformes**
FAMILY	**Laridae**
GENUS AND SPECIES	***Sterna paradisaea***

WEIGHT
3½–4 oz. (100–115 g)

LENGTH
Head to tail: 13–14 in. (33–35 cm); wingspan: 30–34 in. (75–85 cm)

DISTINCTIVE FEATURES
Breeding adult: black cap; light gray underparts and upperwings; blood-red bill; snow-white rump; long, forked tail; long wings

DIET
Marine fish; crustaceans; insects

BREEDING
Age at first breeding: 4 years; breeding season: eggs laid May–June; number of eggs: 1 to 3; incubation period: 20–24 days; fledging period: 21–24 days; breeding interval: 1 year

LIFE SPAN
Oldest ringed bird 34 years

HABITAT
Breeding season: nests on shingle and sand beaches, low rocky shores and peat mosses adjacent to rivers; rough pasture; grassland and heath. Entirely pelagic (occurring on open sea) outside breeding season.

DISTRIBUTION
Breeding season: holarctic range, including Alaska, northern Canada, Greenland, northern fringes of Eurasia. Winter: mainly Antarctic pack ice.

STATUS
Fairly common

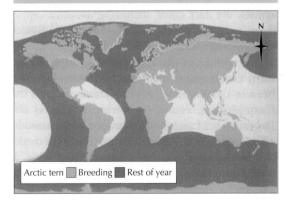

Arctic tern ☐ Breeding ☐ Rest of year

but proof of the incredible journey was given by the recovery of a young Arctic tern that was ringed in Labrador and picked up in South Africa, 11,000 miles (17,600 km) away, less than 3 months after it had learned to fly. By making this long migration, the Arctic tern is able to enjoy almost continuous summer, either in the Antarctic or the Arctic. Ornithologists have estimated that the oldest ringed tern, at 34 years, would have flown at least 600,000 miles (1 million km) on migration, probably more.

Versatile feeders

Terns feed mainly on small fish and crustaceans, which they catch by either skimming low and plucking their prey out of the water or plunge-diving, hovering over their prey and then dropping vertically and half-submerging. Some wade in shallow water in search of food, and the inland terns feed on insects, which they sometimes catch in the air. On a few occasions, terns have been seen following a plow, in a manner reminiscent of gulls, and taking earthworms. Forster's tern has evolved a specialized feeding method due to the fact that it migrates north in the spring. It follows the line of melting ice and feeds on the fish, insects and other small animals that have been frozen in since the previous fall.

Nest site depends on leg length

The breeding habits of terns are very similar to those of gulls, both in routine and in behavior. They nest in colonies, which may be vast: on Ascension Island, for instance, the colonies are so large that the continuous clamor of the sooty tern has earned it the nickname "wideawake." Terns are not as conservative in their choice of breeding sites as gulls. The position of a colony may change from one year to the next and may even be abandoned in mid-season. Sometimes two or more species nest in the same colony, but they occupy different areas. One ornithologist has pointed out that where Arctic, common and roseate terns, *S. dougallii*, nest together, the short-legged Arctic tern nests on bare ground, the long-legged roseate tern nests in quite long grass and the common tern is intermediate in both leg length and in its preference for grass length.

A conspicuous feature of tern courtship is the "fish flight," in which a male flies over the colony with a fish in its bill, calling loudly. It appears to be some form of advertisement, and if the tern is mated, its partner flies in front of it and they may settle, exchange the fish and then fly into the air again. In most species, the nest is no more than a scrape in the sand or gravel, which may not be lined, but the swamp-dwelling terns build floating nests of water plants.

Terns lay one to three eggs. These are effectively camouflaged and incubated by both parents in turn. The chicks leave the nest soon after hatching. Their coloration matches their surroundings so well that they are almost impossible to find except by accident. Their discovery is made less likely by the attentions of the adults, which readily harass even a human intruder en masse, swooping almost vertically down and screaming loudly.

Variable breeding cycles

There is usually little value in reporting the timing of the breeding cycle of a widely distributed bird unless it is possible to give sufficient detail. This is because the start of courtship, egg-laying and other events depends on the climate, which usually varies according to latitude. In a given area, however, the breeding period of most wide-ranging birds usually remains constant from year to year.

One exception to this rule is the sooty tern, which commences nesting on Mariana Island, Hawaii, in April, but on the island of Moks Manu about 10 miles (16 km) away it starts nesting in October. In the Atlantic, another population of sooty terns, the wideawakes of Ascension Island, nest every 7–9½ months, that is to say five times in 4 years. It is possible that on Hawaii the respective tern populations of the two islands may be derived from sooty terns, originally living in opposite hemispheres, which had breeding seasons 6 months apart.

In common with other terns, royal terns, S. maxima, frequent shorelines. They have a white crown for most of the year, acquiring a black cap only during the breeding season.

TROUT-PERCH

The trout-perch is widely distributed in North America, where it favors the backwaters of large, muddy rivers and lakes.

THE TWO SPECIES OF trout-perch live in North America. The blunt-nosed trout-perch, or sandroller, *Percopsis transmontana*, is found in the fresh waters of most of Canada, in Alaska and southward to Virginia, Kentucky, Missouri and Kansas. The second species, called simply the trout-perch, *P. omiscomaycus*, is more localized, being found only in the basin of the Columbia River in western North America. Both species are small, the sandroller measuring up to 6 inches (15 cm) long and the trout-perch reaching 8 inches (20 cm) in length.

Trout-perch have spotted bodies, a fairly pointed head and large eyes and when freshly caught have a distinctive translucent appearance. Although they resemble both trout (family Salmonidae) and perch (family Percidae) in certain respects, trout-perch are related to neither. Among the features they share with perch are their mouth shape and a body that is covered with spiny scales. Trout-perch also have spiny fins like those of a perch, the dorsal, anal and pelvic fins having one or more stout spines in their leading margin. In terms of number of fins, however, trout-perch are like trout. They also have the adipose (fatty) fin and naked head characteristic of all the Salmonidae.

An evolutionary offshoot

Trout-perch are common in the larger streams and in deep, clear lakes, especially those with sandy or gravelly bottoms. They spend the hours of darkness feeding in the shallows and move back into deeper waters during the day. Trout-perch are shoaling species. They eat aquatic insects, fish and small freshwater crustaceans, and are taken in turn by various kinds of predatory fish, including trout and pike (family Esocidae), and as live bait by fishers. At one time the two species were regarded as a kind of missing link between the salmon family and the perch family. However, more recent studies have shown that trout-perch are an evolutionary offshoot of the perch and were probably once much more widespread, with many more species.

In late May or early June in the southern parts of the range (slightly later in the north), trout-perch move to their spawning grounds.

TROUT-PERCH

CLASS	**Osteichthyes**
ORDER	**Percopsiformes**
FAMILY	**Percopsidae**
GENUS AND SPECIES	***Percopsis omiscomaycus***

LENGTH
8 in. (20 cm)

DISTINCTIVE FEATURES
Pale yellowish to silvery body color, frequently nearly transparent; about 10 dark spots in row along midline of back, 10 to 11 spots along lateral line, row of spots high on sides above lateral line; adipose fin; transparent fins transparent; small, weak spines in anal and dorsal fins; pectoral fins extend behind bases of pelvic fins; rough, ctenoid (toothed) scales

DIET
Insect larvae, amphipods and fish

BREEDING
Eggs and milt released in shallow water

LIFE SPAN
4 years

HABITAT
Lakes, rivers and deep-flowing pools of creeks, usually over sand

DISTRIBUTION
Western North America in basin of Columbia River

STATUS
Not threatened

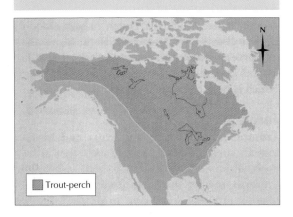

Trout-perch

They spawn in water not more than 3½ feet (106 cm) deep, so in the lakes the shoals move to sandbars, ascending feeder streams when no suitable shallow waters are available. In rivers, trout-perch swim upstream. There is much jostling among the members of the shoal as they sort themselves out, generally with one female attended by two or more males. Remaining close to the surface, the males press close to the female and release their milt as she releases her eggs. Fertilization takes place, and the eggs, 1.4 mm in diameter, sticky and heavier than water, sink to the bottom to adhere to the coarser gravel or rocks. Some populations of trout-perch spawn during the day, others exclusively at night. Trout-perch do not take care of the eggs once they have spawned nor do they look after the fry once they have hatched. Many adults die once spawning is over.

Piratical relative

Closely related to the trout-perch is the pirate-perch, *Aphredoderus sayanus*. It resembles the trout-perch, although it has a deeper body, a more square-ended tail and no adipose fin. Measuring up to 5 inches (13 cm) in length, the pirate-perch has olive-green to brown upper-parts, is yellowish brown on the underside and has dark spots and blotches, usually in rows along the body. The pirate-perch lives in the eastern United States, from New York to Texas, in streams and standing waters. It is said to be very quarrelsome, both with fish of other species and with members of its own. This aggression stems largely from the pirate-perch's strongly territorial nature. The pirate-perch prefers waters with muddy beds, where there are debris and rotting leaves under which it can hide, darting out to take a worm, insect larva or small fish, or to drive away an intruder.

Fat fin mystery

In salmon, trout and other members of the salmon family, the second dorsal fin has been modified to what is called an adipose fin. This is a small flap made up of fatty tissue covered by skin and lacking fin rays or any other supporting skeleton. Some members of the large freshwater family of characins (Characidae) also have an adipose fin, as do the majority of catfish (order Siluriformes), the size of the fin varying from large to small according to the species. In the armored catfish, *Callichthys callichthys*, the adipose fin has a strong spine in front.

Conjecture surrounds the function of the adipose fin. Biologists know that the front dorsal fin of a salmon or trout prevents the fish from rolling and yawing as it moves forward. The pectoral fins, which prevent pitching and rolling, are used in turning and, with the pelvic fins, for braking. The tail fin helps to drive the fish through the water and also acts as a rudder. No one has yet discovered what the adipose fin does. Some ichthyologists believe it has no function, although this is scientifically unsatisfactory.

TUNA

THESE LARGE FISH WERE known as tunny, a term deriving from the Latin *thunnus*, as early as the 15th century in England. It was during the 20th century that the word tuna, derived from Spanish, came into general use.

There are 14 species of tuna in five genera. The northern bluefin tuna, *Thunnus thynnus*, of the Atlantic can reach 15 feet (4.6 m) in length and weigh over 1,500 pounds (680 kg), but few exceed 8 feet (2.4 m). The yellowfin tuna (*T. albacares*) weighs up to 400 pounds (180 kg) and the albacore (*T. alalunga*) up to 80 pounds (36 kg).

The bluefin represents the typical tuna profile. It has a sleek, streamlined body with a large head and mouth and large eyes. The first dorsal fin is spiny, and close behind it is a smaller, soft-rayed second dorsal fin. The anal fin is similar in shape and size to the second dorsal, and behind these two, extending to the crescent-like forked tail, are finlets, nine on the upper tail root and eight on the lower. The pectoral fins are medium sized, as are the pelvic fins, which are level with the pectorals. The back is dark blue, the flanks white with silvery spots and the belly white. The fins are dark blue to black except for the reddish brown second dorsal fin and the yellowish anal fin and finlets. There are three distinctive keels on each side at the base of the tail fin. The bluefin is found across the North Atlantic as far north as Iceland.

Segregated by size
Tuna are oceanic fish that sometimes come inshore but apparently do not enter rivers. They move about in shoals in which individual fish are all approximately the same size. The larger the tuna, the smaller the shoal, and the largest individuals are more or less solitary. They swim near the surface in summer but are found at 100–600 feet (30–180 m) in winter.

Tuna are strongly migratory, their movements being linked with those of the fish on which they feed and on the temperature. They are intolerant of water temperatures below 50–54° F (10–12° C), so although they move into northern waters in summer, they migrate back to warmer seas in the fall. A cold summer limits the extent of the northward migrations. The fish also evidently cross the Atlantic. Tuna tagged off Martha's Vineyard, Massachusetts, in 1954 were caught in the Bay of Biscay, off the coast of Spain, five years later; individuals from North American waters occasionally turn up off the coasts of Norway. Two tagged off Florida in September and October, 1951, were caught off Bergen, Norway, 120 days later, having traveled 4,500 miles (7,200 km).

In common with mackerel, to which they are related, tuna swim with the mouth slightly agape so that their forward movement forces water across the gills. Their oxygen needs are high because of their great muscular activity, which depends on a correspondingly abundant supply of relatively warm blood. Tuna are unique among fish in their ability to maintain their blood at a temperature above that of the surrounding seawater. Owing to their high oxygen requirements, tuna swim more or less continuously, normally at a low cruising speed, though some scientists have reported brief bursts of up to 50 miles per hour (80 km/h).

Feeding frenzy
When they are very young, tuna feed on crustaceans, especially euphausians, but as they mature they eat mainly shoaling fish such as

The skipjack tuna, Katsuwonus pelamis, is found worldwide. It grows to about 3 feet (90 cm) and can weigh more than 45 pounds (20 kg).

herring, mackerel, sprats, whiting, flying fish and sand eels. They also eat some squid and cuttle-fish. When a tuna shoal meets a shoal of prey fish, it is seized with what may be described as a feeding frenzy. It charges through, twisting and turning, often breaking the surface and some-times leaping clear of the water. The commotion usually attracts flocks of seabirds to feed on the smaller fish that are driven to the surface.

Putting on weight

In the Atlantic the bluefin tuna spawns in the Gulf of Cadiz, to the southwest of Spain, and in the Mediterranean in June and July. It spawns off Florida and the Bahamas in May and June.

A shoal of skipjack tuna in Pacific surface waters. Small tuna prey on crustaceans, such as shoaling shrimp, graduating to small fish as they grow.

TUNA

CLASS **Osteichthyes**

ORDER **Perciformes**

FAMILY **Scombridae**

GENUS AND SPECIES **14 species including northern bluefin tuna, *Thunnus thynnus* (detailed below); albacore, *T. alalunga*; yellowfin tuna, *T. albacares***

ALTERNATIVE NAME
Tunny

WEIGHT
1,500 lb. (680 kg)

LENGTH
15 ft. (4.6 m)

DISTINCTIVE FEATURES
Dark blue back, shading to green on upper flanks; silvery-white lower flanks and belly; first dorsal fin yellow or bluish, second dorsal fin reddish brown; dusky yellow anal fin and finlets, edged with black

DIET
Crustaceans; smaller fish, including herring, sprat, pilchard, whiting, sand eel

BREEDING
Breeding season: June–August (Atlantic), April–June (western Pacific); young spend first year in breeding area; mature at 5–6 years

LIFE SPAN
15 years

HABITAT
Oceanic but ventures close to shore; seldom found in waters deeper than 330 ft. (100 m)

DISTRIBUTION
Atlantic Ocean; Mediterranean and Black Seas

STATUS
Not known, owing to migratory habits

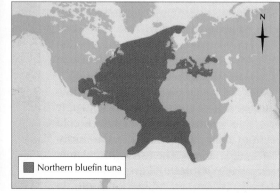

Northern bluefin tuna

Each year an adult female bluefin tuna may produce around 10 million eggs. These are small and float near the surface. They hatch in about 2 days, the new larvae being less than ¼ inch (6 mm) long. The fry grow quickly, weighing 1 pound (450 g) by 3 months and 10 pounds (4.5 kg) at a year old. At 13 years of age they reach a length of 8 feet (2.4 m) and weigh 440 pounds (200 kg).

Ancient fisheries

The many references to the tuna in classical literature reveal it to have been as important to the Mediterranean people as the herring was to the people of northwestern Europe. The fisheries have continued through the centuries. Catching methods have included harpoons, baited hooks and nets. Today, very long nets are used to intercept migrating shoals and guide them into a final compartment. When this is filled with jostling fish, the net floor is raised, the boats close in and the massed fish are clubbed, speared and dragged into the boats. This method became mired in controversy during the late 20th century because an unacceptably high number of dolphins, which habitually follow tuna shoals, became fatally ensnared in tuna nets. The globally important tuna fishing industry was pressed to adopt more dolphin-friendly fishing techniques, such as rod-and-line fishing.

Sport fishing for bluefin tuna also became very popular during the 20th century. A mature fish, played with a rod, is said to give the fisher the ultimate contest, perhaps towing a boat for hours over a distance of several miles before becoming exhausted. The tuna's chief natural predator is the orca or killer whale, *Orcinus orca*.

Wide-ranging tuna

There has long been doubt as to whether the tuna of the American Atlantic is the same species as that on the European side. The fish differ slightly in details of anatomy and in breeding habits. Nevertheless, the tendency now is to treat them as separate populations of a single species.

Other related species have similar wide distributions. A near relative, the Atlantic albacore, up to 4 feet (1.2 m) in length and with long, scythelike pectoral fins, has its counterpart in the Pacific albacore, which ranges from the Pacific coast of North America to Japan and Hawaii. In the yellow-finned albacores or yellowfin tuna, up to 9 feet (2.7 m) long and 400 pounds (180 kg) in weight, the second dorsal and anal fins are also long and scythelike. One species ranges across the tropical and subtropical Atlantic, the other across the Pacific and into the Indian Ocean. It is these fish that make up the bulk of the tuna caught for human consumption.

These bluefins are in a South Australian fish farm. Along with the yellowfin tuna, they have become an immensely valuable commercial species.

TURKEY

Turkeys spend most of their time on the ground, although they are strong fliers and roost in the trees at night.

THE WILD TURKEY, a native of North America, was domesticated by the Aztecs long before Columbus crossed the Atlantic Ocean. The domesticated turkey was brought to Europe and subsequently taken back to what is today the United States.

The male wild turkey is around 43 inches (110 cm) from bill tip to the end of the tail and usually weighs about 16 pounds (7.4 kg), although a weight of 22 pounds (10 kg) has been recorded. The female measures 35 inches (90 cm) and weighs around 9 pounds (4.2 kg). The plumage is mainly metallic green, bronze and copper with white or pale buff in the wings and upper tail coverts. The male, sometimes the female also, has a tuft of bristles near the base of the neck. The reddish legs and feet are strong, and there is a spur, as in other game birds. The head and neck are bare and are decorated with a warty bluish skin, a red throat wattle and a spurlike fleshy caruncle (outgrowth) near the base of the bill.

There are two types of wild turkey: *Meleagris gallopavo*, called simply the wild turkey, and *Agriocharis ocellata*, the ocellated turkey of Yucatan and Guatemala. There are six subspecies of *M. gallopavo*, from Pennsylvania southward. The eastern subspecies of turkey, *M. g. silvestris*, formerly ranging from Canada to Florida, was the one the Pilgrim Fathers ate at Thanksgiving. It is the most numerous wild turkey subspecies, amounting to 2.5 million birds, and the most widespread, being found in 38 states and one Canadian province. In southern Florida lives *M. g. osceola*; Merriam's wild turkey, *M. g. merriami*, lives in the foothills of the Rockies. The fourth subspecies is the Rio Grande turkey, *M. g. intermedia*. The fifth, *M. g. gallopavo*, from which present-day turkeys descended, is native to the highlands of Mexico and is the species that was domesticated by the Aztecs. Gould's wild turkey, *M. g. mexicana*, occurs in Sierra Madre Occidental from northern Chihuahua to southern Jalisco.

Easy targets
Turkeys live in open mixed woodlands, moving over the ground in small flocks by day and roosting in the trees by night. They can fly strongly but seldom stay airborne for more than a quarter of a mile (400 m). The longest turkey flight recorded was 1 mile (1.6 km). They are very shy birds and quickly disappear into the undergrowth on being disturbed. That has not saved them from hunters, however. Turkeys are vulnerable to the shotgun even at night when roosting silhouetted against a moonlit sky.

Habitat destruction
Perhaps the main cause of the decline in turkey numbers, which is particularly marked in some subspecies such as *M. g. silvestris*, has been the destruction of their habitat. The felling of trees

WILD TURKEY

CLASS **Aves**

ORDER **Galliformes**

FAMILY **Meleagrididae**

GENUS AND SPECIES **Meleagris gallopavo**

WEIGHT
(Average) Male: 16 lb. (7.4 kg); female: 9 lb. (4.2 kg); also larger specimens

LENGTH
Male: 43 in. (110 cm); female: 35 in. (90 cm)

DISTINCTIVE FEATURES
Very large; upperparts metallic green, bronze and copper; white or pale buff in wings and upper tail; bare head and neck with warty, bluish skin; red throat wattle; fleshy caruncle (outgrowth) near base of bill

DIET
Seeds, tubers, fruit, leaves, acorns; young fed on insects

BREEDING
Age at first breeding: 1 or 2 years; breeding season: April–July; number of eggs: 10 to 13; incubation period: 28 days; fledging period: young active from hatching: breeding interval: 1 year

LIFE SPAN
Not known

HABITAT
Temperate and subtropical forest to shrub-steppe; also grassland edge and agriculture edge

DISTRIBUTION
Much of United States east of the Rockies and parts of Mexico

STATUS
Not globally threatened; common in parts of range

Wild turkey

and the opening up of the land has everywhere diminished the range of wild turkeys by robbing the birds of cover as well as their natural food. However wild turkeys have been restored to most of their historic range as a result of successful management. This achievement has been brought about by trapping and relocating wild turkeys to suitable habitats, improving the habitat, increasing law enforcement and improving public support and opinion. As a result all wild turkey subspecies in the United States have increased their numbers and range.

Male wild turkeys. Outside the breeding season, males and females form separate flocks, and only the females care for the chicks.

Varied diet
Like pheasants, to which they are closely related, turkeys eat a wide variety of primarily plant foods. However insects, especially grasshoppers, are eaten in large numbers as well, as are seeds and berries, such as dewberries, blackberries and strawberries that grow in the glades and grasslands of the open forests. The turkeys also rely a good deal on acorns and nuts that have fallen from the trees and have accumulated on the forest floor and, until North America's trees were struck by fungal blight, the fruits from chestnuts. Turkeys usually drink twice a day.

Gobblers and their harems
The male turkey, or gobbler, is polygamous (has more than one mate). After mating, the females go their own ways to make their nest in a depression in the ground under low vegetation and in thickets. Each female lays one egg a day, to a total of 10 to 13. The egg is large and lightly spotted with reddish brown.

particularly when the chicks roost on the ground. By September half the turkey chicks have been killed.

The ocellated turkey

The ocellated turkey, which takes its name from the eyes or ocelli on its tail, has fared little better than its more familiar relative, having been wiped out in much of its former range. It now lives only on the Yucatan Peninsula in Mexico and Guatemala, where it is uncommon or rare.

It is smaller than the wild turkey, a male weighing 11 pounds (5 kg) and a female just over half this, and is more colorful than the North American species. It lacks the beard of bristles on the upper breast, and its neck is blue with red caruncles on the head. Its breeding habits are much the same except that the males and females form mixed flocks outside the breeding season, whereas in the wild turkey they separate. Ocellated turkeys also fly more freely when danger threatens, instead of relying on their legs as the wild turkey does.

Turkish merchants

The earliest known record of the domesticated turkey in Europe states that a certain Pedro Nino brought some to Spain in 1500, having bought them in Venezuela for four glass beads each. The turkey is known to have reached England by 1524, and at least by 1558 it was becoming popular at banquets.

In Spain the new bird was often referred to as the Indian fowl, an allusion that is repeated in the French *dindon*, formed from *d'Inde*. The origin of the name turkey is less obvious. One view is that it is from the bird's call *turk-turk-turk*. A more likely explanation is that in the 16th century, merchants trading along the seaboards of the Mediterranean and eastern Atlantic were known as Turks. They probably included the birds in their merchandise and these then became known as turkey fowls.

The colorful ocellated turkey is one of two forms of wild turkey. It is now confined to the Yucatan Peninsula and its numbers are low.

Incubation begins when the clutch is complete and lasts 28 days. The eggs usually hatch in the afternoon, the chicks being led away by the hen, with no help from the male. For the first two weeks the chicks roost on the ground. Then they fly at night to a low branch, where they settle themselves on either side of the mother, who curves her wings over the young in order to protect them.

Infancy is the most dangerous stage of a turkey's life. Predators such as opossums, raccoons and others raid the nests, and after the eggs have hatched there are further losses,

The domesticated breeds of turkeys today range from the Norfolk turkey, known in the United States as the black, through the bronze to several breeds of white turkey, including the small white. Whereas historically people wanted large turkeys to present at the table, today's domestic ovens are much smaller, and as a result the small white has gained popularity.

VAMPIRE BAT

THE REAL-LIFE VAMPIRE BAT is quite unlike the vampire of fiction, apart from the fact that it feeds on blood. True vampires, which are native to tropical and subtropical America, feed only on the fresh blood of mammals and birds. Unlike the human-sized vampires of fable, vampire bats are only 14–18 inches (37–45 cm) long, the weight of an adult varying, according to the different species, from ½–2 ounces (15–50 g). Vampire bats' fur is colored in various shades of brown and the animals have no tail. The ears are small, and the muzzle is short and conical, without a true nose-leaf. There are naked pads on the snout with U-shaped grooves at the tip. Thermosensory organs in these grooves enable vampire bats to sense heat that radiates from their prey. The upper incisor teeth are large and razor-edged, well adapted for gently opening a small wound to take blood. The grooved, muscular tongue fits over a V-shaped notch in the lower lip, forming a tube through which the bat sucks the blood of

its victim. The stomach is also adapted for liquid feeding, the forward end being drawn out into a long tube. The saliva contains an anticoagulant called draculin that prevents the blood from clotting, enabling the bat to obtain a full meal.

Three vampires

There are three genera of vampire bats, each with a single species. The common vampire bat, *Desmodus rotundus*, the most numerous and widespread of the three, is distinguished by its pointed ears, its long thumb with a basal pad and its naked interfemoral membrane. It has only 20 teeth. The species ranges from northern Mexico south to central Chile, central Argentina and Uruguay and is now one of the most common and widespread mammals in eastern Mexico.

The second species, the white-winged vampire, *Diaemus youngi*, is much less numerous. The edges of its wings and part of the wing membrane are white. It has a peculiar short thumb about one-eighth as long as the third finger and

Vampire bat roosts comprise both males and females. Within the roost, the males defend territories against each other by chasing, pushing, fighting and biting.

has a single pad underneath. The white-winged vampire is the only bat known to have 22 permanent teeth. It is mainly confined to the tropical regions of South America from Venezuela and the Guianas south to Peru and Brazil, but it also has been found on Trinidad and in Mexico.

The hairy-legged vampire, *Diphylla ecaudata*, smaller than the common species, is not well known. It has shorter, rounded ears, a short thumb without a basal pad and softer fur. Its interfemoral membrane is well furred. It has 26 teeth and is unique among bats in having a fan-shaped, seven-lobed outer lower incisor tooth that resembles the lower incisor in the order Dermoptera, the gliding lemurs. This species is found in eastern and southern Mexico, Central America and southward to Brazil.

Communal living

During the day vampire bats roost in caves, old mines, hollow trees, crevices in rocks and old buildings. Colonies of the common vampire may consist of as many as 2,000 individuals, but the

average is about 100. The sexes roost together and they may share the caves with other species of bats. They are very agile and can walk rapidly on their feet and thumbs, either on the ground or up the vertical sides of caves. Shortly after dark the bats leave their roosts with a slow, noiseless

The common vampire bat uses its long, well-developed thumb and strong hind legs to bound nimbly over the ground when approaching its prey.

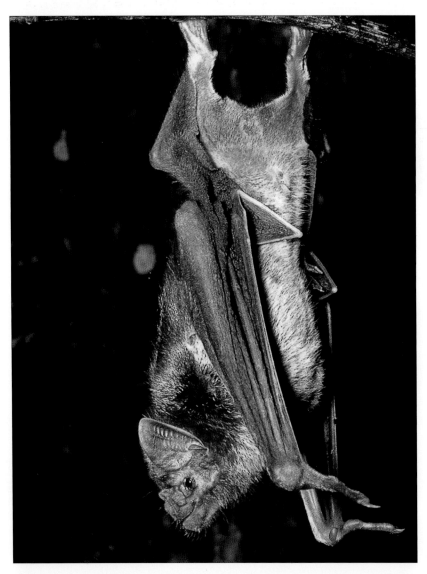

VAMPIRE BAT

CLASS	**Mammalia**
ORDER	**Chiroptera**
FAMILY	**Phyllostomidae**

GENUS AND SPECIES **Common vampire bat, *Desmodus rotundus*; white-winged vampire bat, *Diaemus youngi*; hairy-legged vampire bat, *Diphylla ecaudata***

WEIGHT
½–2 oz. (15–50 g)

LENGTH
Wingspan: 14–18 in. (37–45 cm)

DISTINCTIVE FEATURES
Small ears; chisel-like incisors; well-developed hind legs; heat-sensitive pits in face

DIET
Blood of mammals (*Desmodus rotundus*) or birds (*Diaemus youngi, Diphylla ecaudata*)

BREEDING
(*Desmodus rotundus*) Breeding season: year-round; number of young: usually 1; gestation period: about 210 days; breeding interval: usually 1 year

LIFE SPAN
At least 20 years

HABITAT
Arid and humid regions of Tropics and subtropics. Roosts in caves, buildings and trees.

DISTRIBUTION
Mexico south to central South America

STATUS
Common

Vampire bats

flight, usually only 3 feet (90 cm) above the ground. The bats attack their victims while they sleep, making a quick, shallow bite with their sharp teeth in a place where there is no hair or feathers. They cut away only a very small piece of skin, making a shallow wound from which they lap the blood without a sound, so that the victim does not wake. Unlike other bats, vampires do not cling with their claws but rest lightly on their thumbs and small foot-pads, so lightly that even a human is unlikely to be wakened by their actions. The common vampire bat in particular can consume such large quantities of blood that it is barely able to fly for some time afterward.

The common vampire attacks only large mammals, such as horses, cattle and, occasionally, humans. Cattle generally are bitten on the neck or leg and humans are often bitten on the big toe. The white-winged vampire attacks mainly birds, biting the neck or ankle, and occasionally mammals. The hairy-legged vampire appears to prey mainly on birds such as chickens, but it is possible it may also attack some mammals.

In captivity, vampire bats have been kept alive on defibrinated blood, which has had its clotting agents removed to prevent coagulation. One survived for 13 years in a laboratory in Panama.

Finding their prey

Vampire bats detect their prey primarily by using their thermosensory ability and through smell, although, as in other bats, they may use echolocation (locate objects according to the way sound waves are reflected back from them). Because their source of food is large and relatively stationary, vampires do not have the same difficulty in finding their prey as bats that feed on fast-moving insects or even those that catch fish. Like the New World fruit-eating bats, which also feed on stationary food, their echolocation is by pulses having only one-thousandth of the sound energy of those used by bats feeding on insects or fish. It is notable that vampires very seldom attack dogs, presumably because they have more sensitive hearing than larger mammals such as cattle and are thus able to detect the bat's higher sound frequencies.

Year-round breeding

The breeding habits of the white-winged and hairy-legged vampire bats are still a subject of scientific debate. The common vampire gives birth to a single young, occasionally twins, after a gestation period of about 210 days. They breed throughout the year and it is possible there is more than one birth a year. The young are not carried about by the mother, as is the case in most other bats, but are left in the roost while she goes out foraging.

Disease transmitters

The real danger of vampire bats lies not so much in their feeding on the blood of domestic animals and humans, but in the transmission of disease that results from the bites and risk of secondary infections. Vampires can transmit rabies, which may be fatal to both cattle and humans. They also may transmit the disease to other species of bats and may die of it themselves. In Mexico alone it is necessary to inoculate thousands of head of cattle against the disease each year. The disease is always fatal to uninoculated cattle.

Various control methods have been tried in the past to control vampire bat numbers. These include dynamiting the caves where the bats roost and the use of flamethrowers and poison gas. However, such approaches have been found to be largely ineffective in reducing vampire bat populations and are also highly destructive to other, harmless species of bats. Moreover, although such drastic methods may be successful in killing the bats, they do not help to reduce the overall vampire bat population to a level satisfactory to farmers. The only solution to the problem seems to lie in biological control, including sterilization, habitat management and the use of selective chemical attractants and repellents. A research center has been set up in Mexico City for the ecological study of vampire bats and for research into biological methods of control.

The common vampire bat feeds almost exclusively on the blood from livestock such as horses, cattle, goats, pigs and, as in the picture above, donkeys.

WALRUS

Hunted since the time of the Vikings, sometimes almost to the point of extinction, the walrus has survived and today, with strict conservation measures, some herds are slowly recovering. The two walrus subspecies, the Pacific walrus and the Atlantic walrus, differ only in minor details. The Pacific bulls average 11–11½ feet (3.3–3.5 m) long and weigh slightly more than 2,000 pounds (900 kg) but can reach 13¾ feet (4.1 m) and weigh up to 3,700 pounds (1,665 kg) when they carry maximum blubber. The Atlantic bulls average 10 feet (3 m) long and up to 1,650 pounds (743 kg) in weight but may reach 12 feet (3.6 m) and weigh 2,800 pounds (1,260 kg). The cows of both subspecies are smaller, 8½–9½ feet (2.6–2.9 m) and 1,250 pounds (563 kg), but large Pacific cows may reach almost 12½ ft (3.8 m) and a weight of 1,750 pounds (788 kg).

The walrus is heavily built, adult bulls carrying sometimes 900 pounds (405 kg) of blubber in winter. The head and muzzle are broad and the neck is short, the muzzle being deeper in the Pacific walrus. The cheek teeth are few and simple in shape, but the upper canines are elongated to form large ivory tusks, which may reach 3 feet (0.9 m) in length and are even longer in the Pacific subspecies. The nostrils in the Pacific subspecies are placed higher on the head. The mustache bristles are very conspicuous, especially at the corners of the mouth, where they may reach 4–5 inches (10–12.5 cm). The foreflippers are strong and oarlike, being about a quarter the length of the body. The hind flippers are about 6 inches (15 cm) shorter and very broad, but with little real power in them.

The walrus's skin is tough, wrinkled and covered with short hair, reddish brown or pink in bulls and brown in the cows. The hair becomes scanty after middle age, and old males may be almost hairless, with their hide in deep folds.

The Pacific walrus lives mainly in the waters adjacent to Alaska and the Chukchi Sea in Russia. The Alaskan herds migrate south in the fall into the Bering Sea and Bristol Bay to escape the encroaching Arctic ice, moving northward again in spring when it breaks up.

The Atlantic walrus is sparsely distributed from northern Arctic Canada eastward to western Greenland, with small isolated groups on the eastern Greenland coast, Spitsbergen, Franz Josef Land and the Barents and Kara Seas. It migrates southward for the winter.

Walruses are sociable animals and at one time regularly gathered on remote beaches. Due to persecution by hunters, however, they now tend to gather on less accessible ice floes.

The walrus uses its tusks for hauling itself along on the ice. The family name, Odobenidae, means "those that walk with their teeth."

WALRUS

CLASS	**Mammalia**
ORDER	**Pinnipedia**
FAMILY	**Odobenidae**
GENUS AND SPECIES	***Odobenus rosmarus***

WEIGHT
880–3,740 lb. (400–1,700 kg); male heavier than female

LENGTH
Head and body: 7¼–12 ft. (2.2–3.6 m); male larger than female

DISTINCTIVE FEATURES
Thickset, rotund body; thick, wrinkly skin; broad foreflippers; long tusks; mustache in both sexes

DIET
Crustaceans, especially clams and mussels; fish; rarely seals

BREEDING
Age at first breeding: 7 years (female), 15 years (male); male able to breed earlier but cannot compete with other males until 15 years old; breeding season: mainly January–February; number of young: 1; gestation period: about 14–16 months, including 4–5 months' delayed implantation; breeding interval: 1 calf every 2 years in most productive females

LIFE SPAN
Up to 40 years

HABITAT
Coastal waters in Arctic Ocean and adjoining seas; often found on pack ice

DISTRIBUTION
Arctic Ocean

STATUS
Threatened by hunting; some subspecies regarded as rare or vulnerable

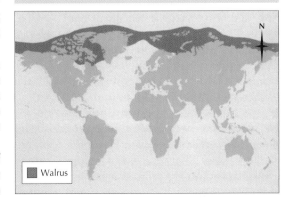

Walrus

Walruses also inhabit the Laptev Sea near Russia and do not migrate in the winter. Scientists believe this herd may be a race midway between the Atlantic and Pacific subspecies.

Sociable lifestyle

Walruses associate in family herds of cows, calves and young bulls of up to 100 individuals. Except in the breeding season the adult bulls usually form separate herds. They live mainly in shallow coastal waters, sheltering on isolated rocky coasts and islands or congregating on ice floes. As a result of persecution by humans, however, walruses avoid land as much as possible and to keep to the ice floes, sometimes far out to sea. They normally are timid but readily become aggressive in the face of danger. There seems to be intense devotion to the young, and the killing of her offspring will rouse a mother to a fighting fury, quickly joined by the rest of the herd.

Walruses can move overland as fast as a human can run, and because of their formidable tusks, hunters, having roused a herd, have often been hard put to keep them at bay. Walruses have even speared the sides of a boat with their tusks or hooked them over the gunwales.

As well as using its large tusks as weapons of offense and defense, the walrus uses them to keep breathing holes open in the ice. It also uses them as anchors for hauling itself out onto the ice, heaving up to bring the foreflippers onto the surface. The horny casing of bare hard skin on the palms of the flippers prevents the walrus from slipping. Some scientists have suggested the tusks are also used to dig for food on the ocean floor, but there is no evidence to support this.

Walruses sunbathe, which turns their skin a pinkish color, and sleep packed close together on the ice floes with their tusks resting on each other's bodies. If the water is not too rough, adult walruses also can sleep vertically in the water by inflating the air sacs under their throats.

Clam grubbers

The walrus's diet consists principally of clams, which it grubs out of the mud with its muzzle, and sea snails. It also takes mussels and cockles. The snout bristles help in detecting the shellfish. In captivity a walrus was seen to suck out clams and discard the shells. A walrus also swallows a quantity of pebbles and stones, possibly to help it crush the food in its stomach. Walruses usually dive for their food in shallow water of about 180 feet (54 m) or less, but occasionally they go down to 300 feet (90 m). As yet, scientist are unsure how walruses deal with pressure problems at this depth, but they must have special physiological adaptations to do so.

Occasionally a walrus, usually an adult bull, will turn carnivorous and feed on whale carcasses or it may kill small ringed or bearded seals. Having sampled flesh, it may continue to eat it in preference to shellfish.

Hitchhiking pup

Most matings take place in January and February, and after a gestation of slightly more than a year one pup is born every alternate year. Birth takes place on an ice floe. The newborn pup is 4 feet (1.2 m) long with a coat of short silver gray hair and weighs 100–150 pounds (45–67.5 kg). It is able to swim immediately, although not very well, and follows its mother in the water. After a week or two it can swim and dive well. Even so, it usually rides on its mother's back for some time after birth, gripping with its flippers. After a month or two the silver gray hair is replaced by a sparser dark brown coat of stiff hairs. The cow nurses the pup for 18 months to two years, but they remain together for several months after weaning. Males become sexually mature at about 8–10 years, the females at about 6–7 years.

Slaughtered by hunters

Killer whales and polar bears attack walruses but not often, the polar bear particularly being wary of attacking an adult bull even when he is ashore and more vulnerable. Walruses have been hunted by humans from early times. Historically, the Inuit and Chukchi relied on the annual kill to supply all their major needs, including meat, blubber, oil, clothing, boat coverings and sled harnesses. Even today they are largely dependent on it. The annual killings by local people, however, had little effect on the numbers of the herds. It was the coming of commercially minded Europeans to the Arctic that started the real population decline. From the 15th century onward they used the walrus's habit of hauling out on the beaches in massed herds to massacre large numbers in the space of a few hours. After 1861, when whales had become scarce, whalers from New England started harpooning walruses. Then they began to use rifles and the Inuit followed suit. More walruses could be killed using a rifle, but many carcasses fell into the water and could not be recovered. An even greater wastage has been caused by ivory hunters, who kill for the tusks and discard the rest of the carcass. By the 1930s the world population of walruses stood at less than 100,000 and only recently have strict conservation measures been enforced. At present, both walrus subspecies are safe from threat.

Inflatable air sacs in their throats enable walruses to float while resting in the water. The sacs also enable them to make special sounds during courtship.

WHALE SHARK

THE WORLD'S LARGEST FISH, yet harmless to humans, the whale shark can grow to a length of about 66 feet (20 m) and weigh up to 20 tons (20,300 kg). It is readily distinguished from any other fish by its prominent color pattern: very dark gray or brownish with white underparts, and the head and body covered in white or yellow spots that are smallest and densest on the head area. Rows of spots on the back are separated by pale vertical stripes. The whale shark has a long, cylindrical body with longitudinal ridges along its back, one down the middle and two or three on each side. Like all sharks, it has a very tough skin, that of a 50-foot (15-m) whale shark being 6 inches (15 cm) thick. The powerful tail is keeled and has an almost symmetrical fin. The head is broad and blunt, and the huge terminal mouth contains hundreds of very small teeth that form a type of rasp. The gape of the mouth is large, at about 5 feet (1.5 m) across in a medium-sized specimen. The eyes are small with small spiracles placed just behind them. The pectoral fins are large and sickle-shaped, and there are two dorsal fins, the second one lying above the anal fin.

One feature of the whale shark that is shared by only one other shark, the basking shark (discussed elsewhere), is the presence of gill rakers. The external gill openings above the base of the pectoral fins are very wide, and within the throat they are covered by close-set rows of sievelike gill rakers, each 4–5 inches (10–12.5 cm) long, growing out from the gill arches. They look like miniatures of the baleen plates of the whalebone whales and have the same function of straining out plankton and small fish.

Whale sharks are found in all the tropical waters of the world. Occasionally individuals have been reported as far north as New York and as far south as Brazil and in Australian waters.

Surface swimmer

The whale shark lives near the surface of the open sea, swimming slowly at around 2–3 knots. It is docile and does not attack swimmers, but it is easily distressed by intruders, and the swish of its tail when fleeing is enough to stun a diver or break ribs. It also likes to bump against small boats, which are then at risk of capsizing. Whale sharks rub themselves deliberately against boats, possibly to get rid of external parasites.

Very few whale sharks have been caught, and they are not often seen except perhaps when basking at the surface. When wounded by a harpoon, the shark will dive straight down or streak away at speed, dragging the boat with it. It has very great powers of endurance and does not give in easily. It is said that if harpooned the whale shark can contract the muscles of its back to prevent the entrance of another spear. While swimming, the whale shark gives out a croaking sound, which is possibly a form of echolocation used in navigation.

Plankton feeder

The whale shark, like the basking shark, feeds on plankton, small schooling fish such as sardines and anchovies, and small crustaceans and squid. It does so by opening its huge mouth. Water rushes out over the gills, leaving the fish sticking to the inner walls of the throat and to the gill rakers. Although the whale shark feeds in this way, it still has numerous small teeth. They are arranged in some 310 rows in each jaw, but only about 10 or 15 rows function at any one time.

Stewart Springer of the U.S. Fishery Vessel *Oregon* once described seeing 30 or 40 whale sharks standing vertically, head up and tail down, during a spell of calm weather in the Gulf of Mexico. They were pumping up and down in the water, feeding on small fish and accompanied by small black-fin tuna that had stirred up the sea all around with their darting and leaping. When actively feeding on zooplankton the whale sharks turn their heads from side to side with part of the head lifted out of the water, opening and closing the mouth and gill slits.

The whale shark, Rhincodon typus, Ningaloo Reef, Australia. Whale sharks can be found singly or in groups of over 100 individuals.

When feeding on plankton the whale shark turns its head from side to side, opening and closing its mouth up to 28 times a minute. The current of swallowed water causes the gill covers to beat in time.

Live young

Whale sharks are ovoviviparous, producing eggs that, when developed, hatch within the mother's body or immediately after emerging. Late-term embryos shed their egg case inside the uterus at a size of 23–25 inches (58-64 cm). The smallest free-swimming young are 21½–22 inches (55–56 cm) long and have umbilical scars. A pregnant female was recently found with 300 embryos inside her, the largest of which measured 23–25 inches (58–64 cm) long.

Few predators

The whale shark has few natural predators. Because of its large size, only the sea's largest carnivores would attempt to attack it, and a blow from its powerful tail would probably be enough to drive away even the largest predator. Commercial exploitation has increased, causing some scientists to press for categorizing this and other sharks as vulnerable.

Gentle giant

The whale shark could truly be called a giant that does not know its own strength, and this is especially illustrated by the following. In 1919 a whale shark became wedged in a bamboo stake-trap set in water 50 feet (15 m) deep in the Gulf of Thailand. It appeared to have made no attempt to break its way out. In the same area in 1950 another whale shark was captured and beached by the local fishermen, and although details of its capture are not at hand, it would seem that the giant fish offered little or no resistance. Prince Chumbhot, reporting this incident, says it was "towed out to deep water and released by fishermen as a matter of luck, with a piece of red rag tied round its tail."

WHALE SHARK

CLASS	**Elasmobranchii**
ORDER	**Orectolobiformes**
FAMILY	**Rhincodontidae**
GENUS AND SPECIES	***Rhincodon typus***

WEIGHT
Maximum 20 tons (20,300 kg)

LENGTH
Up to 66 ft. (20 m)

DISTINCTIVE FEATURES
Huge, blunt-headed shark; terminal mouth; prominent pattern of white or yellow spots and stripes on dark background; spots smaller and closer together on head; gill rakers; numerous rows of small teeth

DIET
Planktonic and swimming prey: small crustaceans, fish and squid

BREEDING
Few details known; ovoviviparous, giving birth to hatched or soon-to-hatch young; embryos up to 23–25 in. (58–64 cm) long

LIFE SPAN
Not known

HABITAT
Usually offshore surface seas, sometimes close inshore in lagoons or coral atolls

DISTRIBUTION
Tropical waters: western Atlantic, from New York through the Caribbean to central Brazil; eastern Atlantic, from Senegal to Gulf of Guinea; Indian Ocean; western Pacific, from Japan to Australia and Hawaii; eastern Pacific, from California to Chile

STATUS
Vulnerable

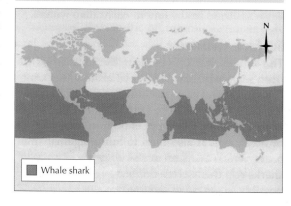

Whale shark

WOODPECKER

N̲O BIRDS ARE BETTER adapted for a life on the branches and trunks of trees than the woodpeckers, family Picidae. There are some 217 species of true woodpeckers, which occur in wooded areas of Eurasia, Africa and both American continents. Some species have common names other than woodpecker, and two groups of these birds are described elsewhere in this encyclopedia under the separate headings of flicker and sapsucker.

Woodpeckers are up to almost 2 feet (60 cm) in length and usually are brightly colored, with patterns of black, white, green or red. A few woodpeckers have crests. The bill is straight and pointed, the legs are short, in most cases with two toes pointing forward and two facing backward, and the tail is made up of pointed feathers with stiff shafts.

Green and pied woodpeckers

The 15 species of green woodpeckers in the genus *Picus* inhabit the woods and forests of Europe and Asia from Britain to Borneo and Java. The green woodpecker, *Picus viridis*, of Europe is 12 inches (30 cm) long and has a green plumage, which is brighter below, a bright yellowish rump and a red crown. The male has a red-and-black stripe under the eye, whereas the female has a plain black stripe.

The pied, or spotted, woodpeckers, genus *Picoides*, form a widespread group of 30-odd species across North America, Eurasia and North Africa. They are mostly black or gray with white patches, bars or mottling. The males often have red crowns. The three-toed woodpeckers, which belong to the pied woodpecker group, also have a circumpolar distribution and are unusual in having only three toes on each foot. The ivory-billed woodpecker, *Campephilus principalis*, of North America and Cuba and the imperial woodpecker, *C. imperialis*, of northern Mexico, were two of the world's largest woodpeckers, both dependent on large forest trees. As a result of habitat destruction and disturbance, both species may be extinct, although sightings have been reported.

Expert tree climbers

Woodpeckers are usually seen as just a flash of color disappearing among the trees. They live solitarily in woodlands and can be identified by their characteristic undulating flight, three or four rapid wingbeats carrying them up, followed by a downward glide. Instead of being seen, they are more likely to reveal themselves by their harsh or ringing calls, such as the loud laugh of

the green woodpecker, or by their drumming, a rapid tattoo that they make with their bills on dead branches or even on metal roofs.

Woodpeckers spend most of their time hopping up tree trunks in spirals, searching for insects. When a woodpecker has examined one tree, it flies to the base of the next and repeats the operation. In climbing vertical trunks, the birds

A young green woodpecker greets its returning parent. The red-and-black mustachial stripe identifies the adult as a male.

The acorn woodpecker, Melanerpes formicivorus, stores acorns in natural or specially excavated holes in trees, the trunks of which can be studded with huge stockpiles of nuts.

are assisted by their sharp claws, two backward-facing toes and stiff tail feathers, which are used as a prop while climbing.

Boring for insects

Woodpeckers feed largely on insects and their larvae. The green woodpeckers often hunt on the ground for ants and sometimes attack beehives, and the red-headed woodpecker, *Melanerpes erythrocephalus*, of North America catches insects on the wing. Usually, though, woodpeckers feed on insects that are pried out of crevices in the bark of trees or drilled out of the wood. The pointed bill is an excellent chisel, and the skull is toughened to withstand the shock of hammering. When they drill, woodpeckers aim their blows alternately from one side and then the other, in the manner of a tree-feller. The birds remove the insects from the hole by using their extremely long tongue, which, in the case of the green woodpecker, can protrude up to 6 inches (15 cm)

HAIRY WOODPECKER

CLASS	**Aves**
ORDER	**Piciformes**
FAMILY	**Picidae**
GENUS AND SPECIES	***Picoides villosus***

WEIGHT
1½–3 oz. (42–80 g); less in south

LENGTH
Head to tail: 6½–10¼ in. (16.5–26 cm), smaller in south

DISTINCTIVE FEATURES
Longish bill, slightly decurved; mostly black-and-white plumage, black on upperparts and white on underparts; small orange-red mark on crown; middle of back white to brown; outer tail feathers white. Plumage and size vary markedly with subspecies.

DIET
Beetles and beetle grubs, crickets, flies, spiders and vegetable matter

BREEDING
Age at first breeding: 1 year; breeding season: February–June, depending on region; number of eggs: 2 to 5; incubation period: 14 days; fledging period: 28–30 days; breeding interval: 1 year

LIFE SPAN
Not known

HABITAT
Wide range of forests, including Douglas fir (*Pseudotsuga taxifolia*) and juniper (genus *Juniperus*)

DISTRIBUTION
North America, except far north and deserts of southwest; highlands of Mexico and Central America south to west Panama

STATUS
Common

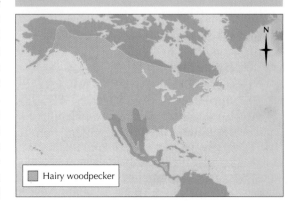

Hairy woodpecker

from the tip of the bill. The tongue is protruded by the same mechanism as that of the piculet (discussed elsewhere), which belongs to the woodpecker family, and is often tipped with barbs or bristles or coated with mucus for brushing up the insects.

Some woodpeckers eat fruit and seeds or drink sap. The red-headed woodpecker and the acorn woodpecker, *Melanerpes formicivorus*, stockpile acorns, drilling separate holes in trees for each one or using natural cavities.

Nesting in holes

Most woodpeckers nest in holes thatthey excavate in trees. They drill into a trunk and then tunnel downward to make a cavity up to 12 inches (30 cm) deep. There is no nest lining, and the two to eight white eggs rest on the bottom of the hole. The eggs hatch in 11–17 days and the chicks fledge in 2–3 weeks, depending on the size of the woodpecker. Both sexes bore the nest hole and take turns at incubating and feeding the chicks. Some woodpeckers excavate nest holes in cacti, and some use the nests of social insects. The rufous woodpecker, *Celeus brachyurus*, of Asia, for example, uses the football-sized nests of ants for its main nest site.

Other woodpecker species, including the African ground woodpecker, *Geocolaptes olivaceus*, dig burrows in the ground for nesting. The same site may be used over several breeding seasons.

Digging too deep

Boring a nest hole several inches across does considerable damage to a tree and may weaken it sufficiently for it to fall. This was the outcome at the nest of one pileated woodpecker, *Dryocopus pileatus*, in the Everglades National Park, Florida. The tree split off at the level of the entrance to the nest, revealing that the trunk had been hollowed to leave a shell only ¼–½ inch (6–13 mm) thick. F. K. Truslow, a bird-watcher working in the area at the time, concealed himself hoping to observe the reactions of the woodpeckers to this development, which took place during the incubation period. About 10 minutes after the trunk split, the female returned to the tree, disappeared into the nest cavity and reappeared with an egg in her bill. She then flew off with it and did not drop it for the 75 yards (70 m) she remained in view. All three eggs were removed in this manner. Truslow's report of the event is one of the few positive records ornithologists have of birds rescuing their eggs by carrying them away.

The great spotted woodpecker, Picoides major, *is a pied woodpecker that occurs in Europe, Asia and North Africa.*

WOOD WARBLER

THE WOOD WARBLERS FORM a large family of small birds confined to the Americas. At present, 116 species are recognized, but it has recently been suggested by some ornithologists that the honeycreepers (discussed elsewhere) belong to the same family and differ only in their adaptations for drinking nectar. Wood warblers range in size from 4–7 inches (10–17.5 cm) long and have narrow, straight bills. The plumage is sometimes dull gray or brown but in many species it is bright, usually yellow, orange or black and white. In tropical America, both male and female are brightly colored, but in temperate latitudes the female's coloration is somber and the male is brightly colored only in the breeding season. The large number of species makes identification difficult; the songs, call notes and male plumage are the most diagnostic features. In Britain, the wood warbler, *Phylloscopus sibilatrix* (discussed elsewhere), is a true warbler in the family Sylviidae.

The yellow warbler, *Dendroica petechia*, in which the sexes are very similarly colored, is widespread. It is buff above, yellow underneath, and yellow and black on the wings and tail, the male having rusty streaks on the breast. The yellow-breasted chat, *Icteria virens*, is the largest wood warbler. It is olive green above and bright yellow below, with white around the eyes. Kirtland's warbler, *D. kirtlandii*, with a yellow breast and black-streaked flanks, is confined to an area of 60 by 80 miles (100 by 130 km) in Michigan, where there are dense growths of jack pines, 3–18 feet (1–5.5 m) high.

Two wood warblers have blue in the plumage. The black-throated blue warbler, *D. caerulescens*, is most the most striking of the two, with bluish gray upperparts, black cheeks and throat and white underparts. The golden-winged warbler, *Vermivora chysoptera*, and the blue-winged warbler, *V. pinus*, interbreed where their ranges overlap. The hybrids, which are fertile, were once considered separate species and were called Brewster's and Lawrence's warblers.

Wood warblers breed from Alaska to southern South America, and about half of the species are found in North America and the Caribbean. Like the vireos (discussed elsewhere), wood warblers occasionally get caught up in weather systems that carry them to Europe.

Impressive migrations

Wood warblers are found mainly in woodland and scrub country, but they have colonized a wide variety of habitats. The northern waterthrush lives in bogs, and others are found in deserts and in tropical rain forests.

The chestnut-sided warbler, *D. pensylvanica*, prefers scrub country, and has benefited from the clearing of forests. Most northern wood warblers are migratory, traveling in flocks to Central America and northern South America, sometimes to Brazil and Chile. These flocks, in which several species of wood warblers fly in company with tits, are one of the most dramatic sights of North American bird-watching.

In the spring, migration is rapid, the black-poll warbler, *D. striata*, taking a month to travel from Florida to Alaska, and flocks of warblers, many in brightly colored breeding plumage, pass through North America. In winter, large flocks of mixed-species wood warblers roam the pine-oak forests of highland regions of Central America and northern South America. The songs of wood warblers are simple when compared with the varied calls of Old World warblers. However, the yellow-breasted chat is a good mimic.

Mainly insect eaters

Almost all wood warblers eat insects, and most feed among the foliage. The waterthrushes, genus *Seiurus*, and the ovenbird, *Seiurus aurocapillus*, feed on the ground, and some wood

Wilson's warbler, Wilsonia pusilla, from California, United States. Although wood warblers live mainly in woodland and scrub areas, they also inhabit bogs and deserts.

A nest of yellow warblers, in Aureolo, Galapagos. Both the male and female yellow warbler are similarly colored.

warblers, like flycatchers, hawk for flying insects. The latter have flattened bills surrounded by bristles for sweeping up their prey.

The black-and-white warbler, *Mniotilta varia*, searches for insects among crevices in bark and has short legs and long claws, which enable it to run up trunks in the manner of a creeper (discussed elsewhere). This warbler is able to stay north in the fall after other wood warblers have migrated because insects hiding in crevices survive longer than those in exposed places. The myrtle warbler, *D. coronata*, survives colder weather because it eats fruit and berries, and can live in areas that have snow in winter.

Varied nest sites

The nests of wood warblers are cup-shaped or domed, some being built 50 feet (15 m) or more up in the tops of trees and others on the ground. The parula warbler, *Parula americana*, builds its nests in hanging skeins of Spanish moss. The nest of the ovenbird, not to be confused with the ovenbirds of the family Furnariidae (discussed elsewhere), is a dome-shaped nest of leaves built on the ground.

The prothonotary warbler, *Protonotaria citrea*, sometimes builds in holes or nest boxes. It is named after the papal secretary, who wears orangish yellow robes. There are usually four to six eggs, the clutch size being lower in tropical America, than in temperate latitudes. The female alone incubates the eggs but both parents feed the chicks. Incubation ranges from 12–14 days and fledging takes about 11 days. The periods are shorter in tropical species than in the northern migratory species.

PROTHONOTARY WOOD WARBLER

CLASS **Aves**

ORDER **Passeriformes**

FAMILY **Parulidae**

GENUS AND SPECIES *Protonotaria citrea*

WEIGHT
⅗ oz. (17 g)

LENGTH
Head to tail: 5½ in. (14 cm)

DISTINCTIVE FEATURES
Male: brilliant golden-yellow head, throat and breast, contrasting sharply with green upperparts, blue-gray wings, blue-gray tail and white undertail. Female: duller than male, especially on head.

DIET
Insects and spiders; occasionally seeds, fruit and nectar

BREEDING
Age at first breeding: 1 year; breeding season: April–June; number of eggs: 4 to 6; incubation period: 12–14 days; fledging period: 11 days; breeding interval: 1 year

LIFE SPAN
Not known

HABITAT
Flooded or swampy mature woodland for breeding; winters mainly in coastal mangroves

DISTRIBUTION
Breeding: lowland areas of U. S., east of the Rockies. Winter: Central America, Caribbean islands, northern Colombia and Venezuela.

STATUS
Fairly common

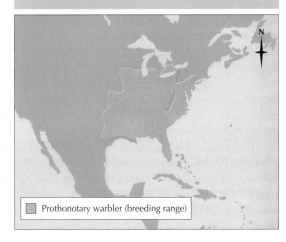

Prothonotary warbler (breeding range)

INDEX